Master Quranic Arabic
In 24 hours

Suhaib Sirajudin

Shield Crest

ISBN   978-1-907629-87-7

MMXIV

Published by
ShieldCrest
Aylesbury, Buckinghamshire,
HP22 5RR
England
www.shieldcrest.co.uk

Glossary

Aakhirah	Hereafter
Abd	Servant
Abqa	Everlasting
Akhlaq	Morals/manners
Alayhis salam	Peace be upon him
Alhumdulillah	All praise is for Allah
Allahu akbar	Allah is the greatest
Azan	The call to prayer
Bid'ah	Innovation in religion
Bukhari	Book of Hadith
Deen	Religion
Dua	Supplication
Dunya	The material (temporal) world
Fatah	Open, victory, or conquest (of Makkah)
Fiqh	Islamic jurisprudence
Hadith qudsi	Sacred hadith
Hajj	Pilgrimage to Mecca
Halal	Permitted
Haram	Forbidden
Ibadah	Worship
Ikhlas	Sincerity
Imaan	Faith
Imam	Scholar
In sha allah	If Allah wills
Jannah	Paradise
Jazakallahu khair	May Allah reward you
Ka'abah	House of Allah
Khair	Good
Khinsab	Name of a devil
Khushu	Concentration in prayer
Khutbah	Speech
Masjid	Mosque
Muslim	Book of Hadith
Quraish	The dominant tribe of Makkah.
Rahman	Most gracious

Rahmatullahi alayi	Allah's mercy be upon him
Rak'ahs	Portion of the salah
Raoof	Most compassionate
Ruku	Bowing down whilst standing
Sajdah	Prostration
Salaf	Pious predecessors
Salah	Prayer
Shaitan	Satan
Subhan allah	Glory be to Allah
Surah	Chapter
Ta'aweez	Talisman or Amulet
Takleef	Burden
Taqwa	God consciousness
Taraweeh	Extra night prayers during Ramadan
Tashreef	Honour
Tawaf	Circumambulating the kabah
Tawheed	Oneness of Allah
Tirmidhi	Book of Hadith

Contents

PART I

Introducing Quranic Arabic

Hour 1

1   An outline of the Course and Masculine
      Pronouns

Hour **1**

At the end of this Hour you will have learnt

6 New Words	**Our Goal 200 Words**
1295 Total words	**Our Goal 25000 Words**

An outline of the course

Welcome to Master Quranic Arabic in 24 Hours. Have you ever wanted to learn the language in which the final revelation (the Quran) was revealed? Maybe you thought learning Arabic was too difficult for you or that you were too old to learn a new language. Well, in fact, not only is learning Quranic Arabic remarkably easy, it can also be fun, as you'll see in this 24-Hour course. Even if you have little or no knowledge of Arabic, you'll find it easy going through these tutorials in the comfort of your home. At the end of each Hour you will be able to put your knowledge into practice and begin to understand Quranic Arabic. After you have completed Hour 1 you will have a basic understanding of the language.

At the end of this Hour, you will have learnt 6 words from the Quran which appear in the Quran no less than 1,295 times. Our goal in this course is to learn 200 words that appear 25,000 times. These words constitute more than 30% of the words in the Quran.

This Hour includes the following:

- Who should read this book
- What this book will do for you
- Whether the book can really teach you to understand the Quran in 24 hours
- Conventions used in the book
- Grammar – Pronouns.

Congratulations! This is your first step in walking towards Allah. In the Hadith, the Prophet (Peace be upon him) cited these words of Allah: "If a servant of Mine comes to Me walking, I come to him running." (Bukhari and Muslim.)

You are probably anxious to get started with your 24-Hour Quranic Arabic course. But first take a few moments to familiarise yourself with the design of this book, which is described in the next few sections.

Who should read this book?

This book is for those who want to learn Quranic Arabic as quickly as possible without compromising the foundations necessary to master the language. Newcomers who don't have any prior knowledge of Arabic will from the very first Hour be able to understand some Quranic Arabic.

The course is also for those who are distracted in their salah causing their mind to wander. Psychologists say that the human mind cannot focus on two different things at the same time. The mind can focus on two things 70% and 30% of the time or 80% and 20% of the time but cannot focus on two different things 100% of the time. So if you focus in your salah on the meaning of what you are reciting, then your mind will never wander 100%

outside of your salah. It may wander by 20% or 30% but the remaining percentage will be focused on your salah. This will In Sha Allah increase your faith, humility, fear and love for Allah and soften your heart.

Some may claim that their mind does not wander in salah. No one can truthfully claim this, and no one should claim this, because in the hadith the Prophet (Peace be upon him) said: "There is a special Shaitan for salah whose name is 'Khinsab' and his job is to distract you from your salah." The moment you begin your salah and say "Allahu Akbar" he will come and distract you and make your mind wander.

What will this book do for me?

You will learn everything you need to begin to understand the Quran. Although this is not a reference book, you will learn virtually everything a beginner or intermediate Arabic learner needs to know to be able to read the Quran for themselves. Most Arabic learners may never need to learn the more advanced material so this book will not waste your time by delving into knowledge unnecessary for basic understanding. I know that you want to become acquainted with Quranic Arabic in 24 Hours and this book will enable you to do so without squandering your time on extra study not essential for understanding the Quran.

Can this book really teach me Quranic Arabic in just 24 Hours?

Yes. With Allah's help everything is possible. You can master each chapter in one hour or less. You will notice the chapters are referred to as 'lessons' or 'Hours', and that they vary in length. However, the material is balanced throughout the course. Each section contains lessons in vocabulary and grammar which are taken directly from the Quran. This will ensure you don't waste time learning vocabulary which you may never need or use. At the end of each Hour, there is a section of advice. This part and section will practically help you in acting upon what you have learnt in each hour.

Conventions used in this book

Each lesson introduces new words and so widens your vocabulary. You will also become familiar with new terms and you will be warned against pitfalls. Furthermore, at the end of each lesson, quiz questions and exercises are provided to consolidate what you have learned.

These are some of the common conventions used in this book to highlight various pieces of information and to make them easily recognisable:

 The first time a new word appears, you will find the New Word icon along with its meaning.

 You'll find numerous tips to enhance your learning of Arabic.

 Warns you about pitfalls and dangers. Reading them will save you getting into trouble.

 Clarifies concepts and meanings.

Your goal in this course

Remember, your goal is not to learn the Arabic Language. Learning Arabic is your means. Frequently, we confuse our means with our goals. For instance, offering salah, giving charity, performing Hajj; all of these rituals are means to get close to Allah. Our goal is Allah. When we confuse our goals with our means we become static, which then becomes a problem in our lives.

So our goal in this course is Allah. In other words, our goal is to understand the message of Allah, ponder it, implement it and spread it. But these goals can only be achieved once we learn and understand Arabic. So let us not mix our means with our goals.

Understanding the Quran is compulsory

We don't have the option of not understanding the Quran. Every human being must understand the message of their creator Allah. You cannot fully understand the Quran unless you read it in Arabic. So it is compulsory for you to learn Quranic Arabic because every human being must understand the message of his creator Allah. Imagine if you were to spend 20, 40, 60 years of your life and on the Day of Judgment Allah says to you: "I sent my message to you. Did you read and understand it?" and you reply "Oh, Allah, I got your message, I read it too, but I never understood a word that you said." How shameful and embarrassing that would be. So, as you cannot fully understand the Quran without knowing Arabic, then this course is compulsory. NO EXCUSES!

The following are some of the excuses for not learning Arabic that are often given by people who do not understand Arabic. They say:

I have no time (or)
I have too many responsibilities

Now, in the comfort of your home, you can complete this course over 24 hours. We have divided simplified Arabic in to 24 one hour easy-to-learn lessons which are delivered in an interactive and entertaining way.

I can read the translation. Isn't that enough?

Yes, you can read the translation, but that does not mean you have read the Quran. By reading the translation, you can only get its overall meaning. The full meaning of the Quran is impossible to access in any other way than through the original Arabic. Once you have read and understood the Quran, it will have an overwhelming impact on you that words cannot adequately describe. Reading the original text will:

- increase your faith;
- increase your *khushu*, humility;
- increase your fear and love for Allah;
- make you cry;
- soften your heart.

Understanding the Quran will mislead me

Allah says in the Quran:

شَهْرُ رَمَضَانَ الَّذِي أُنْزِلَ فِيهِ الْقُرْآنُ هُدًى لِلنَّاسِ وَبَيِّنَاتٍ مِنَ الْهُدَى وَالْفُرْقَانِ

"Ramadan is the (month) in which the Qur'an was sent down as a guide to mankind with clear (Signs) for guidance and judgment (between right and wrong)." (Quran 2:185)

Allah is saying the Quran is a guide for mankind. So will you believe Allah, who is saying it is a guide for mankind, or will you believe those who say it will mislead you? DO NOT FALL INTO THIS TRAP.

I will learn Arabic later on

We don't know how long we will live in this world. Therefore, don't save it for later on. Start today and don't give up!

I don't have anyone to teach me where I'm living

You may be living in an area where you cannot find someone to teach you Arabic. However, this course has been simplified so much that, as you are completing each lesson, you will feel as though I am holding your hand and explaining each lesson until you have completed the course.

We should not try to understand the Quran – it's too difficult, leave it to the scholars

You may think it is difficult to understand the Quran but Allah says:

$$وَلَقَدْ يَسَّرْنَا الْقُرْآنَ لِلذِّكْرِ فَهَلْ مِنْ مُدَّكِرٍ$$

"And we have indeed made the Quran easy to understand and remember: then is there any that will receive admonition?" (Quran 54:17.) In this context, admonition means counsel, advice or teaching.

This verse is mentioned no less than four times in the same chapter of the Quran's Surah Qamar (54:17, 22, 32, 40). So when Allah says "I have made it easy for you to understand," who will you believe? Will you believe yourself that the Quran is too difficult to understand or will you believe what Allah says, that it is easy?

All these excuses are from *Shaitan*. Remember, his aim is to mislead you, to take you away from the Quran. He will always work to prevent you from getting closer to the Quran. So beware of Shaitan, he is your enemy.

Never say the Quran is difficult to understand!

NEVER SAY IT, NEVER THINK IT, AND NEVER AGREE TO IT

THIS IS FROM SHAITAN

Our goal in this course

In the Quran, there are approximately 77,500 words. We will round this figure to 78,000. Most of these words are repeated but 17,000 words are not. However, Arabic is a Semitic language, and in this language family, you are able to form many different words from one root. For example from (عِلْم), which means knowledge, we form the word (عَلِيْم), which means all-knowing. It is possible to have up to nine different words derived from the same root word. So once the root words and their derivatives are set aside, there are only 4,500 unique words in the Quran. *Subhan Allah*. I have mentioned this already, but it is important that you hear and believe this: Allah rightly says in the Quran: "And We have indeed made the Quran easy to understand and remember: then is there any that will receive admonition?". Table 1.1 shows you the number of words in the Quran.

Table 1.1

Words in the Quran	Figure
Total words:	78,000
Non repeated words:	17,000
Unique words:	4,500

In this course, we will In Sha Allah learn 212 vocabulary words that appear in the Quran 25,093 times. We will round this figure to 200 vocabulary words, which appear in the Quran 25,000 times. This represents more than 30% of the words in the Quran. So by the end of 24 Hours you will know the meaning of more than 30% of the words in the Quran.

In addition, you will learn 24 lessons of Arabic grammar. These lessons have been simplified and the concepts will progress from beginner to intermediate as the Hours pass. Advanced Arabic grammar is not taught: it is not needed to understand the Quran. You may never need advanced concepts so we will not waste time on them.

Where do we begin?

We will begin at Surah Fatihah which is the first chapter of the Quran. We start here because we recite these words at least 17 times in our daily salah: it makes sense to start from what we already know and repeat in Arabic every day, instead of starting with unfamiliar words.

We will follow the study of Surah Fatihah with the last 10 Surahs of the Quran and finally the first two *rukus* from Surah Baqrah.

Uniqueness of this course

What makes this course unique is that we don't teach you words which do not appear in the Quran. Our aim is not to teach you spoken Arabic. Communicating in Arabic is not compulsory, but understanding the Quran is compulsory. So we will focus on what is compulsory and that is the vocabulary from the Quran.

Enough! Time is ticking!

Take a Break!

Do you want to master Quranic Arabic? On we go with the Grammar Lesson.

> The CD-ROM accompanying this book includes exercises and quizzes for each hour. We have included it at no charge to you so that you can practice these quizzes as many times as you want. Go through each hour, take a break and then do the quiz.

Grammar – Masculine Pronouns

In this first Hour we will learn six pronouns. Pronouns take the place of a noun and function as the subject of a sentence. These pronouns appear in the Quran 1,295 times and are listed in Table 1.2. Also listed are their meanings and when to use them. These words are used for the masculine gender. We will look at feminine pronouns in the grammar lesson in Hour 4.

Table 1.2

When to use	Meaning	Pronoun
Distant from the speaker (in space or time)	He	هُوَ
Distant from the speaker (in space or time)	They	هُمْ
Close to the speaker	You	أَنْتَ
Close to the speaker	You All	أَنْتُمْ
	I	أَنَا
	We	نَحْنُ

Try to learn these pronouns: it is essential that you know them as they are used frequently in the Quran. Don't worry if you cannot remember the meanings and when to use them as I am sure you will become familiar with them very soon. Go through these pronouns a few times, and practice them by doing the Hour 1 Quiz at the end of this Hour, and provided on the CD-ROM.

Advice and guidance from the author

How to be successful in this course

When you prepare for any task, always follow these three important steps. They are relevant no matter whether the task is religious or secular: as long as you follow these steps, you will be successful. These three steps are:

1. To be successful, first ask for Allah's help: this is the most important step. If we don't ask for Allah's help, how can we be successful? Allah says in the Quran:

$$\text{إِنْ يَنْصُرْكُمُ اللَّهُ فَلَا غَالِبَ لَكُمْ وَإِنْ يَخْذُلْكُمْ فَمَنْ ذَا الَّذِي يَنْصُرُكُمْ مِنْ بَعْدِهِ}$$

$$\text{وَعَلَى اللَّهِ فَلْيَتَوَكَّلِ الْمُؤْمِنُونَ}$$

"If Allah helps you, none can overcome you: if He forsakes you, who is there after that that can help you? In Allah, then, let believers put their trust." (Quran: 3:160)

Allah's help is the most important of all. Without His help, no matter how much effort you put in, you cannot be successful. So first, ask for Allah's help. Make *dua* every day that Allah makes this course easy for you. Show humbleness when making *dua* to Allah: "O Allah, I need your help, without your help I cannot learn Arabic". Allah's help is <u>the</u> most important step for success.

2. The second step for success is to strive and struggle in the path of Allah. Allah says in the Quran:

$$\text{وَالَّذِينَ جَاهَدُوا فِينَا لَنَهْدِيَنَّهُمْ سُبُلَنَا}$$

"And those who strive in Our (Cause), We will certainly guide them to Our paths." (Quran: 29:69)

We must strive and struggle in His path. Some people say "We strive and struggle but we get no results." Allah says that if you strive and struggle in His path He will surely open up your pathways for you. So if your pathways are not open then it is not Allah's fault, it is your fault because you have not put the effort in as you should have. Had you done so, Allah would have surely opened up the pathways for you.

3. The third step for success is the technique, which is the least important. The technique is what we are showing you here, through these lessons and quizzes. Allah says in the Quran:

فَاسْأَلُوا أَهْلَ الذِّكْرِ إِنْ كُنْتُمْ لَا تَعْلَمُونَ

"If ye know this not, ask of those who possess the Message." (Quran: 21:7)

This is the least important of all the three steps to achieve success. However, most people want to know the technique without realising that the technique is the least important. Without Allah's help and without putting the effort in to follow His path, no matter how many techniques you have, it is all useless.

So let us prioritise these steps: firstly, Allah's help; secondly, striving and struggling in His path; and finally the technique, which this book is designed to show you.

Three steps to success

1. Allah's Help **(most important)**
2. Striving and struggling
3. Technique **(least important)**

Summary

This Hour introduced you to the overall structure of this course. You should also be familiar with the frequently used conventions in this book. Make sure you do not forget to follow the three steps for success. Now you understand the course structure, you are ready to begin.

We can summarise this Hour by making the following points:

- It is compulsory to do this course if I do not know Arabic.
- I will be distracted by Shaitan with excuses so I need to approach this course with attentiveness and follow the three steps for success.
- My main goal is to please Allah by implementing the Quran.
- I studied pronouns as part of grammar.

In the next Hour, we will In Sha Allah begin with *Ta'awuz* and *Surah Fatihah*. This will In Sha Allah help you focus more on your salah and prevent your mind from wandering, because you will begin to understand what you are reciting in your salah. Finally, for grammar we will study how to form plurals.

Workshop

The quiz questions and the exercises are provided to further your understanding. Don't worry if you can't answer all of the questions in the quiz. Try your best to answer as many as you can. See Appendix A to check your answers.

Quiz 1

1. Why is it compulsory to understand the Quran?
2. Who should take this course?
3. What is your goal in this course?
4. What is our plan in this course?
5. What are the three steps for success?

Exercise

Insert the CD-ROM accompanying this book into your drive. Select the appropriate folder and do the quiz for this Hour. You may do the quiz as many times as you like in order to further your understanding.

PART II

Ta'awuz and Surah Fatihah

Hours

Hour **2**

At the end of this Hour you will have learnt

13 New Words	**Our Aim 200 Words**
4,479 Total Words	**Our Aim 25,000 Words**

Ta'awuz, Surah Fatihah Verses 1-3 and Making Plurals

In Hour 1, we said we will begin with Ta'awuz and Surah Fatihah. This is the first Surah of the Quran, and it is the Surah which we recite every day in our salah. In the previous Hour we learnt pronouns for grammar and I gave you some tips for being successful at this course. Don't forget the three steps for success: Allah's help, striving and struggling, and the technique.

In this Hour we will learn 7 new words which appear in the Quran 3,184 times. We will study vocabulary words from Ta'awuz and verses 1-3 from Surah Fatihah. For grammar, we will study how to construct plural forms. By the end of this Hour you will have learned 13 words, which appear in the Quran 4,479 times.

The highlights of this Hour include:

- Ta'awuz
- Introduction to Surah Fatihah
- Surah Fatihah verses 1-3
- Grammar – How to form plurals.

Ta'awuz

 Ta'awuz is to seek the protection of Allah from Shaitan.

This is to be read every time we begin reciting the Quran. In our everyday affairs, we are always conscious of safety. When we get into a car, we put on our safety belt and buckle ourselves up. Similarly, Allah tells us to seek safety and His protection.

Table 2.1.1

الرَّجِيمِ	الشَّيْطَانِ	مِنَ	بِاللهِ	أَعُوذُ
the outcast	*Shaitan*	*from*	*in Allah*	*I seek refuge*

Don't worry. We will explain one word at a time. As you can see in Table 2.1.1 there are five words and of those five words you are already familiar with two of them: the word "Allah" and the word "Shaitan". Let us take each word and explain their meanings.

Table 2.1.2

New Word	أَعُوذُ
I seek refuge	
أَ	Means "I".
عُوذُ	"Taking refuge" or "seeking refuge". Here it means to seek protection and help from danger. What danger? Let us find out as we continue with this verse.

Table 2.1.3

New Word	بِاللهِ
in Allah	
بِ	This is a preposition meaning "in". For now, just learn the meaning of this word.

الله	"Allah", our Creator and Sustainer.

Table 2.1.4

New Word	مِنَ الشَّيْطَانِ
	from Shaitan
مِنَ	This preposition means "from". It is so important that it appears in the Quran more than 3,000 times. Again, learn the meaning. Prepositions will be studied in Hours 5 and 6.
الشَّيْطَانِ	"Shaitan" (our implacable enemy).

Table 2.1.5

New Word	الرَّجِيمِ
	the Outcast
الرَّجِيمِ	Means "outcast" or "cursed". It means being separated from all righteousness and expelled from Allah's mercy.

"Outcast" is used deliberately to warn us of the danger of Shaitan.

Lessons derived from this verse

1. Try to ponder over the meaning when you recite this verse.
2. One benefit of reciting this verse is that it cleanses the mouth from any foul speech which it has produced.
3. It purifies the mouth and prepares it to recite the words of Allah.
4. It also requires and demands that we seek Allah's help, and acknowledge His ability to have power over all things.

Surah Fatihah

Al-Fatihah means The Opener of the Book. It has this name because it is the first Surah in the Quran. This is also the Surah with which prayers begin, so no salah is complete without this Surah. We recite this Surah a minimum of 17 times in our daily salah.

This Surah is also known as Umm Al-Kitab (the Mother of the Book), because it contains the core meaning of the entire Quran.

This Surah's third name is Hamd and Salah because the Prophet (Peace be upon him) said: "Allah said, 'The prayer [Surah Fatihah] is divided into two halves between Me and My servants. When the servant says, 'All praise is due to Allah, the Lord of existence, Allah says, 'My servant has praised Me.'" (Tirmidhi, Hadith Qudsi 40:2-3)

Surah Fatihah Verse 1

Table 2.2.1

الرَّحِيمِ	الرَّحْمٰنِ	اللهِ	بِسْمِ
the Most Merciful	the Most Gracious	(of) Allah	In the name

21

Table 2.2.1 shows the first verse of Surah Fatihah. Let us take one word at a time. There are three new words in this verse, because the word "Allah" was covered in Table 2.1.3 above.

Table 2.2.2

New Word	بِاسْمِ
	In the name
بِ	This is a preposition, which means "in". See Table 2.1.3.
اِسْمِ	Means "the name". For example, in Arabic we ask (مَا إِسْمُكَ) which means "What is your name?"

Table 2.2.3

	لله
	Allah
لله	"Allah", Our Creator and Sustainer. See Table 2.1.3.

Table 2.2.4

New Word	الرَّحْمٰنِ
	the Most Gracious
الرَّحْمٰنِ	"The Most Gracious". Think of (رَحْمَة) in Arabic, which means "mercy".

Words formed in this way contain the idea 'extreme'. For instance, (غَفَّار) means "one who is extremely forgiving". This is one of Allah's attributes.

Table 2.2.5

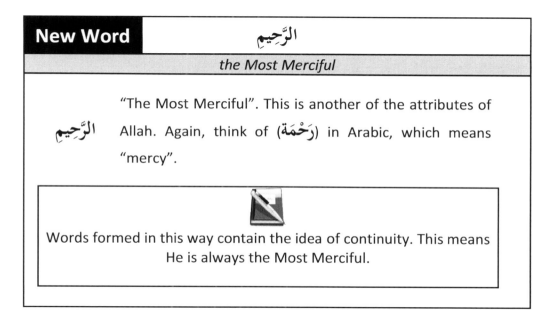

New Word	الرَّحِيمِ
	the Most Merciful

الرَّحِيمِ "The Most Merciful". This is another of the attributes of Allah. Again, think of (رَحْمَة) in Arabic, which means "mercy".

Words formed in this way contain the idea of continuity. This means He is always the Most Merciful.

Lessons derived from this verse

Virtues of this verse

It is recommended we recite this verse before performing any deed such as ablutions (washing ourselves), eating, or any other good deed. As we say it, we strive to feel hopeful and confident at the start of anything we do.

We must say it from our heart, with love for Allah. Whatever we do in our life, when we say "in the name of Allah" we must know that Allah's help is with us. When we have Allah's help, we don't need to look elsewhere for help. As a result, whatever you undertake, you will see that your endeavours will be successful.

Therefore, when you say "in the name of Allah", remember that Allah's help is with you: this will provide good motivation and great support as you study this course.

There are many more lessons to be learned from this verse but we will leave that for later when we go on to advanced study.

Surah Fatihah Verse 2

In this verse Allah is praising Himself.

Table 2.3.1

الْعَالَمِينَ	رَبِّ	لِلّهِ	اَلْحَمْدُ
(of) the worlds.	the Lord	(be) to Allah	(All) the praises and thanks

There are three new words in this verse.

Table 2.3.2

New Word	اَلْحَمْدُ
(All) the praises and thanks	
اَلْحَمْدُ	Means "All praises", "All thanks". We say (اَلْحَمْدُ لِلَّهِ) when we hear good news.

Table 2.3.3

لِلَّه
to Allah
لِ   Means "to", or "for". Prepositions will be studied in Hours 5 and 6.

Table 2.3.4

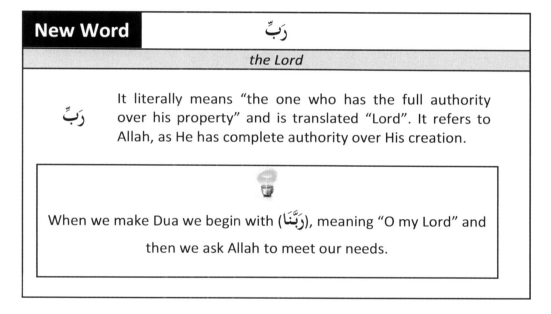

New Word	رَبِّ
	the Lord

رَبِّ	It literally means "the one who has the full authority over his property" and is translated "Lord". It refers to Allah, as He has complete authority over His creation.

When we make Dua we begin with (رَبَّنَا), meaning "O my Lord" and then we ask Allah to meet our needs.

Table 2.3.5

New Word	الْعَالَمِينَ
	the worlds

الْعَالَمِينَ	Means "the worlds". This is the plural form of the Arabic word (عَالَم) which means "world".

Allah used the plural form, "worlds" because there are different creations in heaven and earth. So the meaning is that Allah is NOT ONLY the Lord of humans, He is also the Lord of the Jinns, the Angels, and the entire universe.

Lessons derived from this verse

Don't thank Allah as if you are reading a passage from a book

This verse is a statement of appreciation. Whatever Allah has given to us, we are grateful for it. That's why when a person says "All praise is due to Allah", Allah replies and says "My servant has praised Me".

We must thank Allah from the depths of our hearts, and as we say it, we must mean it. We should not rattle it off as though we are just reading a passage from a book. Suppose someone does you a favour, how do you respond? Do you say "thank you" as if you are reading a passage from a book? No, you don't. You thank that person from your heart. Since Allah has bestowed upon us countless favours, praising Him as though we are reading something is not acceptable. We must thank Him from the depths of our heart and mean it as we say it.

Surah Fatihah Verse 3

In this verse Allah is talking about two of His most beautiful attributes. Allah says:

Table 2.4.1

الرَّحِيمِ	الرَّحْمٰنِ
the Most Merciful.	*the Most Gracious,*

Table 2.4.2

الرَّحْمٰنِ
the Most Gracious,
الرَّحْمٰنِ   "the Most Gracious". See Table 2.2.4.

Table 2.4.3

الرَّحِيمِ
the Most Merciful.
الرَّحِيمِ   "the Most Merciful". See Table 2.2.5.

Lessons derived from this verse

Be merciful to everyone

In the previous verse, Allah stated that He is "the Lord of the worlds". It was a warning from Allah that no one deserves this Lordship except for Allah, so immediately the next verse, verse number 3, is an encouragement from Allah to remember that Allah is "the Most Gracious and the Most Merciful". This verse also teaches us that if we are not merciful to others, Allah will not be merciful to us. In the Hadith, the Prophet (Peace be upon him) said "Allah is not merciful to him who is not merciful to people." (Bukhari, Muslim)

Practice what you have learned

Let us practice what we have learned so far. Practice makes perfect. As it is said, "Practice is a means of inviting the perfection desired." (Martha Graham.)

الرَّجِيمِ	الشَّيْطَانِ	مِنَ	بِالله	أَعُوذُ
the outcast	Shaitan	from	in Allah	I seek refuge

الرَّحِيمِ	الرَّحْمٰنِ	الله	بِسْمِ
the Most Merciful.	the Most Gracious,	(of) Allah	In the name

الْعَالَمِينَ	رَبِّ	لِلّهِ	أَلْحَمْدُ
(of) the worlds	the Lord	(be) to Allah	(All) the praises and thanks

الرَّحِيمِ	الرَّحْمٰنِ
the Most Merciful	The Most Gracious

Revision of vocabulary words studied

Meaning	Arabic Word
I seek refuge	أَعُوذُ
the outcast	الرَّجِيمِ
name	اِسْمِ
the Most Gracious	الرَّحْمٰنِ
the Most Merciful	الرَّحِيمِ
All Praises, all thanks	أَلْحَمْدُ
the Lord	رَبِّ
the worlds	الْعَالَمِينَ

Phew! Alhumdulillah!

So far, we have learnt Ta'awuz and the first three verses from Surah Fatihah. Without Allah's help it would not have been possible, so let's say Alhumdulillah!

Take a Break!

In the next section, you are going to learn Arabic Grammar.

Grammar – forming Plurals

Forming plurals is not difficult at all. The rule is to add the letters (و ن) or

(ي ن) at the end of the noun.

Table 2.5.1

Plural	Singular
مُسْلِمُوْنَ, مُسْلِمِيْنَ	مُسْلِم
مُؤْمِنُوْنَ, مُؤْمِنِيْنَ	مُؤْمِن
صَادِقُوْنَ, صَادِقِيْنَ	صَادِق
ذَاكِرُوْنَ, ذَاكِرِيْنَ	ذَاكِر
صَابِرُوْنَ, صَابِرِيْنَ	صَابِر

Isn't that simple? Don't worry about the meanings of the words, because that is not important for now. Look at the pattern of how plurals are formed, and familiarise yourself with the method. Go through this Table a few times, and practice by doing the Quiz at the end of this Hour.

Advice and guidance from the author

Being good to others is never conditional

We learnt from the above verses that Allah is the Most Gracious, the Most Merciful. We must show mercy in our own homes and to the people with whom we are in contact. Remember, being good is never conditional. We must not have the attitude of, "I will only be good to them as long as they are good to me", or "I will only be good to them as long as they are from the same background as me." Being good to others is not conditional, it has to be unconditional. Irrespective of whether others are good to you or not, we must all be unconditionally good to others all the time.

Shikhul Islam Ibn Taymiyyah (*Rahmatullahi Alayhi*) said "a sincere person is he when he is being appreciated or not, for the favours he has done upon others, for him both is the same". However, when someone does a favour for us we must say (*Jazakallahu Khair*) and appreciate it. If we do a favour for someone else, whether the person appreciates it or not, we should not be concerned about their ingratitude, because the reward for it comes from Allah, and we did that favour for the sake of Allah and not for appreciation from others.

Four principles when dealing with your loved ones

Remember these four extremely important principles when dealing with your loved ones:

1. The person is more important than the point. Sometimes we put so much emphasis on the point that we end up losing the person. What good is the point when you have lost that person? So we want to delay making the point but save the person.
2. Being kind is more important than being right. Yes, you may be right but that's not it. Because in the process, if you are right it does not mean you are kind. So as we are right, we must also be kind in the process.
3. Mean what you say and say what you mean.
4. Don't be harsh. When Allah told Moosa Alayhi Salam to deliver his message to pharaoh, Allah told Moosa Alayhi Salam to speak to him softly and to be gentle. So be gentle when dealing with your loved ones.

Being good to someone who is good to you does not make you a good person, but being good to someone who is not good to you makes you a really good person.

Summary

In this Hour, you have learned Ta'awuz and the first three verses from Surah Fatihah. Let's ponder over what we have learnt so far in our daily salah and let's mean what we recite from our hearts, and not just read it like reading a book. Once we start to ponder over what we recite in our salah, we will start to see the difference in our salah after only Hour 2 of this course. Starting from the next salah you perform you will begin to feel an increase in your faith and in your humility towards Allah, if you ponder over the verses as you recite them.

Remember the three steps to success formula: Allah's help, striving and struggling in the path of Allah and finally the technique. So stay focused, be committed and don't lose faith in Allah. Allah will make this course easy for you. Allah has chosen you for this course because He cares for you, so let us thank Allah and say Alhumdulillah!

So far, we have learnt 13 new words that appear in the Quran 4,479 times. We have also learnt how to form plurals. Alhumdulillah!

Workshop

The quiz questions and the exercises are provided to further your understanding. Don't worry if you can't answer all of the questions in the quiz. Try your best to answer as many as you can. See Appendix A to check your answers.

Quiz 2

1. What are the benefits of reciting Ta'awuz?
2. What are the different names for Surah Fatihah?
3. How do we form plurals in Arabic Grammar?
4. Form the plurals for the following words:

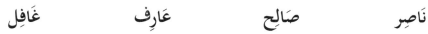

غَافِل   عَارِف   صَالِح   نَاصِر

5. What are the important principles when dealing with our loved ones?

Exercise

Insert the CD-ROM accompanying this book into your drive. Select the appropriate folder and do the quiz for this Hour. You may choose to do the quiz as many times as you like in order to further your understanding.

Hour **3**

At the end of this Hour you will have learnt

19 New Words	**Our Aim 200 Words**
5,958 Total Words	**Our Aim 25,000 Words**

Surah Fatihah Verses 4-5 and Possessive Adjectives

In Hour 2, we started with Surah Fatihah and studied verses 1-3. We also learnt how to form plurals, and at the end of the Lesson I gave you some advice on being kind and showing mercy to others. Remember, kindness is not only beautiful when you *talk* about it; kindness is truly beautiful when you *do* it.

In this Hour, we will learn 6 new words which appear in the Quran 1,479 times. We will extend our vocabulary by learning words from Surah Fatihah verses 4-5 and in the grammar section we will study Possessive Adjectives. At the end of this Hour you will have learned a total of 19 words which appear in the Quran almost 6,000 times.

The highlights of this Hour include

- Surah Fatihah, verses 4-5
- Grammar – Possessive Adjectives
- Advice and guidance

Surah Fatihah Verse 4

In this verse, Allah speaks about His sovereignty on the day of Resurrection.

Table 3.1.1

الدِّين	يَوْم	مَالِك
(of) judgment	*(of) the day*	*Master*

There are three new words in this verse.

Table 3.1.2

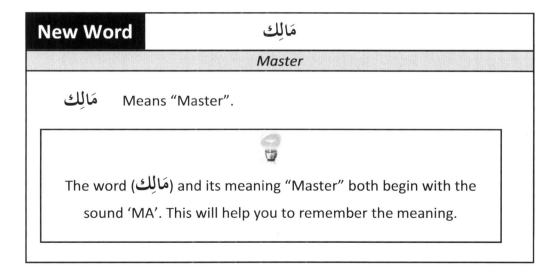

New Word	مَالِك
Master	

مَالِك   Means "Master".

The word (مَالِك) and its meaning "Master" both begin with the sound 'MA'. This will help you to remember the meaning.

Table 3.1.3

New Word	يَوْم
	day

يَوْم   Means "day".

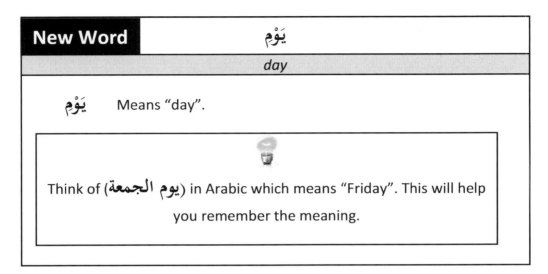

Think of (يوم الجمعة) in Arabic which means "Friday". This will help you remember the meaning.

Table 3.1.4

New Word	الدِّين
	judgment

الدِّين   Means "way of life", "religion", "judgment".

This word has three meanings. In this verse, Allah is referring to the day of Judgment.

In another verse, (Quran 3:19), Allah says the only way of life acceptable to Him is Islam. So in that context the word means "way of life".

Lessons derived from this verse

Who is the wise man?

The Day of Judgment is *the* most important day, and we have been sent into this world to prepare ourselves for that Day. In the Hadith, the Prophet (Peace be upon him) said: "The wise person is he who reckons himself and works for (his life) after death." (Musnad Ahmed, Ibn Majah, Hakim.) So begin now to prepare yourself for death before it's too late.

Does this verse mean Allah is not the Master of this world, He is only the Master of the Day of Judgment?

No. When Allah specifies that He is the Master of the Day of Judgment, it does not mean He is not the Master of this world. The reason Allah mentions the Day of Judgment is because, in this world, people claim ownership of certain things: their car, their house, and so forth. However, on the Day of Judgement, Allah says that He alone will claim ownership of everything.

Power of pondering over this verse

When you offer your salah and recite this verse, imagine you are standing in front of Allah on the Day of Judgment and accountable for all your deeds. Imagine if you do this for only one day. That means you will recite this a minimum of 17 times in your salah, and all 17 times, if you imagine that you are standing in front of your Creator on the Day of Judgment and you are accountable for all your deeds, you will begin to realize the impact this will have on your life. This concentration during your salah will surely make you more obedient to Allah and so be ruled by His commands.

Surah Fatihah Verse 5

In this verse Allah speaks about the importance of worshipping Him alone and asking for His help only and no one else.

Table 3.2.1

نَسْتَعِينُ	وَإِيَّاكَ	نَعْبُدُ	إِيَّاكَ
we ask for help	and you alone	we worship	You alone

There are three new words in this verse.

Table 3.2.2

New Word	إِيَّاكَ
	You alone
إِيَّا	Means "alone".
كَ	Means "You". This is a Possessive Adjective letter used in Arabic. We are explaining Possessives in the grammar section of this Hour.

Table 3.2.3

New Word	نَعْبُدُ
we worship	
نَ	Means "we". See Table 1.2.
عْبُدُ	Means "worship". It comes from the Arabic root word (عبد) which means "servant".
	Think of (عبادة) in Arabic which means "worship". Think of the names (عَبْدُ اللّه) and (عَبْدُ الرَّحْمَن) which mean "servant of Allah", and "servant of the Most Gracious". This will help you remember this word.

Table 3.2.4

وَإِيَّاكَ	
and you alone	
وَ	Means "and". This letter in Arabic is mainly used for conjunction.
إِيَّا	Means "alone". See Table 3.2.2.
كَ	Means "you". See Table 3.2.2.

Table 3.2.5

New Word	نَسْتَعِينُ
	we ask for help

نَ	Means "we". See Table 1.2.
سْتَعِينُ	Means "asking for help".

⚠️

Do not seek help from anyone except Allah

Lessons derived from this verse

What is worship?

Worship means following the commands of Allah with the utmost love, humility and fear. Whatever Allah commands you to do is worship and whatever He tells you to abstain from, abstention from it is worship of Allah.

We must worship Allah not only in our salah, but also outside salah. For example, being good and kind to your spouse, being kind to your parents and your neighbours. All these are acts of worship.

There are two conditions for any act of yours to be true worship:

1. You must have sincerity, i.e. *Ikhlas.*
2. You must perform that act the way the Prophet Muhammad (Peace be upon him) performed it.

If you follow the above two rules, any act of yours is in fact an act of worship.

Does this mean we cannot ask a human being to help us?

The rule is that if a human being has the ability to help you, you can ask him to help, but if he does not have that ability, then you cannot.

For example, you are not allowed go to a grave and ask a dead person to do something for you because he is not able to help you. Similarly, believing that a saint or an imam living on the other side of the world can resolve your problems is not allowed because he is not there with you to help you. Therefore asking a human being to help you when he cannot physically help you is not allowed. So, you can ask for help but only if that human being is capable of providing exactly that help.

Talismans and Amulets

Do not wear talismans and amulets. All these are considered to be seeking help from someone or something other than Allah. When a person seeks help from a source other than Allah then they are committing shirk, which is worshipping another entity that shares in the names and attributes of Allah. Shirk is the biggest sin in Islam. So if you are wearing talismans or amulets i.e. *Ta'aweez*, then stop wearing them. The Prophet (Peace be upon him) said: "Talismans and amulets are forms of shirk." (Ibn Majah).

Three points to remember when asking help from others

When we ask for help from others in our everyday life, remember three things. Firstly, only ask for help if there is a need. Secondly, the person helping you must be happy to help you, and thirdly there should be no sin involved in whatever you need help with.

Practice what you have learnt

Now practice what you have learnt so far. "Practice creates the master." (Miguel Ruiz).

مَالِك	يَوْم	الدِّين
Master	(of) the day	(of) judgment

إِيَّاكَ	نَعْبُدُ	وَإِيَّاكَ	نَسْتَعِينُ
You alone	we worship	and you alone	we ask for help

Don't forget to ponder over the meaning in your next salah. Pause after every verse, imagine the response from Allah, and try to build humility and love for Allah in your salah.

Revision of vocabulary

Meaning	Arabic Word
Master	مَالِك
day	يَوْم
way of life, judgment	الدِّين
You alone	إِيَّاكَ
we worship	نَعْبُدُ
we ask for help	نَسْتَعِينُ

Phew! Alhumdulillah!

So far, we have learnt verses four and five from Surah Fatihah. Without Allah's help it would not have been possible, so let us say Alhumdulillah!

Take a Break!

In the next section, you are going to learn Arabic Grammar.

Grammar – Possessive Adjectives

Possessive Adjectives are suffixes (added at the end of words). They are not separated as they are in English. For example, in English we say "listen to me" whereas in Arabic, the word 'me' is attached to the word 'listen'. The next Table shows examples of common possessive adjectives. These are masculine. We will study feminine possessives in the Hour 4 grammar lesson. We have used the Arabic word (كِتَاب) meaning 'book' for these examples.

Table 3.3.1

	Example	Meaning	Possessive Adjective
his book	كِتَابُهُ	His	هُ __
their book	كِتَابُهُمْ	Their	هُمْ __
your book	كِتَابُكَ	Your (S)	كَ __
your book	كِتَابُكُمْ	Your (P)	كُمْ __
my book	كِتَابِيْ	My	ي __
our book	كِتَابُنَا	Our	نَا __

Abbreviations: (S) means 'Singular', (P) means 'Plural'.

Don't worry if you cannot memorize them all. Study the pattern and the examples given. When you have done the exercise for this Hour, with the help of Allah you will master this grammar lesson.

Advice and Guidance from the Author

Did you know we only use 5% of our brain?

Did you know that? The other 95% is inactive. You often hear the phrase "use it or lose it". So either we use that 95% or we lose it. What better use can we make of the brain than learning the language in which the Last and the Final Revelation was revealed? If 95% of our brain is empty, why not use it to learn the Quran?

Are you doing this course with sincerity?

We must have sincerity as we learn Arabic because it is an act of worship. We must not do this course for fame, money, or to show off. We must do it for the sake of Allah and to please Him. Remember, our goal is to understand the Quran, implement it in our lives, and spread the words of Allah.

Many people ask how we can attain sincerity. The answer is that initially our intention must be to become closer to Allah, and as we progress through the course, we must constantly ask Allah to give us sincerity. That you are asking Allah to give you sincerity is a sign that In Sha Allah you have sincerity in you.

You can do the same for other acts of worship, such as patience, gratitude, and so forth. If a calamity befalls you and you desire greater patience, ask Allah to grant you more of this grace, and doing this is a sign, In Sha Allah, that you have patience within you.

Don't forget the two conditions that can make any act of yours into worship: sincerity and following the footsteps of Prophet Muhammad (Peace be upon him).

Summary

In this Hour, you have learnt Verses 4-5 from Surah Fatihah. By now, you will have started to ponder the verses which we have studied. You will have begun to feel an increase in your faith, and a better connection to Allah. As we continue studying these verses, let us also ponder the response from Allah.

We have put our brains to work so we may improve our understanding of the Quran. And there is no better purpose for our brains than to understand the message of Allah. So: stay focused, be committed, and Allah will make this course easy for you.

We have now learnt 19 words that appear in the Quran 5,958 times. We have also learnt the grammar and use of possessive adjectives. Alhumdulillah!

Workshop

The quiz questions and the exercises are provided to further your understanding. Don't worry if you can't answer all of the questions in the quiz. Try your best to answer as many as you can. See Appendix A to check your answers.

Quiz 3

1. Who is a wise person according to the Hadith of the Prophet Muhammad (Peace be upon him)?
2. What does worship mean?
3. What are the conditions of worship?
4. Is it allowed to wear talismans and amulets?
5. Form possessive adjectives for the following words.

طَعَام   صَلٰوة   قَلَم   رَبّ

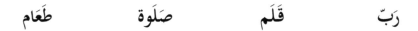

Exercise

Insert the CD-ROM accompanying this book into your drive. Select the appropriate folder and do the quiz for this Hour. You may do the quiz as many times as you like in order to further your understanding.

3

Hour **4**

At the end of this Hour you will have learnt

25 New Words   Our Aim 200 Words

9,086 Total Words   Our Aim 25,000 Words

Surah Fatihah Verses 6-7 and the Feminine Gender

In Hour 3, we studied Verses 4-5 from Surah Fatihah and we are now coming to the end of this Surah. We studied possessive adjectives in the grammar section of Hour 3. We also said we should pause between verses in our salah and imagine Allah's response to us.

In this Hour, we will learn 6 new words which appear in the Quran 3,128 times. We will extend our vocabulary by learning words from Surah Fatihah verses 6-7, and we will study grammar relating to the feminine gender. By the end of this Hour you will have learnt 25 words which appear in the Quran 9,086 times. Let's make Dua to Allah and approach this Hour in the firm belief that Allah will make it easy for us.

The highlights of this Hour include

- Surah Fatihah verses 6-7
- Grammar – related to the Feminine Gender
- Advice and guidance

Surah Fatihah Verse 6

In this verse, we are making Dua to Allah to guide us to the straight path.

Table 4.1.1

الْمُسْتَقِيمَ	الصِّرَاطَ	اهْدِنَا
the straight	*(to) the path*	*Guide us*

There are three new words in this verse.

Table 4.1.2

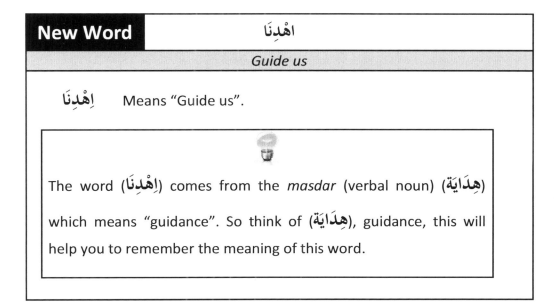

New Word	اهْدِنَا
Guide us	

اِهْدِنَا   Means "Guide us".

The word (اِهْدِنَا) comes from the *masdar* (verbal noun) (هِدَايَة) which means "guidance". So think of (هِدَايَة), guidance, this will help you to remember the meaning of this word.

> **New Term**
>
> A *masdar* is a verbal noun, and it holds the meaning of 'the act of doing that verb'. In English the form is verb + ing, for example, writing, reading, praying and so on.

Table 4.1.3

New Word	الصِّرَاطَ
the path	

صِّرَاطَ   Means "path".

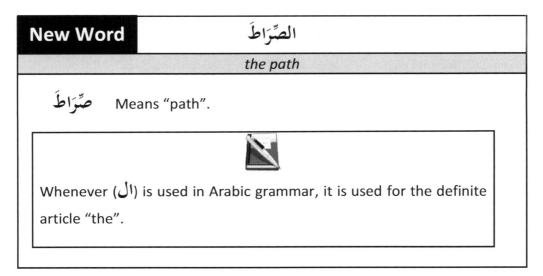

Whenever (ال) is used in Arabic grammar, it is used for the definite article "the".

Table 4.1.4

New Word	الْمُسْتَقِيمَ
the straight	

مُسْتَقِيمَ   Means "straight".

Lessons derived from this verse

1. This is the best way to seek help, by first praising the One from whom help is being sought, and then asking for His aid for one's self.

2. When we are asking for guidance in our salah, we are not asking for it only during our salah, but also for whatever we do after our salah.

3. As Muslims we are already guided, so why are we asking Allah to guide us? Guidance is of two types. The first is the guidance of Islam, and the second is guidance of firmness and continuity in performing the deeds that help one remain on the path of faith.

4. "The straight path" firstly means the path of Allah and His Prophet Muhammad (Peace be upon him). The Quran and the Sunnah are the sources of guidance. So if we don't make an honest effort to try to understand them then we are not sincere.

   Imagine a student in class who wants to pass his exams, but he does not study the resources and the material for his exam. Would you say he is sincerely trying? How will he pass his exams?

   So when we ask Allah to guide us on the path of the Quran and the Sunnah, we must take time out to understand them so that we *can* be guided.

5. "The straight path" secondly means the path of worshipping Allah. Allah says in the Quran:

وَأَنِ اعْبُدُونِي هَذَا صِرَاطٌ مُسْتَقِيمٌ

"And that you must worship Me (because) this is the straight path." (Quran: 36:61)

Surah Fatihah Verse 7a

In this verse, Allah describes the characteristics of the path of the people who are accepting guidance.

Table 4.2.1

صِرَاطَ	الَّذِينَ	أَنْعَمْتَ	عَلَيْهِمْ
(The) path	(of) those	You (have) bestowed favours	on them

There are two new words in this verse.

Table 4.2.2

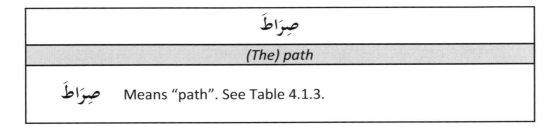

صِرَاطَ
(The) path
صِرَاطَ   Means "path". See Table 4.1.3.

Table 4.2.3

New Word	الَّذِينَ
	(of) those
الَّذِينَ	Means "those". This word appears in the Quran 1,080 times. It is a relative noun and we will cover these in the Hour 8 grammar lesson.

Table 4.2.4

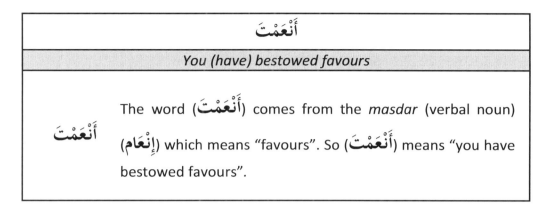

أَنْعَمْتَ
You (have) bestowed favours
أَنْعَمْتَ   The word (أَنْعَمْتَ) comes from the *masdar* (verbal noun) (إِنْعَام) which means "favours". So (أَنْعَمْتَ) means "you have bestowed favours".

Table 4.2.5

New Word	عَلَيْهِمْ
	on them
عَلَى	Means "on". This word is used over 1000 times in the Quran. See the Hour 6 grammar lesson on Prepositions.
هِمْ	Means "them".

Lessons derived from this verse

1. This verse is an explanation of the previous verse. It gives a definition of the straight path. The straight path is the path of those people upon whom Allah has bestowed His favours. It is the path of prophets of Allah, the truly faithful, martyrs and righteous people.

2. What was the path of the prophets? Their path was to act upon the message of Allah, to purify themselves, spread the message and demonstrate it in their own lives.

Surah Fatihah Verse 7b

In this verse, Allah describes the characteristics of the path of the people who are not receiving or accepting guidance.

Table 4.3.1

الضَّالِّينَ	وَلاَ	عَلَيْهِمْ	الْمَغْضُوبِ	غَيْرِ
(of) those who go astray	and not	on them	(of) those who earned (Your) wrath	not

There are three new words in this verse.

Table 4.3.2

New Word	غَيْرِ
	not
غَيْرِ	Means "not", "other than". This word comes in the Quran 147 times.

New Word	الْمَغْضُوبِ
	(of) those who earned (Your) wrath
مَغْضُوب	Means "(of) those who earned (Your) wrath" It comes from the *masdar, (verbal noun)* (غَضَب) which means "anger and wrath".

54

Allah is referring to the Jews here. However (مَغْضُوْب), are those people who know the truth, yet they turn away from it and disobey Allah.

Table 4.3.3

عَلَيْهِمْ
on them
عَلَيْهِمْ   Means "on them". See Table 4.2.5.

Table 4.3.4

New Word	وَلاَ
	and not
وَ	Means "and".
لاَ	Means "not".

New Word	الضَّآلِّينَ
	(of) those who go astray
ضَآلِّينَ	Means "(of) those who go astray". This is a plural form

of (ضَالّ) and it comes from the *masdar (verbal noun)*

(ضَلَال) which means "going astray", "straying from the right path", "error".

Allah is referring to the Christians here. However, (ضَآلِّينَ) are those people who don't know the truth, and have gone astray.

Lessons derived from this verse

Do not follow culture if it goes against the Quran and the Hadith

Sometimes we know the truth, but we don't follow it. One of the main reasons for this is because of our family culture. We don't want to go against what our forefathers used to do, even if they were in error. For example, to say, "My forefathers used to act this or that way: how can they be wrong, how can I go against them?" We need to be firm and strict in following Allah and His Messenger (Peace be upon him) even if we have to go against family tradition or culture.

The kind of attitude we must have, is that I don't mind going against my culture, but I do mind going against Allah and his Prophet Muhammad (Peace be upon him).

Practice what you have learned

الْمُسْتَقِيمَ	الصِّرَاطَ	اهْدِنَا
the straight	(to) the path	Guide us

عَلَيْهِمْ	أَنْعَمْتَ	الَّذِينَ	صِرَاطَ
on them	You (have) bestowed favours	(of) those	(The) path

الضَّآلِّينَ	وَلاَ	عَلَيْهِمْ	الْمَغْضُوبِ	غَيْرِ
those who go astray	and nor of	on them	(of) those who earned (Your) wrath	not

Don't forget to ponder over the meaning in your next salah. Pause after every verse, imagine the response from Allah, and try to build humility and love for Allah in your salah.

Revision of Vocabulary words studied

Meaning	Arabic Word
guide us	اهْدِنَا
path	صِرَاطَ
straight	مُسْتَقِيمَ
those	الَّذِينَ
you bestowed favours	أَنْعَمْتَ
not	غَيْرِ
those who earned wrath	مَغْضُوبِ
those who go astray	ضَآلِّينَ

Phew! Alhumdulillah!

We have completed Surah Fatihah. Imagine, in just four Hours you have understood not only the translation of Surah Fatihah, you have understood the message given by Allah to you in this beautiful Surah. Until now, you have been reciting it without understanding it. Now you understand it, you are able to ponder over it, implement it and hopefully spread it. Without Allah's help, it would not have been possible, so let's say Alhumdulillah!

Take a Break!

In the next section, you are going to learn Arabic Grammar.

Grammar – Feminine Gender

Pronouns

Pronouns take the place of a noun and function as the subject of a sentence. In Hour 1's grammar lesson, we studied masculine gender pronouns. In this lesson, we will study pronouns, the methods for forming plurals, and possessive adjectives specifically related to the feminine gender. The reason we are treating feminine gender pronouns separately is so you do not mix them up with the masculine ones. By now, you should already have practiced and so be familiar with the grammar specific to masculine gender. You will notice that there is only a slight change in the words relating to the feminine gender.

Table 4.4.1

When to use	Meaning	Pronouns
Distant from the speaker (in space or time)	She	هِيَ
Distant from the speaker (in space or time)	They	هُنَّ
Close to the speaker	You	أَنْتِ
Close to the speaker	You All	أَنْتُنَّ

Study the above table a few times, and you will notice that there are only a few changes of letters compared with the masculine pronouns.

Plurals

In Hour 2's grammar lesson, we showed you how to make plurals. We said that simply by adding the letters (و ن) or (ي ن) we can form plurals. However, forming plurals for the feminine gender is different. Instead of adding the letters (و ن) or (ي ن) the rule is to add (ات) at the end. Here are some examples to help you practice this rule.

Table 4.4.2

Plural	Singular
مُسْلِمَاتٌ	مُسْلِم
مُؤْمِنَاتٌ	مُؤْمِن
صَادِقَاتٌ	صَادِق
ذَاكِرَاتٌ	ذَاكِر
صَابِرَاتٌ	صَابِر

That's how simple it is to form plurals for the feminine gender. Don't worry about the meanings of these words for now, you just need to understand the pattern of plural formation.

Possessive Adjectives

In Hour 3, you learnt how to use possessive adjectives. In this section, we will study possessive adjective formation for the feminine gender. To recap, we said that possessive adjectives are suffixes that are attached to the verb. Here are possessive adjectives in the feminine gender.

Table 4.4.3

	Example	Meaning	Possessive Adjectives
her book	كِتَابُهَا	Her	هَا ــ

their book	كِتَابُهُنَّ	Their	ـ هُنَّ
your book	كِتَابُكِ	Your (S)	ـ كِ
your book	كِتَابُكُنَّ	Your (P)	ـ كُنَّ

Abbreviations: (S) means 'Singular', (P) means 'Plural'.

Don't worry too much for now. I know this grammar lesson has been a bit longer than usual, but I'm sure you have enjoyed it. Once you do the exercise and practice a few times you will master it just as you mastered masculine-related grammar earlier in the course. Remember, Allah's help is always with you.

Advice and guidance from the author

Which group do you belong to?

In this Surah, Allah mentions three groups of people. And every human being belongs to one of these three groups. The first group is the group that Allah has bestowed His favours upon, the second group consists of those that have earned Allah's wrath, and the third group are those who have gone astray.

Every time you say Surah Fatihah in your salah, ask yourself to which group you belong. We need to ask Allah to place us amongst the group whom He has favoured. Only when we are aware of the danger of the other two groups will we be more vigilant.

Are you as good a Husband, Father, and Son as Muhammad (Peace be upon him)?
Are you as good a Wife, Mother and Daughter as Khadijah (R.A.)?

The group favoured by Allah is the group of the Prophets of Allah, the truly faithful, the martyrs, and righteous people. We have a very important question to ask ourselves: What does it mean to follow the Prophets of Allah, loving them and following in their footsteps?

Unfortunately, most of us have only made an imam of Muhammad (Peace be upon him) and limited him in the masjid, and in our salah. Do we offer salah the same way he offered? Do we give khutbah the same way he gave khutbah? The minute we step outside of masjid, we do not take his teachings with us, instead we leave him in the masjid.

As a result, what happens is that our imitation of Muhammad (Peace be upon him) becomes very physical. Do we look like the way Muhammad (Peace be upon him) looked? Do not misunderstand me, it is very important to imitate his physical appearance, but his physical appearance reflected his moral character, and for us to focus on his appearance rather than his character is wicked and despicable.

How much effort does it take to grow a beard? Just don't shave, that's all. But do you limit your practice of the teachings of Muhammad (Peace be upon him) to just growing your beard? Thus we have only made an imam out of Muhammad (Peace be upon him). The minute we step out of the masjid into our business dealings, we do not deal as he taught. As husbands, when we go home we are not the same husbands as Muhammad (Peace be upon him). As fathers, as sons, as brothers, as employers, as employees, we forget that part of his teaching is to personify his teachings wherever you are.

So let us follow Muhammad (Peace be upon him) not only in his physical appearance but also in his moral values.

Summary

In just four Hours, we have completed Surah Fatihah, the first Surah of the Quran. Allah rightly says in the Quran, "And we have indeed made the

Qur'an easy to understand and remember." Let's start to ponder over what we have learnt so far in our salah, and let's follow the paths of the prophets according to the Quran and Hadith.

We have also studied grammar related to the feminine gender. You should by now be familiar with pronouns, plurals, and possessive adjectives for both genders.

So far, we have learnt 25 words that appear in the Quran 9,086 times. Alhumdulillah!

There are so many lessons and messages from Allah given to us in Surah Fatihah, that's why Shaitan does not want us to understand it.
SO BEWARE OF Shaitan
HE IS AN IMPLACABLE ENEMY TO ALL

4

Workshop

The quiz questions and the exercises are provided to further your understanding. Don't worry if you can't answer all of the questions in the quiz. Try your best to answer as many as you can. See Appendix A to check your answers.

Quiz 4

1. What is a *masdar*?
2. When we are already guided and offering Salah, why are we asking Allah to guide us?
3. What are the three groups mentioned in this Surah?
4. Who are the people upon whom Allah has bestowed his favour?
5. Make the feminine plural for each of the following words.

مُشْرِك   مُتَصَدِّق   خَاشِع   قَانِت

6. Make possessive adjectives for each of the following words.

طَعَام   صَلٰوة   قَلَم   رَب

Exercise

Insert the CD-ROM accompanying this book in your drive. Select the appropriate folder and do the quiz for this Hour. You may do the quiz as many times as you like in order to further your understanding.

PART III

Last 10 Surahs of the Quran

Hour

Hour 5

At the end of this Hour you will have learnt

31 New Words	**Our Aim 200 Words**
9,673 Total Words	**Our Aim 25,000 Words**

Surah Nas and Prepositions

Now that you've completed Surah Fatihah, which you recite daily in your salah, we will study other Surahs which we recite frequently in our salah. The last ten Surahs of the Quran are those recited more often than the other Surahs. We will begin with Surah Nas. As you learn the new vocabulary from this Surah, you are building a range of words from the Quran which are enriching your knowledge of the Quran. Here's a short review of this Surah:

1. This is the last Surah in the Quran. It is a Surah for protection from Shaitan, and it informs us that we need to fight him constantly while we live.

2. We must protect ourselves from Shaitan, since he does not leave anyone. He didn't even leave the Prophet Adam (Peace be upon him) alone so how can we hope to be immune?

3. Shaitan's goal is to mislead human beings and beautify evil deeds. No wonder alcohol bottles and cigarette packets are beautifully presented in stores.
4. This Surah is a protection from black magic. There is no better cure for black magic than this Surah and the one before it, Surah Falaq. Both of these Surahs will protect us from black magic.
5. Prophet Muhammad (Peace be upon him) would recite Surah Nas, Surah Falaq and Surah Ikhlas, blow on his hands and then wipe his hands over his body before going to bed at night.

Let's make Dua to Allah and approach this Hour in the firm belief that Allah will make this Hour easy for us.

Beware of Shaitan - He is our **WORST** enemy

The highlights of this hour include:

- Surah Nas verses 1-6
- Grammar – Prepositions
- Advice and guidance

Surah Nas Verse 1

Table 5.1.1

النَّاسِ	بِرَبِّ	أَعُوذُ	قُلْ
(of) mankind	*in the Lord*	*"I seek refuge*	*Say,*

This verse contains four words. Only two words are new.

Table 5.1.2

New Word	قُلْ
Say,	
قُلْ	Means "say". This word is much used in the Quran.

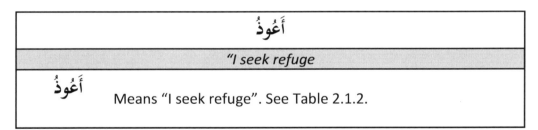

The word (قُلْ) appears in the Quran hundreds of times. The Quran is a book of dialogue between the disbelievers and the believers. In many places, Allah says the disbelievers say *this*, and O'Muhammad (Peace be upon him) tells them *that*.

Table 5.1.3

أَعُوذُ
"I seek refuge
أَعُوذُ   Means "I seek refuge". See Table 2.1.2.

Table 5.1.4

بِرَبِّ
in the Lord
بِ   Means "in". Prepositions are coming up in Hours 5 and 6.
رَبِّ   Means "Lord". See Table 2.3.4.

Table 5.1.5

New Word	النَّاسِ
	Mankind
نَاسٍ	Means "mankind", "people". An easy way to remember this word is to think of the word (إِنْسَان) which means "human being", "man".

Lessons derived from this verse

Why is Allah asking us to say this out loud?

We need to realise that we are weak and we are in great need of Allah's help. When we accept this, we should say and feel that only Allah the most powerful can help.

The reason that Allah is commanding us to say it is that when we say it aloud, it has more effect on us. That's why Allah is commanding us to speak it out loud.

Also, voicing it aloud increases your obedience to Allah. After all, how can you disobey Him when you say such words out loud? That's another reason why Allah is commanding us to declare these words out loud.

Surah Nas Verses 2 and 3

In these verses, Allah describes Himself as King of all Kings, and the God of mankind.

Table 5.2.1 and Table 5.3.1

النَّاسِ	إِلٰهِ	النَّاسِ	مَلِكِ
(of) mankind	(the) God [3]	(of) mankind	(The) King [2]

There are two new words in this verse.

Table 5.2.2

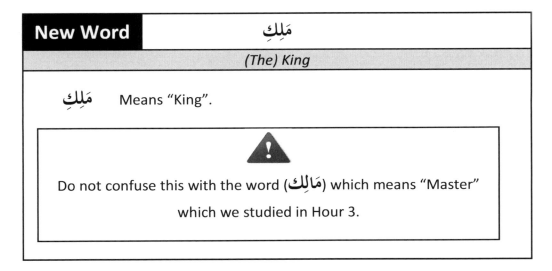

New Word	مَلِكِ
	(The) King

مَلِكِ   Means "King".

Do not confuse this with the word (مَالِك) which means "Master" which we studied in Hour 3.

Table 5.2.3

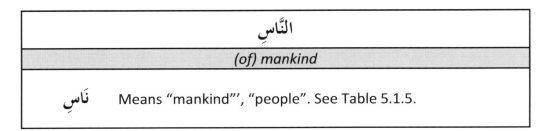

النَّاسِ
(of) mankind

نَاسِ   Means "mankind"', "people". See Table 5.1.5.

Table 5.3.2

New Word	إِلَهِ
	(the) God
إِلَهِ	Means "God", "One who deserves to be worshipped". That is Allah.

Table 5.3.3

النَّاسِ
(of) mankind
نَاسٍ — Means "mankind", "people". See Table 5.1.5.

Lessons derived from these verses

Obey Allah if we really believe He is the King of all Kings

As Allah is the King and God of mankind, we should follow Him and obey Him. If we don't follow and obey Him, then we don't actually believe in our hearts that this is so.

Suppose your country has a King: you would obey and follow everything he says, wouldn't you? So, as Allah is the King of all Kings, and the God of all mankind, then if we don't obey and follow Him, we really don't believe in our hearts that Allah is the King of mankind.

Surah Nas Verse 4

After a beautiful introduction of Allah made by Allah himself, what do you think the next part is going to be? Let's study the next verse and see.

Table 5.4.1

الْخَنَّاسِ	الْوَسْوَاسِ	شَرِّ	مِنْ
the one who withdraws after whispering	(of) the whisperer,	(the) evil	From

There are three new words in this verse.

Table 5.4.2

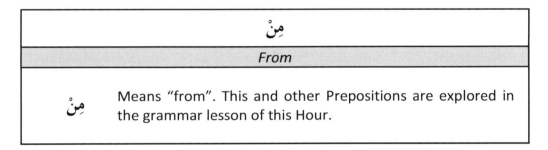

مِنْ	
From	
مِنْ	Means "from". This and other Prepositions are explored in the grammar lesson of this Hour.

Table 5.4.3

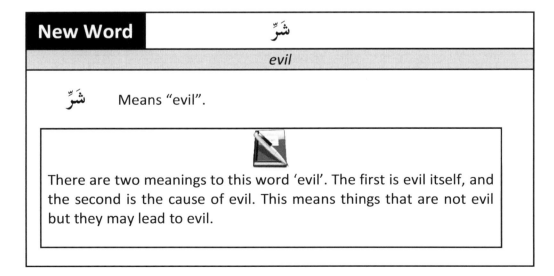

New Word	شَرِّ
evil	
شَرِّ	Means "evil".

There are two meanings to this word 'evil'. The first is evil itself, and the second is the cause of evil. This means things that are not evil but they may lead to evil.

72

Table 5.4.4

New Word	الْوَسْوَاسِ
	(of) the whisperer
وَسْوَاسِ	Means "whisperer", "one who puts evil thoughts in the heart". Here it refers to Shaitan.

Table 5.4.5

New Word	الْخَنَّاسِ
	the one who withdraws after whispering
خَنَّاسِ	Means "the one who withdraws after whispering".

Lessons derived from this verse

Shaitan will withdraw from you, every time you remember Allah

Shaitan is either whispering or he is withdrawing after whispering. When you forget Allah he will whisper, but the moment you remember Allah again, he will withdraw. So let us remember Allah in every action of ours. This does not mean that voicing the remembrance of Allah is sufficient, but also whatever actions we perform as husbands, wives, sons, daughters, employees, employers and so on, must be according to the Quran and the Sunnah. This is the real meaning of remembering Allah. If we are remembering Allah with our voices, but our heart and actions are not following the Quran and the Sunnah, then this is nothing but lip service and Allah is not interested in lip service.

Surah Nas Verse 5

In the previous verse, Allah warned us against the whisper of Shaitan. In this verse, Allah continues to warn us of the whispers of Shaitan so that we can protect ourselves.

Table 5.5.1

الَّذِي	يُوَسْوِسُ	فِي	صُدُورِ	النَّاسِ
Who	whispers	into	(the) chests	(of) mankind

There are two new words in this verse.

Table 5.5.2

الَّذِي
Who
الَّذِي   Means "who". This is a relative noun and we will cover this topic in detail in Hour 8.

Table 5.5.3

يُوَسْوِسُ
(he) whispers
يُوَسْوِسُ   Means "whispers". It comes from the same root word as (وَسْوَاس) which means "the one who whispers". This is in the present tense form, meaning "he whispers".

Table 5.5.4

New Word	فِي
	into
فِي	Means "in" or "into". This preposition appears in the Quran many times, and we will learn Prepositions in Hours 5 and 6.

Table 5.5.5

New Word	صُدُورِ
	(the) chests
صُدُورِ	Means "chests". The word (صُدُورِ) is a plural form for (صَدْرٌ) which means "chest".

Table 5.5.6

النَّاسِ
mankind
نَاسِ   Means "mankind", "people". See Table 5.1.5.

Lessons derived from this verse

Where does Shaitan attack us?

Shaitan tries to attack our hearts within our chests, and Allah has given us a remedy for this. The Quran is the cure for what is wrong in the chest.

Shaitan tries to attack, and no one can escape him, so what can we do?

The remedy is the **QURAN**
READING, UNDERSTANDING, IMPLEMENTING

Surah Nas Verse 6

In this verse, Allah is describing the two categories of Shaitan. The Jinn kind and human kind are the two types of Shaitan.

Table 5.6.1

وَالنَّاسِ	الْجِنَّةِ	مِنَ
and mankind	*among Jinns*	*From*

There is only one new word in this verse, the other two words are repeated words.

Table 5.6.2

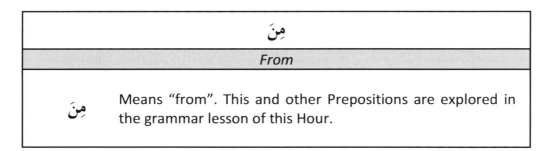

مِنَ
From
مِنَ   Means "from". This and other Prepositions are explored in the grammar lesson of this Hour.

Table 5.6.3

New Word	الْجِنَّةِ
	(among) Jinns

جِنَّةٍ   Means "Jinns". This is a plural form of (جِنِّيٌّ) which means "Jinn".

The word (جِنَّةٍ) and its meaning "Jinns" both words start with the sound "Jin". This will help you to remember the meaning of this word.

Table 5.6.4

وَالنَّاسِ
and mankind

وَ	Means "and". It is used often for conjunction.
نَاسِ	Means "mankind", "people". See Table 5.1.5.

Lessons derived from this verse

1. Allah is warning us to beware of Shaitan, not only Jinn Shaitans, but He is also warning us about the human Shaitans.
2. Choose to be in good company, and avoid bad company.
3. Only join bad company if you are able to encourage and enjoin what is good and forbid what is wrong. If you can do this, then go and stop the evil. If you cannot do this, then stay away from bad company.

Stay away from bad company,
UNDERLINE__UNLESS__ you are able to encourage what is good and forbid what is wrong.

Practice what you have learned

النَّاسِ	بِرَبِّ	أَعُوذُ	قُلْ
(of) mankind,	in the Lord	"I seek refuge	Say,

النَّاسِ	إِلـٰهِ	النَّاسِ	مَلِكِ
(of) mankind	(the) God	(of) mankind	(The) King

الْخَنَّاسِ	الْوَسْوَاسِ	شَرِّ	مِنْ
the one who withdraws after whispering	(of) the whisperer,	(the) evil	From

78

الَّذِي	يُوَسْوِسُ	فِي	صُدُورِ	النَّاسِ
Who	(he) whispers	into	(the) chests	(of) mankind

مِنَ	الْجِنَّةِ	وَالنَّاسِ
From	(among) Jinns	and mankind.

Don't forget to ponder over the meaning in your next salah. Pause after every verse, imagine the response from Allah, and try to build humility and love for Allah in your salah.

Revision of vocabulary words studied

Meaning	Arabic Word
say	قُلْ
mankind	نَاسِ
evil	شَرِّ
whisperer	وَسْوَاسِ
one who withdraws after whispering	خَنَّاسِ
he whispers	يُوَسْوِسُ
chests	صُدُورِ
Jinns	جِنَّةِ

Phew! Alhumdulillah!

We have completed Surah Nas. Without Allah's help, it would not have been possible, so let's say Alhumdulillah! Let's start to ponder over what we have learned so far in our salah, and let's use the Quran as the cure for what is in our hearts. Remember to read this surah before going to sleep at night, understand it, ponder over it, implement it and spread it.

Take a Break!

Refreshed? Good.

In the next section, you are going to learn Arabic Grammar.

Grammar – prepositions

Prepositions like 'from', 'to', and 'with' function in Arabic in exactly the same way as they do in English. There are four shown below in Table 5.7.1. Learn and master them, as they occur frequently in the Quran.

Table 5.7.1

Translation	Example	Meaning	Prepositions
For him	لَهُ		
For you	لَكَ	For / To	لَ, لِ
For me	لِيْ		
From / Against him	مِنْهُ		
From / Against you	مِنْكَ	From / Against	مِنْ
From / Against me	مِنِّيْ		
With / About them	عَنْهُمْ		
With / About you	عَنْكُمْ	With / About	عَنْ
With / About us	عَنَّا		
With them	مَعَهُمْ		
With you	مَعَكُمْ	With	مَعَ
With me	مَعِيْ		

Study the prepositions, along with their examples, and see if you can come up with a few examples of your own.

Advice and guidance from the author

Have you ever wondered how powerful thoughts are?

Shaitan will not stop tempting you until you leave this world. He will follow you and try to mislead you until your last breath. His wickedness can be seen in his communication with those who he leads astray, and on the Day of Judgment he will say to them, "Allah's promise was truth, I too promised you but I broke my promise, I only invited you, it was you who accepted my invitation." (Quran 14:22) So he will not leave you until your death.

The thoughts that come in to your heart are very powerful, because your thoughts determine your destiny. Here is what they say about thoughts:

Watch your thoughts; they become your words,
Watch your words; they become your actions,
Watch your actions; they become your habits,
Watch your habits; they become your character,
Watch your character, which becomes your destiny.

So we need to watch out for our thoughts, because they determine our destiny. However, since we don't have any control over our thoughts, and no one can escape the thoughts that come into their hearts, what can we do?

We do not have control over what kind of thoughts come into our mind, but we definitely have control over what kinds of thoughts we choose to dwell on.

Sometimes an evil thought will come into our mind and sometimes a good thought will come. Although we don't have control over what kind of thoughts are coming in to us, what we do with those thoughts is the real question. Let us choose to dwell on those thoughts that come into us that will impact positively on our lives, and not choose those thoughts that will impact our lives negatively.

Summary

In this Hour, we have completed Surah Nas, Alhumdulillah! Let's continue pondering what we have learned so far in our salah. Remember, this surah is a protection from Shaitan, and the Prophet Muhammad (Peace be upon him) would recite this surah before going to bed every night, so try and make this your habit too.

We cannot avoid Shaitan whispering to us. However, the moment he whispers we must remember Allah. If we remember Allah, then Shaitan withdraws from us. As for the thoughts that come into our mind, we do not have control over those thoughts, so let us choose wisely as to what kind of thoughts we choose to dwell on, since our thoughts determine our destiny.

For grammar, we studied Prepositions. We will continue with this topic in the grammar lesson in the next Hour.

So far, we have learnt 31 words that appear in the Quran 9,673 times. Alhumdulillah!

Workshop

The quiz questions and the exercises are provided to further your understanding. Don't worry if you can't answer all of the questions in the quiz. Try your best to answer as many as you can. See Appendix A to check your answers.

Quiz 5

1. Name some virtues of Surah Nas.
2. What is the solution to an evil thought from Shaitan?
3. What is the cure for black magic?
4. Why would Shaitan withdraw after whispering?

Exercise

Insert the CD-ROM accompanying this book into your drive. Select the appropriate folder and do the quiz for this Hour. You may do the quiz as many times as you like in order to further your understanding.

Hour **6**

At the end of this Hour you will have learnt

38 New Words	**Our Aim 200 Words**
12,115 Total Words	**Our Aim 25,000 Words**

Surah Falaq and Prepositions

You will have noticed from the study of Surah Nas that there are many words repeated in the Quran. There will continue to be repeated words as we look at further Surahs. Surah Falaq is the last-but-one Surah in the Quran. Here is some information about Surah Falaq before we look at the verses themselves:

1. Surah Falaq and Surah Nas were revealed in Madinah and they are known as 'muawwizatayn'.

New Term	Muawwizatayn refers to the last two Surahs in the Quran because we seek protection in them from Shaitan.

2. Surah Falaq and Surah Nas are a protection for mankind from Shaitan - and all of us want protection and safety.
3. Prophet Muhammad (Peace be upon him) would recite Surah Nas, Surah Falaq and Surah Ikhlas, and blow on his hands, and then wipe his hands over his body before going to bed at night. This shows the importance of these Surahs.

The highlights of this Hour include:

- Surah Falaq verses 1-5
- Grammar – Prepositions
- Advice and guidance

Surah Falaq Verse 1

Table 6.1.1

الْفَلَقِ	بِرَبِّ	أَعُوذُ	قُلْ
(of) the daybreak	in the Lord	"I seek refuge	Say,

There is only one new word in this verse.

Table 6.1.2

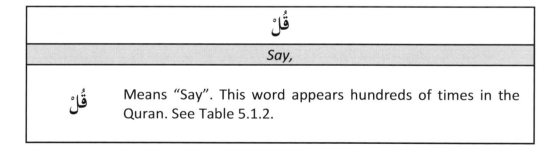

قُلْ	
Say,	
قُلْ	Means "Say". This word appears hundreds of times in the Quran. See Table 5.1.2.

Table 6.1.3

أَعُوذُ
I seek refuge
أَعُوذُ   Means "I seek refuge". See Table 2.1.2.

Table 6.1.4

بِرَبِّ
in the Lord
بِ   Means "in". This is a Preposition which we will cover in detail in the grammar lesson at the end of this Hour.
رَبِّ   Means "Lord". See Table 2.3.4.

Table 6.1.5

New Word	الْفَلَقِ
(of) the daybreak	
فَلَقِ Means "daybreak".	

6

Lessons derived from this verse

Why is Allah asking us to say this out loud?

When we voice this aloud, it has more effect on us. That's why Allah is commanding us to say it.

Also, speaking the words out loud increases your obedience to Allah. After all, how can you disobey Him when you voice such words? This is another reason why Allah is commanding us to utter these words.

As we say this verse, we remind ourselves that we are weak and we are in great need of Allah's help. When we realise this, we should say and feel that only Allah the most powerful can help us. We must feel the greatness and the power of Allah by contemplating His creations – the sun, the earth, the sunrise, and realise how weak we are.

Surah Falaq Verse 2

In this verse, Allah points out the first thing the human being must seek protection from.

Table 6.2.1

خَلَقَ	مَا	مِنْ شَرِّ
He created	(of) what	From (the) evil

There are two new words in this verse.

Table 6.2.2

مِنْ شَرِّ	
From (the) evil	
مِنْ	Means "from". This is a Preposition. See the grammar lesson of Hour 5.
شَرِّ	Means "evil". See Table 5.4.3.

Table 6.2.3

New Word	مَا
	(of) what
مَا	This word has two meanings. 1) Not. 2) What? If the word (مَا) is preceded by a preposition or a present tense, then it will mean 'not'. Otherwise it will mean 'what' - as in this case. Don't worry for now about tenses, as we will study them in future grammar lessons.

One of the questions we will be asked after we are buried in our graves is (مَا دِيْنُك) meaning "What is your religion?"

Be prepared for your Aakhirah. Don't let Shaitan deceive you.

Table 6.2.4

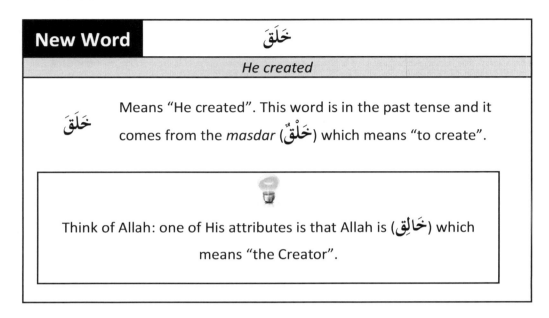

New Word	خَلَقَ
	He created

خَلَقَ Means "He created". This word is in the past tense and it comes from the *masdar* (خَلْقٌ) which means "to create".

Think of Allah: one of His attributes is that Allah is (خَالِق) which means "the Creator".

Lessons derived from this verse

Did Allah create evil?

There is nothing that Allah has created which is 100% pure evil. Some things are 100% good. For example, The Books of Allah, Messengers, and so forth are 100% good, and not evil. Certain things that Allah has created are evil but there is yet some goodness in them. For example, alcohol: there is some goodness in it but it contains more evil.

There is some goodness in Shaitan, but also evil. You may wonder what is good about Shaitan. Well, you can enter Jannah by not obeying him. So everything that is evil has yet some goodness in it. Allah has created nothing that is 100% evil.

Surah Falaq Verse 3

In this verse, Allah tells of the second thing for human beings to seek protection from.

Table 6.3.1

وَقَبَ	إِذَا	غَاسِقٍ	وَ مِنْ شَرِّ
it becomes intense	*when*	*(of) darkness*	*and from (the) evil*

There are three new words in this verse.

Table 6.3.2

وَ مِنْ شَرِّ
and from (the) evil

مِنْ	Means "from". This is a Preposition. See the grammar lesson in Hour 5.
شَرِّ	Means "evil". See Table 5.4.3.

Table 6.3.3

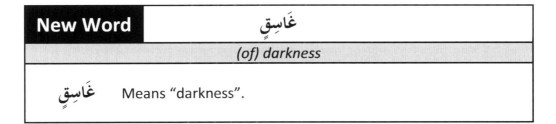

New Word	غَاسِقٍ
	(of) darkness

غَاسِقٍ	Means "darkness".

Table 6.3.4

New Word	إِذَا
	when
إِذَا	Means "when".

Table 6.3.5

New Word	وَقَبَ
	it becomes intense
وَقَبَ	Means "it became intense". This word is in the past form.
إِذَا وَقَبَ	However, when there is (إِذَا) preceding a past tense, it changes the meaning to the present tense, like in this verse. So here it means "it becomes intense".

Lessons derived from this verse

Why are we asking for protection from the evil of the night?

The reason for this is because most evil happens at night. Clubs, cinemas, and other evils, are mainly open at night time. Also, evil can attack us more easily at night than during the day. Therefore, we are told to seek protection from the evil of the night.

Surah Falaq Verse 4

In this verse, Allah mentions the third thing which we are asked to seek protection from.

Table 6.4.1

الْعُقَدِ	فِي	النَّفَّاثَاتِ	وَ مِنْ شَرِّ
(the) knots	in	(of) those who blow	and from (the) evil

There are two new words in this verse.

Table 6.4.2

وَ مِنْ شَرِّ
and from (the) evil
مِنْ   Means "from". This is a Preposition. See the grammar lesson in Hour 5.
شَرِّ   Means "evil". See Table 5.4.3.

Table 6.4.3

New Word	النَّفَّاثَاتِ
	(of) those who blow
نَفَّاثَات	Means "those women who blow". (نَفَّاثَة) is the singular form meaning "woman who blows".

(نَفْثٌ) is the *masdar* which means "to blow".

Table 6.4.4

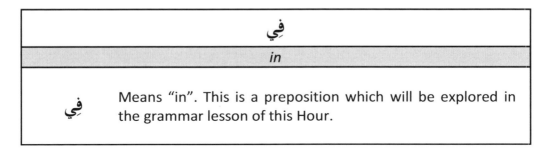

فِي
in
فِي	Means "in". This is a preposition which will be explored in the grammar lesson of this Hour.

Table 6.4.5

New Word	الْعُقَدِ
	(the) knots
عُقَدِ	Means "knots". (عُقْدَة) is the singular form meaning "knot".

Lessons derived from this verse

Why did Allah mention women who blow knots and not men?

It does not mean that men are shielded from blowing knots. The reason why Allah mentioned women who blow knots is because it is mostly women who are involved in blowing knots, and in black magic.

Black magic and its connection with this Surah

This Surah is a protection from black magic, anyone affected by black magic must hold onto this Surah.

We should not deny black magic, because it does exist. The Prophet (Peace be upon him) was affected by black magic, and Surah Falaq and Surah Nas were revealed as a protection against black magic, and an antidote for it. So the best cure for black magic is the Quran.

Path Of Allah: Through reciting the Quran
Path Of Shaitan: Quran is too holy for you so go and get a *Ta'aweez*, talisman or amulet.

Surah Falaq Verse 5

In this verse Allah mentions the fourth and the last thing that human beings need protection from.

Table 6.5.1

إِذَا حَسَدَ	حَاسِدٍ	وَ مِنْ شَرِّ
when he envies	*(of) the envier*	*and from (the) evil*

There is only one new word in this verse.

Table 6.5.2

وَ مِنْ شَرِّ
and from (the) evil
مِنْ   Means "from". See the Hour 5 grammar lesson.

شَرٌّ	Means "evil". See Table 5.4.3.

Table 6.5.3

New Word	حَاسِدٍ
	(of) the envier
حَاسِدٍ	Means "envier". (حَسَدٌ) is the *masdar* which means "to envy".

Table 6.5.4

إِذَا حَسَدَ	
when he envies	
إِذَا	Means "when". See Table 6.3.4.
حَسَدَ	Means "he envies". See Table 6.5.3.

Lessons derived from this Verse

Envy is only allowed in two cases

Envy is prohibited in Islam, although it is acknowledged in two cases:

1. Envy of those to whom Allah has given knowledge of the Quran and the Hadith, and they spread it day and night.

2. Envy of those on whom Allah has bestowed wealth, who gives it away in the path of Allah day and night.

Other than in these two situations, envy is prohibited.

You poison your own ambition by being envious of other people's accomplishments or possessions. Instead of envying them, STOP! And ask yourself, what is it that you love most in this world?

The thing that you love most in this world is the thing you will be envious about!

Practice what you have learned

قُلْ	أَعُوذُ	بِرَبِّ	الْفَلَقِ
Say,	"I seek refuge	in the Lord	(of) the daybreak

مِنْ شَرِّ	مَا	خَلَقَ
From (the) evil	(of) what	He created

وَ مِنْ شَرِّ	غَاسِقٍ	إِذَا	وَقَبَ
and from (the) evil	(of) darkness	when	it becomes intense

وَ مِنْ شَرِّ	النَّفَّاثَاتِ	فِي	الْعُقَدِ
and from (the) evil	(of) those who blow	in	(the) knots

إِذَا حَسَدَ	حَاسِدٍ	وَ مِنْ شَرِّ
when he envies	(of) the envier	and from (the) evil

Don't forget to concentrate on the meaning during your next Salah. Pause after every verse, imagine your response from Allah, and try and build humility and love for Allah in your Salah.

Revision of Vocabulary words studied

Meaning	Arabic Word
daybreak	فَلَقِ
he created	خَلَقَ
darkness	غَاسِقٍ
when	إِذَا
it becomes tense	وَقَبَ
those who blow	نَّفَّاثَاتِ
knot	عُقَدِ
envier	حَاسِدٍ

Phew! Alhumdulillah!

We have completed Surah Falaq. Without Allah's help it would not have been possible, so let's say Alhumdulillah. Let us ponder over what we have learnt so far in our salah, and ask Allah to save us from the evils mentioned in this Surah. If you know someone who is affected by black magic, tell them to recite Surah Falaq as a cure, so spread this message as much as you can. Remember to read this surah before going to sleep at night, understand it, ponder over it, implement it in your life, and spread it.

Take a Break!

Refreshed? Good.

In the next section, you are going to learn Arabic Grammar.

Grammar – prepositions

In Hour 5 we studied four Prepositions. In this Hour, we will look at four more which are frequently used in the Quran.

Table 6.6.1

Translation	Example	Meaning	Preposition
In him	بِهِ		
In you	بِكَ	In	بِ
In me	بِي		
In him	فِيْهِ		
In you	فِيْكَ	In	فِيْ
In me	فِيَّ		
On them	عَلَيْهِمْ		
On you	عَلَيْكُمْ	On	عَلَى
On us	عَلَيْنَا		
To them	إِلَيِهِمْ		
To you	إِلَيْكُمْ	To	إِلَي
To me	إِلَيَّ		

Study these prepositions along with their examples, and see if you can come up with a few examples of your own.

Advice and Guidance from the Author

Do you know how precious we humans are?

In this surah Allah has mentioned some of the evil things that human beings do, like blowing knots and being envious or jealous and so forth. However, please bear this in mind: Allah gave us much more honour when creating us than He did when he created everything else. Allah created us human beings with His own hands which suits His Majesty. This in itself is a great honour from Allah. Therefore even if someone is involved in evil, do not look down upon them.

We humans do not lose our value

As people we don't lose our value. No matter what circumstances we are in, no matter what difficult times we go through, no matter how much we have failed, no matter how crumpled we may be, no matter how many people may have stepped on us, we don't lose our value. No one loses their value. No matter how poor you are, you must not allow anyone to degrade you because of your circumstances. Equally as important is that you do not degrade or rob people of their human dignity and integrity no matter what their situation or circumstances, even if you believe they are guilty of evildoing!

The difference between the person and the performance

People may be guilty of wrong actions but they do not lose their human dignity and value. Every time you deal with any person, make sure you recognize the difference between these two things: the person and the performance. We can criticize the performance, yes, it was definitely an evil deed, but the person himself does not lose his human dignity and value, whether he is muslim or non-muslim. This is what the Quran says:

6

وَلَقَدْ كَرَّمْنَا بَنِى ءَادَمَ

"... we have honoured the children of Adam ..." Quran (17:70) If you are a human being, you are one of those who have been honored by Allah.

We are always talking about our rights,
And that is really not the issue.
The issue is not 'what are the rights of humans?',
The issue is 'who are humans?'

Summary

In this Hour we have completed Surah Falaq, Alhumdulillah. Continue pondering what we have learnt so far in our salah. Remember this Surah is a cure for black magic. So if you know someone who has been affected by black magic, try to help them by teaching them this surah.

For grammar we studied prepositions. Try to master these prepositions as they are present in thousands of places in the Quran.

So far we have learnt 38 words that occur in the Quran 12,115 times. Alhumdulillah!

Workshop

The quiz questions and the exercises are provided to further your understanding. Don't worry if you can't answer all of the questions in the quiz. Try your best to answer as many as you can. See Appendix A to check your answers.

Quiz 6

1. What are the 4 things we are asking for protection from in this Surah?
2. Why did Allah create evil?
3. What are the two situations in which envy is permissible?
4. Why are people envious?

Exercise

Insert the CD-ROM accompanying this book into your drive. Select the appropriate folder and do the quiz for this Hour. You may do the quiz as many times as you like in order to further your understanding.

6

Hour **7**

At the end of this Hour you will have learnt

54 New Words	**Our Aim 200 Words**
13,374 Total Words	**Our Aim 25,000 Words**

Surah Ikhlas and Demonstrative Pronouns

In this Hour we will study Surah Ikhlas. This is one of the shortest Surahs in the Quran. A review of Surah Ikhlas before we begin the study:

1. It is the third from the last Surah of the Quran.
2. It was revealed in Makkah.
3. One of the companions of the Prophet (Peace be upon him) would constantly recite this surah, and when the Prophet (Peace be upon him) was informed of this, the Prophet (Peace be upon him) said: "your love for this Surah will enter you into Jannah".
4. It is equivalent to one third of the Quran.
5. The Prophet Muhammad (Peace be upon him) would read it every night before going to bed.
6. It was a reply to the disbelievers of Makkah when they asked the Prophet (Peace be upon him) who is Allah? This Surah,which gives a description of Allah, was revealed.

Whichever God you worship, He **MUST** fit the description of Surah Ikhlas – Don't let Shaitan deceive you!

Let's make Dua to Allah and approach this Hour in the firm belief that Allah will make this Hour easy for us.

The highlights of this Hour include:

- Surah Ikhlas verses 1-4
- Grammar – Demonstrative Pronouns
- Advice and guidance

Surah Iklas Verse 1

In this verse Allah is giving us a description of Himself, explaining who Allah is.

Table 7.1.1

أَحَدٌ	اللّٰهُ	هُوَ	قُلْ
One	(is) Allah	He	Say,

There is only one new word in this verse.

Table 7.1.2

قُلْ	
Say,	
قُلْ	Means "Say". See Table 5.1.2.

Table 7.1.3

هُوَ	
He	
هُوَ	Means "He". See the Hour 1 grammar lesson.

Table 7.1.4

اللهُ	
(is) Allah	
اللهُ	Means "Allah". See Table 2.1.3.

Table 7.1.5

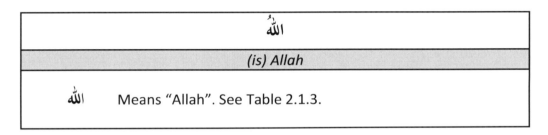

New Word	أَحَدٌ
One	
أَحَدٌ	Means "One". In Arabic (وَاحِد) also means "one". (أَحَد) can only be used for Allah, if the sentence is positive. If the sentence is formed as a negative, then it can be used for someone other than Allah.

Lessons derived from this verse

Do we really make Allah the One true God?

Allah says that He is One. We have a very important question to ask ourselves, and that is, do we make Allah the One or do we make gods other than Allah by following and obeying our priests and leaders? In the Hadith a person once said to the Prophet Muhammad (Peace be upon him) that we do not make our priests into Lords. Prophet Muhammad (Peace be upon him) replied: "Don't they (the priests) decide the Halal (allowed matters) Haram (disallowed matters) and the Haram Halal, which you follow?" He agreed. Prophet Muhammad (Peace be upon him) said: "That is worshipping them." (Hadith). So when we say 'Allah is One' we must obey Him and Him alone.

How many times do we follow our own desires and Shaitan, although we say Allah is One, and we only worship Allah? So we need to increase our obedience to Him in order to truly worship Allah alone.

Why is Allah telling us to say 'Allah is One'?

Since we Muslims already say 'Allah is One', why is Allah telling us to "Say 'Allah is One.' "? The reason why Allah is telling us to "say" that Allah is One, is because it increases our obedience to Allah. When you are voicing these words, how can you disobey Him? That's why Allah is commanding us to "Say".

Another reason is that it is a command from Allah to go and correct the people who say Allah is more than One.

Surah Ikhlas Verse 2

In this verse Allah continues giving His own description as to who Allah is.

Table 7.2.1

اَللّٰهُ الصَّمَدُ
Allah the Self-Sufficient

There is only one new word in this verse.

Table 7.2.2

New Word	الصَّمَدُ
	the Self-Sufficient
صَمَدُ	This word (صَمَد) cannot easily be described in English.. It means an entity who is self-existing; He's eternal, He's absolute, everything is dependent on Him, and He is independent of anything and everything. It has many nuances of meaning.

Lessons derived from this verse

Allah does not need us, we need Allah

If everything is dependent on Him, He is independent of anything and everything, then we all need Allah. Allah does not require us, neither does He require our worship. When we worship Allah, it only benefits us, it does not benefit Allah. When we say *Allahu Akbar*, Allah is the greatest, it does not make Allah great. Allah will always be the greatest, whether we say it or not. So when we worship Allah, it only benefits us humans.

Do we run to Allah or to this world?

When we all need Allah, then do we really run to him? Or do we run after money, wealth, status and so forth? Let's show through our actions that we run to Allah. We need Allah, so let's run to him. If we run to him, you will get the success of this world and the next world (hereafter). (Hadith)

If we run to *dunya*, and make *dunya* our primary concern, then the Prophet (Peace be upon him) said, "Allah will put poverty between your eyes, and your worldly affairs will become scattered. If you run to Allah, then Allah will put contentment in your heart, and Allah will give you this *dunya* as well as *aakhirah*, this world and the hereafter."

Your actions **MUST** show that you run to Allah and not to this world. If you just mouth the words but your actions do not show that you run to Allah, then our religion becomes nothing but a philosophy and nice words – **AND NO ONE IS INTERESTED IN NICE WORDS, WE ALL WANT TO SEE ACTION.**

Surah Ikhlas Verse 3

In this verse Allah gives a third description of Himself.

Table 7.3.1

يُولَدْ	وَلَمْ	يَلِدْ	لَمْ
is He begotten	*and did not*	*He beget*	*Did not*

[This is a literal translation of the Arabic: the verse means "He begetteth not, nor is He begotten."]

There are two new words in this verse.

Table 7.3.2

New Word	لَمْ
Did not	
لَمْ	Means "not". This word occurs over 170 times in the Quran.

Table 7.3.3

يَلِدْ
He beget
يَلِدْ   Means "he beget". It comes from the *masdar* (وِلَادَة) which means "birth".

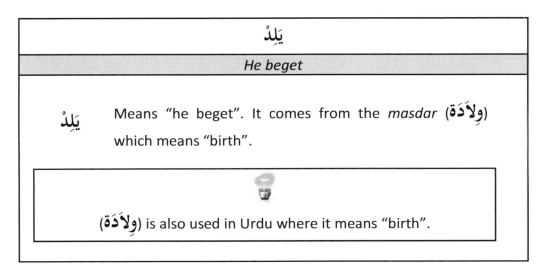

(وِلَادَة) is also used in Urdu where it means "birth".

Table 7.3.4

وَلَمْ يُولَدْ
and did not is he begotten
وَلَمْ	Means "and not". See Table 7.3.2.
يُولَدْ	Means "is he begotten". It is derived from the same *masdar* as (يَلِدْ) but this is the Present Passive Tense. Don't worry about this term for now, as we will cover this in future

grammar lessons.

Lessons derived from this verse

Look how merciful Allah is!

This is a message to those people who say Allah has begotten a son, and they claim that Jesus (Peace be upon him) is a son of Allah. (We seek Allah's protection from such belief.) Yet even for those who claim that Allah has a son, Allah provides them with provisions and cures them. How merciful Allah is!

Many of us cannot see how merciful Allah is. We think our sins are so great that Allah won't forgive us.

Path of Allah: Allah's mercy is far greater than our sins.
Path of Shaitan: Our sins are too many, Allah won't forgive.

Surah Ikhlas Verse 4

In this verse Allah mentions the fourth description of Himself.

Table 7.4.1

أَحَدٌ	كُفُوًا	لَّه	وَ لَمْ يَكُن
(no) one	like	to Him	and (there) is not

There are two new words in this verse.

7

Table 7.4.2

New Word	وَ لَمْ يَكُن
	and (there) is not
وَ لَمْ	Means "and not". See Table 7.3.2.
يَكُن	Means "is". This is a present tense of the word (كَانَ) which means "was". These two words occur in the Quran 333 times.

Table 7.4.3

لَّهُ
to Him
لَهُ — Means "to Him". See the grammar lesson in Hour 5.

Table 7.4.4

New Word	كُفُوًا
	like
كُفُوًا	Means "like". It also means "equal".

Table 7.4.5

أَحَدٌ		
(no) one		
أَحَدٌ	Means "one". See Table 7.1.5. Because of the (لَمْ) at the beginning of this sentence, it has the meaning of "no-one".	

Lessons derived from this verse

How to understand human qualities attributed to Allah in the Quran?

The moment you can compare anything to Allah, He is not Allah. There is none like unto Him. However there are verses in the Quran that speak about Allah's hands, about His speech and so forth. So how do we understand these verses? Aren't they human qualities attributed to Allah?

The answer is yes: speech, hands etc. all these are human qualities. However when Allah says, "Allah spoke to Moosa (Peace be upon him)" and other similar verses, then if you say that Allah spoke the way we human beings speak, then that is not Allah (وَلَمْ يَكُن لَّهُ كُفُوًا أَحَدٌ) and there is nothing like unto Him. Allah spoke, He surely spoke, but how did He speak? Only Allah Himself knows. Allah's hands, mentioned in the Quran, we do not deny, because Allah says 'Allah's hands'. These are surely not like the hands of human beings, but only Allah Himself knows.

7

Imam Malik (May Allah's mercy be upon him)'s Statement

The best reply regarding the verses in the Quran that speak about Allah's hands and so on is the reply given by Imam Malik (May Allah's Mercy be upon him). He said: "Allah is on His throne, this is known. How He is, is unknown. Believing in it is obligatory, and asking questions regarding this is an innovation".

Practice what you have learned

أَحَدٌ	اللهُ	هُوَ	قُلْ
One	(is) Allah	He	Say,

الصَّمَدُ	اَللهُ
the Self-Sufficient	Allah

يُولَدْ	وَلَمْ	يَلِدْ	لَمْ
is He begotten	and did not	He beget	Did not

أَحَدٌ	كُفُوًا	لَّه	وَلَمْ يَكُن
(no) one	like	to Him	and (there) is not

Don't forget to ponder over the meaning in your next salah. Pause after every verse, imagine the response from Allah, and try to build humility and love for Allah in your salah.

Revision of Vocabulary words studied

Meaning	Arabic Word
One	أَحَدٌ
Self-Sufficient	صَمَد
not	لَمْ
He beget	يَلِدْ
like	كُفُوًا

Phew! Alhumdulillah!

We have completed Surah Ikhlas. Without Allah's help it would not have been possible, so let's say Alhumdulillah! Let's start to ponder over what we have learnt so far in our salah, and let's increase our knowledge of Tawheed [the Oneness of Allah] and improve our obedience to Allah. Remember to read this surah every night before going to sleep, understand it, ponder over it, implement it in your life, and spread it.

Take a Break!

Refreshed? Good.

In the next section, you are going to learn Arabic Grammar.

7

Grammar – Demonstrative Pronouns

Demonstrative Pronouns are pronouns that are used to point at something, just as they are used in English. However in Arabic there are more forms than there are in English because of the gender duality, also because there are singular, dual, and plural forms.

Demonstrative Pronouns are generally used in two ways:

- To point at something in the near distance
- To point at something in the far distance

The singular and plural forms of Demonstrative Pronouns occur in the Quran more times than the dual forms do. However, try and master all three to help you understand the Quran better.

Table 7.5.1 Near Distance

Meaning	*Gender/Numbers*	*Demonstrative Pronoun*
This	Masculine / Singular	هَٰذَا
	Feminine / Singular	هَٰذِهِ
These two	Masculine / Dual	هَٰذَانِ
	Feminine / Dual	هَٰاتَانِ
These all	Masculine + Feminine / Plural	هَٰؤُلَاءِ

Table 7.5.2 Far Distance

Meaning	Gender/Numbers	Demonstrative Pronoun
That	Masculine / Singular	ذَلِكَ
	Feminine / Singular	تِلْكَ
Those two	Masculine / Dual	ذَانِكَ
	Feminine / Dual	تَانِكَ
Those all	Masculine + Feminine / Plural	أُوْلَئِكَ

Study these Demonstrative Pronouns and see if you can come up with a few examples of your own from the vocabulary you have learnt so far. If you cannot remember any, go back and see if you can find any words as examples of Demonstrative Pronouns.

Advice and Guidance from the Author

What does "Allah is One." mean?

We say Allah is One. But what do we mean by this? When we say Allah is One and He is unique, it means Allah is unique in three things:

1. One and Unique in His Lordship
2. Unique in His Names and Attributes
3. Unique in His Worship.

These three things constitute Tawheed.

7

Unique in His Lordship

Allah is the creator, cherisher, and sustainer of the entire universe, without any need from it or for it. Allah is One: He has neither sons nor parents, He is self-sufficient, and there is no-one and nothing like Him.

Unique in His Names and Attributes

This is divided in to five sub-categories:

1. Allah should be referred to in the ways Allah Himself or the Prophet (Peace be upon him) has described Allah, without explaining His names and attributes, unless explanation was given by Allah Himself or the Prophet (Peace be upon him).
2. Allah must be referred to in the way that Allah has referred to Himself. For instance, the Quran says Allah gets angry, but we cannot attribute that Allah is the angry one (we seek Allah's protection from this), because Allah did not refer to Himself as the angry one.
3. We cannot give any human attributes to Allah. We cannot say Allah made a mistake, (we seek Allah's protection from this) because to make mistakes is a human attribute.
4. We cannot give any attributes of Allah to His creation. For example, (الرّحْمن) the Most Merciful. We cannot give this attribute to a human being.
5. Names of Allah cannot be given to any of His creatures. Some names that are indefinite form [would have the indefinite article 'a/an'] can be given like "Raoof". However in the definite forms [would have the definite article 'the'] like Ar Raoof, Ar Rahman, can only be used if you add 'Abd' before it, which means 'slave'. For example, Abd Raoof, Abd Raheem.

Unique in His worship

Meaning "maintaining the unity of worship" worshipping Allah alone and no one else. This includes all acts of worship, for example:

- Being patient at the decree of Allah
- Having trust Only in Allah and no one else
- Making Dua Only to Allah and no one else
- Seeking blessings Only from Allah and no one else
- Seeking help Only from Allah and no one else, instead of seeking it from Charms, Talismans and Amulets.

All these acts of worship must be for Allah alone and no one else. All three categories of Tawheed are equally important, and if any one of them is missing, it is referred to as shirk. shirk is the biggest sin in Islam, and if anyone dies committing shirk Allah will never forgive him.

Summary

In this Hour we have completed Surah Ikhlas, Alhumdulillah! Let's continue pondering what we have learnt so far in our salah. Remember this Surah is the one which gives the best description of Allah. After we are buried in our graves our first question will be (مَنْ رَبُّكَ) who is your Lord? This shows how important this Surah is, that it gives you the description of Allah.

For grammar we studied Demonstrative Pronouns. Try to master these, as they occur thousands of times in the Quran.

So far we have learnt 54 words that are used in the Quran 13,374 times. Alhumdulillah!

7

Workshop

The quiz questions and the exercises are provided to further your understanding. Don't worry if you can't answer all of the questions in the quiz. Try your best to answer as many as you can. See Appendix A to check your answers.

Quiz 7

1. Give the four descriptions that Allah gave of Himself in Surah Ikhlas.
2. What is our belief regarding verses which give a human attribute to Allah?
3. What are some of the virtues of this Surah?
4. Why are there certain words in Arabic (like the word (صَمَد))that cannot be accurately translated into English?

Exercise

Insert the CD-ROM accompanying this book into your drive. Select the appropriate folder and do the quiz for this Hour. You may do the quiz as many times as you like in order to further your understanding.

Hour **8**

At the end of this Hour you will have learnt

73 New Words	**Our Aim 200 Words**
13,713 Total Words	**Our Aim 25,000 Words**

Surah Masad and Relative Pronouns

In this Hour we will study Surah Masad. This Surah was revealed in response to Abu Lahab. One day Prophet Muhammad (Peace be upon him) went out to the valley of Al Batha and he ascended the mountain and invited his people to Allah. Abu Lahab said to Prophet Muhammad (Peace be upon him) "Is this why you gathered all of us here? May you perish!" So Allah revealed this Surah in response to Abu Lahab.

A quick review of this Surah before studying it:

1. It is fourth from the last Surah of the Quran
2. It was revealed in Makkah
3. It talks about the destruction of Abu Lahab and his wife.

DO NOT become the enemy of Allah and His messenger, like Abu Lahab and his wife did.

8

The highlights of this Hour include:

- Surah Masad verses 1-5
- Grammar – Relative Pronouns
- Advice and guidance

Surah Masad Verse 1

In this verse Allah is talking about the destruction of Abu Lahab.

Table 8.1.1

وَتَبَّ	أَبِي لَهَبٍ	يَدَا	تَبَّتْ
and perish he.	*(of) the father of flame*	*the two hands*	*Perish*

There are three new words in this verse.

Table 8.1.2

New Word	تَبَّتْ
Perish	
تَبَّتْ	Means "perish". It is used in this sentence as a curse. It comes from the *masdar* (تَبَّ) which means "perish", "to be destroyed".

Table 8.1.3

New Word	يَدَا
	the two hands
يَد	Means "hand". (يَدَانِ) means "two hands". The letter (ن) has been dropped from the end, so it becomes (يَدَا) meaning "two hands".

Table 8.1.4

New Word	أَبِي لَهَبٍ
	(of) the father of flame
أَب	Means "father".
لَهَبٍ	Means "flame".

Abu Lahab was the Uncle of the Prophet Muhammad (Peace be upon him). His real name is Abdul Uzza, but he was called Abu Lahab because of the brightness of his face. He was a strong enemy of Islam.

Table 8.1.5

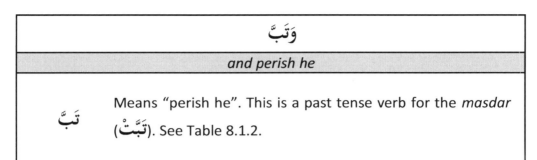

وَتَبَّ
and perish he
تَبَّ   Means "perish he". This is a past tense verb for the *masdar* (تَبَّتْ). See Table 8.1.2.

Lessons derived from this verse

Allah destroyed Abu Lahab and his Plans

Allah did not simply ruin Abu Lahab's plans to hurt (and eventually to destroy) the Prophet Muhammad (Peace be upon him). Abu Lahab and his plans were totally destroyed by Allah.

Do we feel we are being destroyed by Allah through calamities?

We have a very important question to ask ourselves. Do we also feel we are being destroyed by Allah when calamities befall us? Well, guess what, for those who believe in Allah, calamities are a blessing from Him. However they are a punishment from Allah for the non-believers.

Prophet Muhammad (Peace be upon him) said: "Anything that befalls a believer, be it grief, be it worry, be it sadness, be it sickness, Allah will forgive his sins because of the calamity." (Hadith). So calamities are a blessing from Allah for a true believer in Allah.

Always be optimistic even in times of calamities. The Prophet (Peace be upon him) said: (اَلْفَأْلُ حُسْنُ الْخُلُق) that being optimistic is the best of character.

Surah Masad Verse 2

In this verse Allah continues to talk about Abu Lahab's destruction, saying that neither his wealth nor his children will benefit him.

Table 8.2.1

كَسَبَ	وَمَا	مَالُهُ	عَنْهُ	أَغْنَى	مَا
he earned	and what	his wealth	to him	(will) benefit	Not

This is a long verse with some new words. Let us explain the meaning of each word separately.

Table 8.2.2

مَا	
Not	
مَا	This word has two meanings, "not" and "what". In this sentence it means "Not". This word occurs hundreds of times in the Quran. See Table 6.2.3.

Table 8.2.3

New Word	أَغْنَى
	(will) benefit
أَغْنَى	Means "he benefits". It is a past tense verb, and it comes from the *masdar* (إِغْنَاءٌ) which means "to avail" and "to benefit". We begin to look at tenses in Hour 9, just learn this for now.

Table 8.2.4

New Word	عَنْهُ
	to him
عَنْ	Means "to". This word comes many times in the Quran and it is usually a verb prefix.
هُ	Means "him".

Table 8.2.5

New Word	مَالُهُ
	his wealth
مَال	Means "wealth". The same word is also used for wealth in other languages, like Urdu. This word occurs in over 50 different places in the Quran in different forms.

(مَال) is the Singular form (أَمْوَال) is the Plural form.

Table 8.2.6

وَمَا
and what
مَا   In this sentence it means "what". See Table 6.2.3.

Table 8.2.7

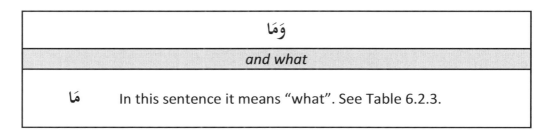

New Word	كَسَبَ
	he earned
كَسَبَ	Means "he earned" it comes from the *masdar* (كَسْبٌ) which means "to earn". In this context it means his children (Tafsir Ibn Kathir). Meaning, his children will not benefit him.

Lessons derived from this verse

Wealth and children is a test from Allah

If a person deserves hell fire in the hereafter, neither his wealth nor his children will benefit him. We think money can buy everything, but remember to always acquire money only for those things money can buy.

8

Things money can buy:

- Money can buy you a bed but it cannot buy you sweet dreams
- It can buy you a house but it cannot buy you a home
- It can buy you fame but it cannot buy you true friends
- It can buy you books but it cannot buy you knowledge
- It can buy you food but it cannot buy you health
- It can buy you a clock but it cannot buy you time.

So you only want money for the things money can buy. It is dangerous when we acquire money to buy things money can<u>not</u> buy. At that point, no matter how much of it we have we will always feel - and be - poor.

<u>REMEMBER:</u> Islam does not prohibit having a lot of money. The question is, "How are you going to earn it? And what are you willing to sacrifice in the process?"

Don't let Shaitan take you away from Allah with your wealth and children. Use your wealth and children to get closer to Allah.

Surah Masad Verse 3

In this verse Allah is stating what will happen to Abu Lahab.

Table 8.3.1

لَهَبٍ	ذَاتَ	نَارًا	سَيَصْلَى
flame	blazing	(in) a fire	Soon he will enter

128

There are three new words in this verse.

Table 8.3.2

New Word	سَيَصْلَى
	Soon he will enter
سَ	Means "Soon". This letter occurs many times in the Quran and it is usually a verb prefix.
يَصْلَى	Means "he will enter" it is a present tense verb. It comes from the *masdar* (صَلًى) which means "to enter".

Table 8.3.3

New Word	نَارًا
	(in) a fire
نَار	Means "fire". This word occurs in the Quran more than 135 times.

Table 8.3. 4

New Word	ذَاتَ
	blazing
ذَاتَ	Means "blazing". The meaning of this word changes depending upon the verb it follows. It has the same meaning

> as the verb but in an active participle form. e.g. (ذَاتَ الْيَمِيْنِ)
>
> which means "right side".
> Just learn it for now.

Table 8.3.5

لَهَبٍ
flame
لَهَبٍ Means "flame". See Table 8.1.4.

Lessons derived from this verse

Seek Protection from Hell Fire?

Allah is describing to us in this verse how severe the punishment of Hell Fire is. We need to ask ourselves a very important question: are we asking Allah to protect us from Hell Fire? Below is a Dua from the Hadith of the Prophet Muhammad (Peace be upon him) for protection from Hell Fire:

اللَّهُمَّ إِنِّي أَعُوذُ بِكَ مِنْ عَذَابِ الْقَبْرِ، وَمِنْ عَذَابِ جَهَنَّمَ، وَمِنْ فِتْنَةِ الْمَحْيَا وَالْمَمَاتِ، وَمِنْ شَرِّ فِتْنَةِ الْمَسِيحِ الدَّجَّالِ

"O Allah, I seek refuge in You from the punishment of the grave, and from the punishment of Hell Fire, and from the trials of life and death, and from the evil of the trial of the False Messiah." (Bukhari and Muslim)

Shaitan is trying to fill Hell with Jinns and humans.
He made an oath to Allah that he will fill it up with Jinns and humans,
and he will fulfill his promise.
SO SEEK PROTECTION FROM HELL FIRE

Surah Masad Verse 4

In this verse Allah is talking about the destruction of Abu Lahab's wife.

Table 8.4.1

الْحَطَبِ	حَمَّالَةَ	وَامْرَأَتُهُ
wood	(who) carries	and his wife (too)

There are three new words in this verse.

Table 8.4.2

New Word	وَامْرَأَتُهُ
	and his wife (too)
امْرَأَة	(امْرَأَة) means "woman". In this context it means wife. (رَجُل) means "man".

Table 8.4.3

New Word	حَمَّالَةَ
	(who) carries
حَمَّالَةَ حَمَّالَةَ	Means "female one who carries" "the female carrier". (حَمَّالَةَ) is "a female carrier". (حَمَّال) is "a male carrier".

Table 8.4.4

New Word	الْحَطَبِ
	wood
حَطَبِ Means "wood".	

Surah Masad Verse 5

In this verse Allah continues talking about the punishment of Abu Lahab's wife.

Table 8.5.1

مِنْ مَسَدٍ	حَبْلٌ	فِي جِيدِهَا
from palm fibre	*(will be) a rope*	*In her neck*

Table 8.5.2

New Word	فِي جِيدِهَا

In her neck	
فِي	Means "In". See the Hour 6 grammar lesson. [English would use 'around' in this context.]
جِيد	Means "neck".
هَا	This is the Pronoun for the feminine gender. See Table 4.4.3.

Table 8.5.3

New Word	حَبْلٌ
(will be) a rope	
حَبْلٌ	Means "rope".

Table 8.5.4

New Word	مِنْ مَسَدٍ
from palm fibre	
مِنْ	Means "from". See the Hour 5 grammar lesson. [English would use the word 'of' in this context.]
مَسَدٍ	Means "fibre". It also refers to rope made from fibres or palm leaves.

8

Lessons derived from this verse

Do we make creation happy or our Creator?

No one can help us on the Day of Judgment. The Quran says, a person will be running away from his brother, sister, mother, father, spouse in fear that they may ask for their rights.

Abu Lahab's wife would do anything to please her husband, to the point of hurting Prophet Muhammad (Peace be upon him). We need to ask ourselves, do we also make our spouses happy in spite of our actions making our Creator upset with us?

The Prophet (Peace be upon him) said: "whoever makes Allah angry by making people happy, Allah will be angry with him and He will also make people angry with him; but if a person makes Allah happy by making the people angry, Allah will be happy with him, and He will also make people happy with him." (Hadith)

DO NOT make the Creator angry by making creation happy.

Practice what you have Learned

وَتَبَّ	أَبِي لَهَبٍ	يَدَا	تَبَّتْ
(and) perish he	(of) the father of flame	the two hands	Perish

كَسَبَ	وَمَا	مَالُهُ	عَنْهُ	أَغْنَى	مَا
he earned	and what	his wealth	to him	(will) benefit	Not

لَهَبٍ	ذَاتَ	نَارًا	سَيَصْلَى
flame	blazing	(in) a fire	Soon he will enter

الْحَطَبِ	حَمَّالَةَ	وَامْرَأَتُهُ
wood	(who) carries	and his wife (too)

مِنْ مَسَدٍ	حَبْلٌ	فِي جِيدِهَا
from palm fiber	(will be) a rope	In her neck

Don't forget to ponder over the meaning in your next Salah. Pause after every verse, imagine the response from Allah, and try to build humility and love for Allah in your Salah.

8

Revision of vocabulary words studied

Meaning	Arabic Word
perish	تَبَّتْ
two hands	يَدَا
father	أَبِي
flame	لَهَبٍ
benefit	أَغْنَى
wealth	مَالُ
he earned	كَسَبَ
soon	سَ
he will enter	يَصْلَى
fire	نَارً
blazing	ذَاتَ
woman/wife	امْرَأَتُ
carrier	حَمَّالَةَ
wood	حَطَبٍ
neck	جِيدِ
rope	حَبْلٌ
palm fibre	مَسَدٍ

Phew! Alhumdulillah!

We have completed Surah Masad. Without Allah's help it would not have been possible, so let's say Alhumdulillah! Let's start to ponder over what we have learnt so far in our salah, and let's continue to seek protection from Hell Fire and let us not please our spouses, families and friends, in a way displeasing to Allah.

Take a Break!

In the next section, you are going to learn Arabic Grammar.

8

Grammar – Relative Pronouns

Relative Pronouns are used as conjunctions, to join nouns and verbs to other nouns and verbs. They are used to link a noun that previously came in the sentence to it's description provided by another full sentence. For example: 'I read the book that you gave me.' In this sentence 'that' is a relative pronoun. 'You gave me' is describing the book. Look at Figure 8.1 below for a better understanding.

Figure 8.1

This is an example of a relative pronoun:

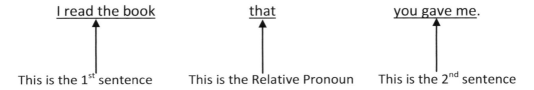

We will study six relative pronouns. Mastering these will help you to understand the Quran much better.

Table 8.6.1

Meaning	Gender/Numbers	Relative Pronoun
Who/That	Masculine / Singular	الَّذِي
	Feminine / Singular	الَّتِي
Those two/Who (dual)	Masculine / Dual	اللَّذَانِ
	Feminine / Dual	اللَّتَانِ
These all	Masculine / Plural	الَّذِينَ
	Feminine / Plural	اللائِي

Study the above Relative Pronouns, and see if you can come up with some examples of your own from the vocabulary you have learnt so far. If you cannot think of any, you may go back, and see if you can find any words to use with these Relative Pronouns.

Advice and Guidance from the Author

What will benefit you when you die?

As Allah said that neither Abu Lahab's wealth nor his children would benefit him or his wife. Similarly no matter how much wealth we have, how big our bank balance, how many properties we own, they will not benefit us in the hereafter. After a person dies Prophet Muhammad (Peace be upon him) said 'only three things will benefit him':

The three things that will benefit you after you die:

1. Continued Charity
2. Knowledge that you left behind which people are benefitting from
3. Pious children that you leave behind, who pray for you.

Do you know the best way to make use of your wealth?

I am not saying that it is prohibited to have wealth in your hands. There are four categories of people who acquire wealth.

1. A person who cannot afford expensive clothes, an expensive house, expensive possessions and so forth, yet he borrows money, or takes out a loan to buy expensive items. This is extravagance, which is prohibited.

8

2. Allah has given you the means and he has given you wealth, but your wealth is in your heart, instead of being in your hand. Meaning you cannot live without expensive possessions; then this is also prohibited.

3. Allah has given you the means, he has given you the wealth, but the wealth is not in your heart, and with the wealth you own these luxury things, then this is permissible. We have the example of Sulaiman (Alayhis Salam).

4. Allah has given you the means, the power, the fame, but you don't use it, and instead you use it in the path of Allah. Like the example of Prophet Muhammad (Peace be upon him), the power he had, the fame he had, the command he had, he used it all in the path of Allah. This is the best category of them all.

Have *dunya* in your hand and not in your heart.

How do I know if a calamity is a blessing from Allah or a punishment from Him?

Allah destroyed Abu Lahab and his plans to harm Prophet Muhammad (Peace be upon him). This calamity upon him was a punishment from Allah. The question is: how do we know if a calamity is a blessing from Allah or a punishment from Him? The calamity itself does not determine whether it is a blessing from Allah or a punishment from Him, in fact it is our response to that calamity that makes the difference. The way we respond to that event renders it a blessing from Allah or a punishment from Him. For example, a person has some financial loss, he can complain to Allah and say 'Oh Allah why did you put me through this calamity and why did you choose me for this calamity?' and so on. This kind of response will make this calamity a punishment from Allah. The same calamity can be responded to by the person saying to himself, 'Whatever Allah gave me, that all belongs to Allah.' He is grateful for what Allah has given him, he is patient and does not complain. This kind of response will make the calamity into a blessing from Allah. So how you respond to any calamity determines whether it is a blessing or a punishment from Allah.

I find it difficult to bear calamity, what should I do?

Here are some important points: if you think of these things then In Sha Allah it will be easy for you to bear any calamity.

1. One of the most important things you should do is to say this Dua:

اِنَّا للَّهِ وَإِنَّا إِلَيهِ رَاجِعُونَ اللَّهمَّ أجِرني في مُصِيبَتي ، وَاخْلُف لي خَيْراً)

(مِنْها

The meaning is 'Verily to Allah we belong and unto Him is our return. O Allah, reward me for my affliction and compensate me with something better.' The Prophet (Peace be upon him) said that if any one says this Dua then Allah will provide something better.

Umm Salmah (May Allah be pleased with her) made this Dua after her husband died, and she was provided with someone better than her husband: she married Prophet Muhammad (Peace be upon him).

2. Allah has stored for that person rewards greater than whatever has been lost, and if Allah wanted, He could have made the calamity even greater.

3. Think about those people who have been hit harder than the calamity which has befallen you.

4. Panicking will not help, so do not panic. It will just make matters worse. Panicking makes Allah angry and makes Shaitan happy.

8

5. Missing out on the reward from Allah for being patient through a calamity is a bigger loss than the calamity itself.

6. We will see the reward for being patient through our calamities on the Day of Judgment. One of the salaf said: 'Were it not for the calamities of this world, we would come empty-handed on the Day of Resurrection.'

7. Allah did not send this calamity to cause you pain or to destroy you; Allah is testing to see whether, after sending this calamity, you still continue praying to Allah and continue making Duas to Allah.

8. If Allah hadn't sent these calamities to us, we might become arrogant, which could lead to our doom in this world and in the hereafter. So Allah in His wisdom puts us through calamities so we do not suffer any of the diseases of the heart, such as jealousy or arrogance.

9. Bitterness in this world is the essence of sweetness in the Hereafter, as Allah will turn the former into the latter. Similarly the sweetness of this world is the essence of bitterness in the Hereafter. It is better to move from temporary bitterness to eternal sweetness than the other way round. In the Hadith the Prophet (Peace be upon him) said: "Paradise is surrounded with difficulties, and Hell is surrounded with desires."

A calamity that makes you turn to Allah is better for you than a blessing which makes you forget the remembrance of Allah. (Ibn Taymiyyah)

What a person dislikes may be better for him than what he likes, because what he dislikes causes him to call upon Allah, whereas what he likes may make him heedless.

'What can my enemies do to me? My garden is in my heart: wherever I go it is with me and never leaves me. My detainment is seclusion (an opportunity for worship), my being killed is martyrdom, and being expelled from my city is a journey.' (Ibn Taymiyyah)

Summary

In this Hour we have completed Surah Masad, Alhumdulillah! Let's continue pondering what we have learnt so far in our salah. This Surah tells us the outcome for two people who disobeyed Allah, and Allah is describing their punishment in the hereafter. So be obedient to Allah and seek protection from Hell Fire. May Allah protect us all from Hell Fire.

For grammar we studied Relative Pronouns. Try to master these, as they occur in hundreds of places in the Quran.

So far we have learnt 73 words that come in the Quran 13,713 times. Alhumdulillah!

Workshop

The quiz questions and the exercises are provided to further your understanding. Don't worry if you can't answer all of the questions in the quiz. Try your best to answer as many as you can. See Appendix A to check your answers.

8

Quiz 8

1. Why did Allah punish Abu Lahab and his wife?
2. Does Islam prohibit earning a lot of wealth?
3. How do we know if a calamity is a punishment from Allah or a blessing from Him?
4. How can your children be a blessing for you in the hereafter?

Exercise

Insert the CD-ROM accompanying this book into your drive. Select the appropriate folder and do the quiz for this Hour. You may do the quiz as many times as you like in order to further your understanding.

Hour 9

At the end of this Hour you will have learnt

83 New Words	Our Aim 200 Words
14,522 Total Words	Our Aim 25,000 Words

Surah Nasr and the Past Tense

In this Hour we will study Surah Nasr. A bit of review of Surah Nasr before studying it:

1. This is the last Surah to be revealed to Prophet Muhammad (Peace be upon him)
2. It is fifth from the last Surah of the Quran
3. It was revealed in Madinah
4. It is equivalent to one fourth of the Quran.

Let's make Dua to Allah and approach this hour in the firm belief that Allah will make this hour easy for us.

The highlights of this hour include:

- Surah Nasr verses 1-3
- Grammar – the Past Tense
- Advice and guidance

Surah Nasr Verse 1

Table 9.1.1

وَالْفَتْحُ	نَصْرُاللهِ	جَاءَ	إِذَا
and victory	the help of Allah	comes	When

There are three new words in this verse.

Table 9.1.2

إِذَا
When

إِذَا	Means "when". See Table 6.3.4.

Table 9.1.3

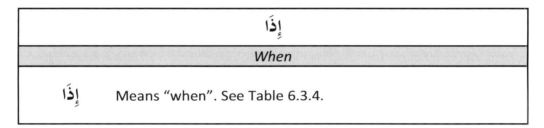

New Word	جَاءَ
	comes

جَاءَ	Means "came". This is a past tense verb. However because of the word (إِذَا) before it, it changes the meaning from past to present. So the meaning here is "when comes" and not "when came".

Table 9.1.4

New Word	نَصْرُ
help	
نَصْرُ	Means "help". It comes from the *masdar* (نَصْرُ) which means "to help".

Table 9.1.5

New Word	وَالْفَتْحُ
and victory	
فَتْحُ	Fatah means "open", "victory" or "conquest".

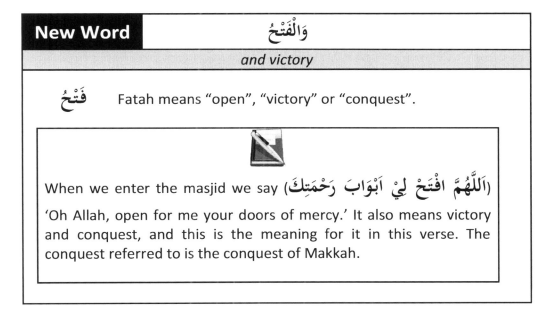

When we enter the masjid we say (اَللَّهُمَّ افْتَحْ لِيْ اَبْوَابَ رَحْمَتِكَ) 'Oh Allah, open for me your doors of mercy.' It also means victory and conquest, and this is the meaning for it in this verse. The conquest referred to is the conquest of Makkah.

Lessons derived from this verse

After every difficulty there is ease, so don't be sad.

After all the effort and calamities Prophet Muhammad (Peace be upon him) went through, Allah gave him victory in conquering Makkah, whereby many people accepted Islam.

A very important lesson we can learn here is that with every difficulty and calamity there comes also an easier time. Not only that: sometimes the calamity itself can be a blessing from Allah which we may not be able to see at the time.

Did you know that even the worst of illnesses (like cancer) can be a blessing from Allah?

Any kind of calamity that befalls a believer can be a blessing from Allah. It is all to do with our response to that calamity.

A relative of mine had incurable cancer, and the doctors only gave him 6 months to live. As a believer, when you know you will not live for long, you start to prepare yourself and strive even more for the hereafter. So that is what he did. Just four months later he passed away. This was not because of cancer, it was due to a fatal heart attack

If you just consider this incident, if Allah had not given him cancer, he probably would not have prepared himself in the way he did when he expected he would not live for much longer. So this cancer was a blessing for him. Again, it all depends how we look at calamities. It has to do with our response.

If a calamity befalls you, it is because Allah loves you.
Prophet Muhammad (Peace be upon him) said:
'When Allah loves a servant he puts him through tests.'

Surah Nasr Verse 2

In this verse Allah mentions that after the conquest of Makkah people will be entering into Islam in crowds. This is exactly what happened. Not even two years passed and the whole of the Arabian peninsula was laden with faith.

Table 9.2.1

أَفْوَاجًا	دِينِ اللَّهِ	فِي	يَدْخُلُونَ	النَّاسَ	وَرَأَيْتَ
(in) crowds	the religion of Allah	in	entering	the people	and you see

There are three new words in this verse.

Table 9.2.2

New Word	وَرَأَيْتَ
	and you see
رَأَيْتَ	Means "you saw". This is a Past Tense verb. It comes from the *masdar* (رُؤْيَةٌ) which means "to see" and (رُؤْيَا) means "dream". In this verse because of the word (إِذَا), it changes the meaning from past to present. So the meaning in this verse is "you see" and not "you saw".

Table 9.2.3

النَّاسَ
the people
نَاسَ Means "people." See Table 5.1.5.

Table 9.2.4

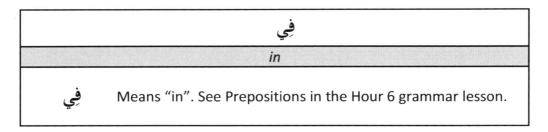

New Word	يَدْخُلُونَ
	entering
يَدْخُلُونَ	Means "entering". This is a present tense verb. It comes from the *masdar* (دُخُوْل) which means "to enter".

Table 9.2.5

فِي
in
فِي Means "in". See Prepositions in the Hour 6 grammar lesson.

Table 9.2.6

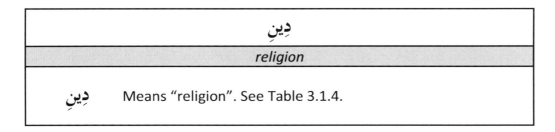

دِينِ
religion
دِينِ Means "religion". See Table 3.1.4.

Table 9.2.7

New Word	أَفْوَاجًا
	(in) crowds

Means "crowds". This is the plural form of (فَوْج).

أَفْوَاج   (فَوْج) means crowd (singular).

(أَفْوَاج) means crowds (plural).

Lessons derived from this verse

Allah's help is so powerful that you can see it continuing right up to today

When Allah's help came, within two years the whole of the Arabian peninsula was filled with faith. It did not stop there, in fact to this very day, people are accepting Islam and it continues to grow. So let's be amongst those who invite others to the religion of Allah.

Shaitan's aim is to take you away from the religion of Allah.
<u>SO BEWARE!</u>

Surah Nasr Verse 3a

In this verse Allah commands Prophet Muhammad (Peace be upon him) to praise Allah and ask forgiveness.

Table 9.3.1

وَاسْتَغْفِرْهُ	رَبِّكَ	بِحَمْدِ	فَسَبِّحْ
and ask His forgiveness	(of) your Lord	with praises	so glorify

There are two new words in this verse.

Table 9.3.2

New Word	فَسَبِّحْ
	so glorify

فَ	Means "so". This letter occurs in the Quran in many places, and often behaves as a prefix.
سَبِّحْ	Means "glorify". This is an imperative tense.

Think of (تَسْبِيْح) in which we glorify Allah. This will help you remember the meaning of this word.

Table 9.3.3

بِحَمْدِ
with praises

بِ	Means "with". See the Hour 5 grammar lesson.

حَمْدِ	Means "praises". See Table 2.3.2.

Table 9.3.4

رَبِّكَ
(of) your Lord
رَبٌّ   Means "Lord". See Table 2.3.4.
كَ   Means "your". This is the singular possessive adjective, see the grammar lesson of Hour 3.

Table 9.3.5

New Word	وَاسْتَغْفِرْهُ
	and ask His forgiveness

اسْتَغْفِرْهُ	Means "ask His forgiveness". It comes from the *masdar* (إِسْتِغْفَار) which means "to ask forgiveness".

> Think of the word (إِسْتِغْفَار), when we ask Allah for forgiveness. This will help you remember the meaning of this word.

Lessons derived from this verse

How much should we ask Allah to forgive us?

Allah is telling Prophet Muhammad (Peace be upon him) to glorify Allah and ask His forgiveness, even though Prophet Muhammad (Peace be upon him) was already forgiven by Allah: all his past sins were forgiven. So how much more should we be glorifying Allah and asking Him to forgive us, when we commit so many sins every day. We need to plan to Glorify Allah and ask His forgiveness.

Signs of Accepted Repentance

1. You do not commit the same sin again, your good deeds increase and your bad deeds decrease.
2. You have fear of Allah.
3. You are remorseful and keep on asking Allah for forgiveness.
4. You are humble and you always address Him with humility.

Signs of Unacceptable Repentance

1. The person's repentance is deficient, he remembers the pleasures of his sins and he gets proud and continues to sin.
2. He is arrogant in being 100% sure that his repentance is accepted.
3. He does not cry and his heart is hardened.
4. There is no increase in his good deeds.

Are you prepared for your death?

All good deeds end with prayers and a request for forgiveness. For example when we offer Salah, we complete our Salah with Duas and a plea for forgiveness. So when Allah is telling Prophet Muhammad (Peace be upon him) to ask for forgiveness, it's a reminder to Prophet Muhammad (Peace be upon him) that he will die. Allah is telling him that he should prepare to meet his Lord by glorifying Him and asking Him for forgiveness.

We need to ask a very important question of ourselves here: Allah is telling Prophet Muhammad (Peace be upon him) to prepare himself to meet his Lord - how much do you think we should prepare ourselves to meet Allah?

Death comes unannounced, so prepare for your death.
<u>DON'T DELAY!</u>

Surah Nasr Verse 3b

In this verse Allah tells us that one of his attributes is that he is 'Oft-Returning'.

Table 9.3.6

تَوَّابًا	كَانَ	إِنَّهُ
Oft-Returning	*is*	*Indeed He*

There are three new words in this verse.

Table 9.3.7

New Word	إِنَّهُ
	Indeed He

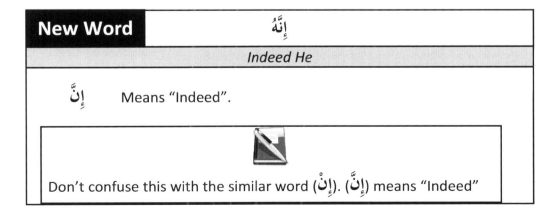

إِنَّ   Means "Indeed".

Don't confuse this with the similar word (إِنْ). (إِنَّ) means "Indeed" and (إِنْ) means "if". These words are frequently used in the Quran.

هُ   Means "He".

Table 9.3.8

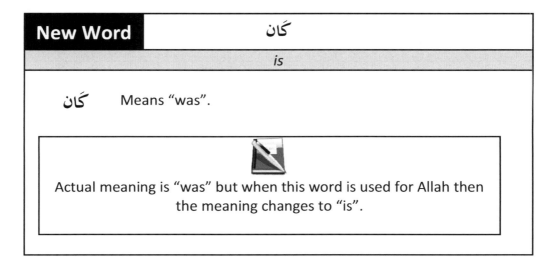

New Word	گَان
is	

گَان   Means "was".

Actual meaning is "was" but when this word is used for Allah then the meaning changes to "is".

Table 9.3.9

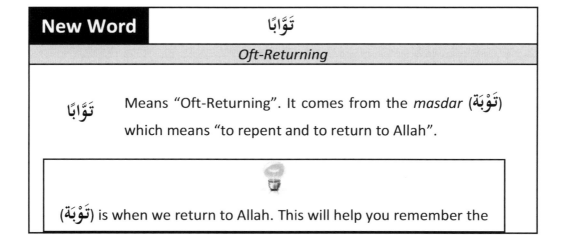

New Word	تَوَّابًا
Oft-Returning	

تَوَّابًا   Means "Oft-Returning". It comes from the *masdar* (تَوْبَة) which means "to repent and to return to Allah".

(تَوْبَة) is when we return to Allah. This will help you remember the meaning of this word.

Lessons derived from this verse

Why do you despair?

Many of us find it difficult to come back to the straight path. We think we have committed so many sins, how can Allah forgive us? We forget that Allah's mercy is greater than our sins. So don't despair: instead turn to Allah with sincere repentance.

Practice what you have learned

وَالْفَتْحُ	نَصْرُاللهِ	جَاءَ	إِذَا
and victory	the help of Allah	comes	When

أَفْوَاجًا	دِينِ اللَّهِ	فِي	يَدْخُلُونَ	النَّاسَ	وَرَأَيْتَ
(in) crowds	the religion of Allah	in	entering	the people	and you see

وَاسْتَغْفِرْهُ	رَبِّكَ	بِحَمْدِ	فَسَبِّحْ
and ask His forgiveness	(of) your Lord	with praises	so glorify

تَوَّابًا	كَانَ	إِنَّهُ
Oft-Returning	is	Indeed He

Don't forget to ponder over the meaning in your next Salah. Pause after every verse, imagine the response from Allah, and try to build humility and love for Allah in your Salah.

Revision of Vocabulary words studied

Meaning	Arabic Word
came	جَاءَ
help	نَصْرُ
victory	فَتْحُ
you see	رَأَيْتَ
they enter	يَدْخُلُونَ
crowds	أَفْوَاجًا
so	فَ
glorify	سَبِّحْ
ask his forgiveness	اسْتَغْفِرْهُ
indeed	إِنَّ
is	كَانَ
Oft-Returning	تَوَّابًا

Phew! Alhumdulillah!

We have completed Surah Nasr. Without Allah's help it would not have been possible, so let's say Alhumdulillah! Let's start to ponder over what we have learnt so far in our salah, and let's increase our repentance to Allah and praise Him for what He has given us.

Take a Break!

In the next section you are going to learn Arabic Grammar. You will learn the Arabic Root Letter system and the Past Tense.

Grammar – Past Tense

In Arabic, unlike English, there are only three tenses. These are:

1. Past Tense
2. Present Tense
3. Imperative Tense.

The present tense expresses both the present and future tenses. In this Hour we will focus on the Past Tense.

Understanding the Arabic Root Letter/Word System

Before we look at the Past Tense, we need to understand how the Arabic root system works. The Arabic language is based on root letters, and from those root letters we can form many words that mean many different things. For example, let's take the Arabic Root word (درس). Table 9.4.1 shows how minor changes using the same root word produces many words.

Table 9.4.1

Arabic Root word (درس)		
مَدْرَسَة	دَرَّسَ	دَرَسَ
a place to study i.e. school	to teach	to study

As you can see, one root word produces other words with related meanings.

Past Tense

Now you have seen how the root system works, let's come back to our topic for this lesson, which is how to form Past Tenses. For example in English we say, He wrote, He sat, He helped and so on. These are Past Tense inflections in English. We also have Past Tense forms in Arabic.

Different Number of Root Letters

The number of letters in Arabic root words is not constant: sometimes a root word consists of three letters, sometimes four, sometimes five letters.

Different Past Tense patterns

The formation of the Past Tense in Arabic depends on the number of letters in the Root Word. You will understand this in stages as you go along. In Three Root Letter Words there are three patterns used to make the past tense.

Table 9.4.2

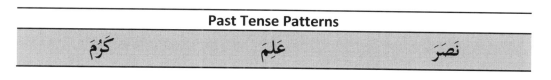

Past Tense Patterns		
كَرُمَ	عَلِمَ	نَصَرَ

Pay attention to the middle letter's vowel sign, that is the only one to change in all three patterns.

Past Tense Form

In this lesson we will form the Past Tense using the first pattern. Table 9.4.3 shows you the Past Tense form for the masculine gender using the first Past Tense pattern which is (نَصَرَ). Study these, paying close attention to the suffixes of the pronoun and the Past Tense form. For example the Past Tense form (كَتَبَا) and the Pronoun (هُمَا) both have the same suffixes. This will make it easy for you to study since you are already now master of these Pronouns.

Table 9.4.3

Past Tense Pattern: نَصَرَ		Gender: Masculine
Pronoun	**Past Tense Form**	**Meaning**
هُوَ	كَتَبَ	He wrote (Singular)
هُمَا	كَتَبَا	They wrote (Dual)
هُمْ	كَتَبُوا	They wrote (Plural)
أَنْتَ	كَتَبْتَ	You wrote (Singular)
أَنْتُمَا	كَتَبْتُمَا	You wrote (Dual)
أَنْتُمْ	كَتَبْتُمْ	You wrote (Plural)

Table 9.4.4

Past Tense Pattern: نَصَرَ	Gender: Feminine

Pronoun	Past Tense Form	Meaning
هِيَ	كَتَبَتْ	She wrote (Singular)
هُمَا	كَتَبَتَا	They wrote (Dual)
هُنَّ	كَتَبْنَ	They wrote (Plural)
أَنْتِ	كَتَبْتِ	You wrote (Singular)
أَنْتُمَا	كَتَبْتُمَا	You wrote (Dual)
أَنْتُنَّ	كَتَبْتُنَّ	You wrote (Plural)

Table 9.4.5

Past Tense Pattern: نَصَرَ		*Gender:* Both (Masculine and Feminine)
Pronoun	**Past Tense Form**	**Meaning**
أَنَا	كَتَبْتُ	I wrote
نَحْنُ	كَتَبْنَا	We wrote

SIGNS TO SHOW THAT A WORD IS A PAST TENSE VERB

1. The verb comes without any suffixes, i.e. (كَتَبَ) which has the same letters as its *masdar*.

2. The verb comes with suffixed pronouns, i.e. (تُ، تَ، تِ) as in (كَتَبْتُ، كَتَبْتَ، كَتَبْتِ).

3. The verb comes with the plural of these pronouns (نَا، تُمْ، تُنَّ) i.e. (كَتَبْنَا، كَتَبْتُمْ، كَتَبْتُنَّ).

Study these Past Tense formations a few times, and see if you can come up with a few examples of your own from the vocabulary you have learnt so far. If you cannot remember any, you may go back and see what words you can find to use as further practice in forming the Past Tense.

This grammar lesson has been slightly longer than usual, but don't worry, we have dedicated the next Hour's grammar lesson to Past Tense formation as well.

Advice and Guidance from the Author

Are you really Grateful to Allah?

In this Surah, Allah reminds us that His blessings on Prophet Muhammad (Peace be upon him) included the conquest of Makkah. He then tells the Prophet (Peace be upon him) to glorify Him with praises. Allah has given us so many bounties and blessings: are we really grateful to Him?

How should you start your day?

The moment we wake up in the morning, our day starts with complaints. We complain about clothes not ironed, food not right, not feeling well, not enough money, house too small and so on and so forth. Look at Muhammad (Peace be upon him): the moment he opens his eyes in the morning from his sleep, the first words on his lips are "All praise to Allah, Who revived us to life after giving us death and to whom we shall return" The first words on the lips of Muhammad (Peace be upon him) were praising Allah for his life.

Components of being a Grateful Servant of Allah

1. Pondering and reflecting over his bounties in your heart. i.e. you visualize the bounty and you are fully aware of it.
2. As you visualize gratitude, it must manifest itself in what is being said, so you are constantly engaged in praising Allah.

3. Using these bounties only in ways that are pleasing to Allah.

What happens when you constantly complain?

We live in a time of constantly complaining. We complain about back ache when we get up in the morning, about the weather not being right, traffic, and so on. We are always complaining. And they say that a person who is constantly complaining creates a negative atmosphere around them. There are people who do not acknowledge, who do not see, what is beautiful. Instead they can only see negativity and so they complain all the time.

A person who is constantly complaining is telling us that his eyes are always focused on what is wrong and what is missing, they do not see or appreciate that which is right and beautiful. And the result is a very negative atmosphere and environment, which is not what we want.

Did you know?

1. In the Quran the opposite of (شكر) gratitude is (كفر) disbelief.
2. Allah says in the Quran "Very few of my servants are really grateful to me." (Quran 34:13).
3. There are only two servants of Allah whom Allah praises in the Quran who were full of gratitude: Prophet Nuh (Alayhis Salam) and Prophet Ibrahim (Alayhis Salam).

Summary

In this Hour we have completed Surah Nasr, Alhumdulillah! Let's continue considering what we have learnt so far in our salah. Remember to constantly be grateful to Allah for what He has given you.

> People are so bothered about what they *don't* have that they forget to enjoy what they *do* have.

For grammar we studied the Past Tense. Try to master how to form the Past Tense. I can assure you that with Allah's help you will get used to the process.

So far we have learnt 83 words that come in the Quran 14,522 times. Alhumdulillah!

Workshop

The quiz questions and the exercises are provided to further your understanding. Don't worry if you can't answer all of the questions in the quiz. Try your best to answer as many as you can. See Appendix A to check your answers.

Quiz 9

1. What are some of the virtues of Surah Nasr?
2. How does the Arabic root word system work?
3. How did Prophet Muhammad (Peace be upon him) start his day?
4. What happens when you constantly complain?
5. Form Past Tenses for the following verbs. Don't worry about the meanings of the words. They use the pattern (نَصَرَ).

دَخَلَ   خَرَجَ   ضَرَبَ

Exercise

Insert the CD-ROM accompanying this book in your drive. Select the appropriate folder and do the quiz for this Hour. You may do the quiz as many times as you like in order to further your understanding.

Hour 10

At the end of this Hour you will have learnt

85 New Words	Our Aim 200 Words
17,510 Total Words	Our Aim 25,000 Words

Surah Kafiroon and the Past Tense

As Hour 10 begins of this course your vocabulary from the Quran continues to increase. A review of the Surah before beginning its study:

1. It is the sixth from the last Surah of the Quran.
2. It was revealed in Makkah.
3. Prophet Muhammad (Peace be upon him) would recite this Surah and Surah Ikhlas in the two *Rak'ahs* of *Tawaf*.
4. It is equivalent to one fourth of the Quran.
5. Prophet Muhammad (Peace be upon him) would tell his companions to read it before going to sleep because this Surah is a protection from shirk.

The highlights of this Hour include:

- Surah Kafiroon verses 1-6

- Grammar – Continuation of Past Tense forms
- Advice and guidance

Surah Kafiroon Verse 1

In this verse Allah is telling Prophet Muhammad (Peace be upon him) to give this message to the disbelievers.

Table 10.1.1

الْكَافِرُونَ	يَا أَيُّهَا	قُلْ
disbelievers	"O	Say

There are two new words in this verse.

Table 10.1.2

قُلْ
Say
قُلْ Means "Say". See Table 5.1.2.

Table 10.1.3

New Word	يَا أَيُّهَا
	"O
يَا أَيُّهَا	Means "O" It is used to call someone. There are other similar words used for calling someone in Arabic. For example:

(يَا) is used for masculine and feminine gender

(يَا أَيُّهَا) is used for masculine gender

(يَا أَيَّتُهَا) is used for feminine gender.

All three words have the same meaning, "O".

Table 10.1.4

New Word	الْكَافِرُونَ
	disbelievers
كَافِرُونَ	Means "disbelievers". This is the plural form for (كَافِر) which means "disbeliever". It comes from the *masdar* (كفر) which means "to cover", and because the disbeliever covers the truth that's why a person who covers and hides the truth is called a (كَافِر).

Lessons derived from this verse

Do we also hide the truth?

When the truth is presented to us, do we sometimes hide it by not following it? We say 'I understand, but my parents have taught me so and so,' or 'My teacher has taught me so and so,' or 'Because of my culture I don't want to follow what you say.' We need to be careful about this.

Do not think that this verse is referring to other human beings who hide the truth. For every single verse from the Quran, you must ask yourself, what message does Allah have for me in this verse? So ask yourself, when the path of Allah and His Prophet Muhammad (Peace be upon him) is presented to me, am I following it or not? Or am I following my own desires and culture?

Surah Kafiroon Verse 2

In this verse Allah tells Prophet Muhammad (Peace be upon him) the message to give to the disbelievers.

Table 10.2.1

مَا تَعْبُدُونَ	لَا أَعْبُدُ
what you worship	*I do not worship*

There are no new words in this verse.

Table 10.2.2

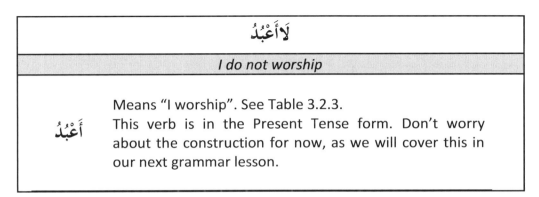

لَا أَعْبُدُ
I do not worship
أَعْبُدُ   Means "I worship". See Table 3.2.3. This verb is in the Present Tense form. Don't worry about the construction for now, as we will cover this in our next grammar lesson.

The root word for this word is (عبد). This word is in several places in this Surah in different forms. As we have said above, this is the Present Tense form.

Table 10.2.3

مَا تَعْبُدُونَ
what you worship

مَا	Means "what". See Table 6.2.3.
تَعْبُدُونَ	Means "you worship". It comes from the root word (عَبَد). This is a Present Tense Plural Form.

Surah Kafiroon Verse 3

In this verse Allah continues with His message to give to the disbelievers.

Table 10.3.1

مَا أَعْبُدُ	عَابِدُونَ	وَلَا أَنْتُمْ
(of) what I worship	*(are) worshippers*	*And not you*

There are no new words in this verse.

Table 10.3.2

وَلَا أَنْتُمْ	
And not you	
وَ	Means "and". This is a conjunction.
لَا	Means "not".
أَنْتُمْ	Means "you all". See the Hour 1 grammar lesson.

Table 10.3.3

عَابِدُونَ	
(are) worshippers	
عَابِدُونَ	Means "worshippers". It comes from the root word (عَبَد). This is an Active Participle Plural Form. We will study this in a future grammar lesson.

Table 10.3.4

مَا أَعْبُدُ	
(of) what I worship	
أَعْبُدُ	Means "I worship". It comes from the root word (عَبَد). This is a Present Tense Form.

Surah Kafiroon Verse 4

In this verse Allah further continues to give His message to the disbelievers.

Table 10.4.1

مَا عَبَدْتُمْ	عَابِدٌ	وَلَا أَنَا
(of) what you worship	a worshipper	And not I am

There are no new words in this verse.

Table 10.4.2

وَلَا أَنَا	
And not I am	
أَنَا	Means "I". See the Hour 1 grammar lesson.

Table 10.4.3

عَابِدٌ	
a worshipper	
عَابِدٌ	Means "worshipper". It comes from the root word (عَبَد). This is an Active Participle Singular Form.

Table 10.4.4

مَا عَبَدْتُمْ
(of) what you worship
عَبَدْتُمْ   Means "you worship". It comes from the root word (عَبَد). This is a Present Tense Plural Form.

Surah Kafiroon Verse 5

In this verse Allah further continues to give His message to the disbelievers.

Table 10.5.1

مَا أَعْبُدُ	عَابِدُون	وَلَا أَنْتُمْ
(of) what I worship	*are worshippers*	*And not you*

There are no new words in this verse.

Table 10.5.2

وَلَا أَنْتُمْ
And not you
وَلَا أَنْتُمْ   Means "and not you". See Table 10.3.2.

Table 10.5.3

عَابِدُون
(are) worshippers

عَابِدُون	Means "worshippers". It comes from the root word (عَبَد). This is an Active Participle Plural Form. We will study Active Participle in future grammar lessons.

Table 10.5.4

مَا أَعْبُدُ
(of) what I worship

أَعْبُدُ	Means "I worship". It comes from the root word (عَبَد). This is a Present Tense Form.

Lessons derived from this verse

Can I follow my culture and customs?

We should never compromise our religion. However when we are living in a particular culture, if it does not go against our religion, then there is no problem in living in that way. When it comes to those things which Allah has prohibited, we cannot compromise in those things. Our obedience firstly goes to Allah, since He is our creator.

Don't let Shaitan make you compromise your religion, that's his initial step.

Surah Kafiroon Verse 6

In this verse Allah further continues to give His message to the disbelievers.

Table 10.6.1

دِينِ	وَلِيَ	دِينُكُمْ	لَكُم
(is) my religion	*and for me*	*(is) your religion*	*For you*

There are no new words in this verse.

Table 10.6.2

لَكُم
For you
لَكُم   Means "for you". The letter (ل) is a preposition which we covered in the grammar lesson in Hour 5.

Table 10.6.3

دِينُكُمْ
your religion
دِينُ   Means "religion". See Table 3.1.4.
كُمْ   Means "your". See the grammar lesson in Hour 3.

Table 10.6.4

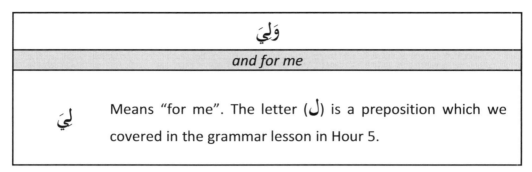

وَلِيَ
and for me
لِيَ   Means "for me". The letter (ل) is a preposition which we covered in the grammar lesson in Hour 5.

Table 10.6.5

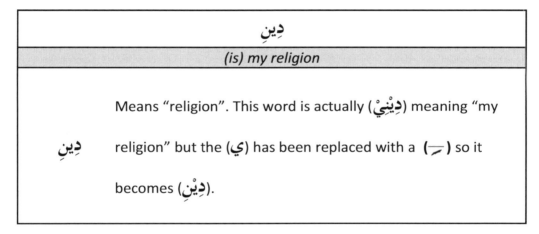

دِينِ
(is) my religion
دِينِ   Means "religion". This word is actually (دِيْنِي) meaning "my religion" but the (ي) has been replaced with a (ـِ) so it becomes (دِيْنِ).

Lessons derived from this verse

The best way to convey Allah's message

When we convey Allah's message to others, we must deliver it with wisdom and beautiful preaching. We must continue to pass on Allah's message until that message is not welcome. If after conveying Allah's message they are still not guided, then we say "your way is yours and my way is mine." What we must not do is use this verse 'for you is your religion and for me is my religion' as our first response. Instead, we must deliver Allah's message and as a last resort, Allah says, tell them "your way is yours and my way is mine."

Practice what you have Learned

الْكَافِرُونَ	يَا أَيُّهَا	قُلْ
disbelievers	"O	Say

مَا تَعْبُدُونَ	لَاأَعْبُدُ
what you worship	I do not worship

مَا أَعْبُدُ	عَابِدُونَ	وَلَا أَنْتُمْ
(of) what I worship	(are) worshippers	And not you

مَا عَبَدْتُمْ	عَابِدٌ	وَلَا أَنَا
(of) what you worship	a worshipper	And not I am

مَا أَعْبُدُ	عَابِدُون	وَلَا أَنْتُمْ
(of) what I worship	are worshippers	And not you

دِينِ	وَلِيَ	دِينُكُمْ	لَكُمْ
(is) my religion	and for me	(is) your religion	For you

Don't forget to ponder over the meaning in your next Salah. Pause after every verse, imagine the response from Allah, and try to build humility and love for Allah in your Salah.

179

Revision of Vocabulary words studied

Meaning	Arabic Word
O	يَا أَيُّهَا
disbelievers	كَافِرُونَ
I worship	أَعْبُدُ
you worship	تَعْبُدُونَ
worshippers	عَابِدُونَ
worshipper	عَابِدٌ
you worship	عَبَدْتُمْ
religion, way of life	دِين

Phew! Alhumdulillah!

We have completed Surah Kafiroon. Without Allah's help it would not have been possible, so let's say Alhumdulillah! Let's start to ponder over what we have learnt so far in our salah. Let's increase our knowledge of shirk, and the wrong path, so that we can stay away from it. Remember to read this surah before going to sleep at night, understand it, ponder over it, live by it and also spread it.

Take a Break!

Grammar – Past Tense

Recap of the Grammar Lesson in Hour 9

Our last lesson was about Arabic Root Words. We also learnt one way to form the Past Tense. We said there are three patterns for Past Tense and we used the first pattern (نَصَرَ). In this Hour we will look at the second pattern which is (عَلِمَ). There are three Tables because the formation produces different words depending on gender.

Table 10.7.1

Past Tense Pattern: عَلِمَ		Gender: Masculine
Pronoun	**Past Tense Form**	**Meaning**
هُوَ	عَلِمَ	He knew (Singular)
هُمَا	عَلِمَا	They knew (Dual)
هُمْ	عَلِمُوا	They knew (Plural)
أَنْتَ	عَلِمْتَ	You knew (Singular)
أَنْتُمَا	عَلِمْتُمَا	You knew (Dual)
أَنْتُمْ	عَلِمْتُمْ	You knew (Plural)

Table 10.7.2

Past Tense Pattern: عَلِمَ		Gender: Feminine
Pronoun	**Past Tense Form**	**Meaning**
هِيَ	عَلِمَتْ	She knew (Singular)
هُمَا	عَلِمَتَا	They knew (Dual)
هُنَّ	عَلِمْنَ	They knew (Plural)
أَنْتِ	عَلِمْتِ	You knew (Singular)
أَنْتُمَا	عَلِمْتُمَا	You knew (Dual)
أَنْتُنَّ	عَلِمْتُنَّ	You knew (Plural)

Table 10.7.3

Past Tense Pattern: نَصَرَ		Gender: Both (Masculine and Feminine)
Pronoun	**Past Tense Form**	**Meaning**
أَنَا	عَلِمْتُ	I knew
نَحْنُ	عَلِمْنَا	We knew

SIGNS TO SHOW THAT A WORD IS A PAST TENSE VERB

1. The verb has no suffixes such as (عَلِمَ), which is exactly the same as the *masdar*.

2. The verb has suffixed pronouns such as (تُ، تَ، تِ) as in (عَلِمْتُ، عَلِمْتَ، عَلِمْتِ)

3. The verb comes with the plural of these pronouns (نَا، تُمْ، تُنَّ) as in (عَلِمْنَا، عَلِمْتُمْ، عَلِمْتُنَّ)

Study these Past Tense forms a few times, and see if you can come up with some examples of your own from the vocabulary you have learnt so far. If you cannot remember any, you may go back and see if you can find some words to practice forming Past Tenses.

Advice and Guidance from the Author

No Compromise in Religion

When it comes to faith, Tawheed, the basic and the fundamental teachings of Islam, there is no compromise permitted. We should NEVER compromise these beliefs and behaviours. However, when it comes to fiqh issues, we should not forget that we are dealing with other human beings. There are times in the process that we forget this, and as a result, we end up crushing each other's souls and spirits, and that is not acceptable.

Fiqh issues - for example whether we should pray 20 Rak'ah Taraweeh or 8 Rak'ah; should we follow the local moon sighting or the Saudi moon sighting - are all minor issues. Allah is not going to punish anyone for having minor fiqh variations, but to raise voices or fight about them: this is prohibited. Do what is good, because these differences are utterly trivial and In Sha Allah everything you do has good in it. So compromise is permitted in matters of fiqh, but never in Tawheed.

When dealing with fiqh differences, remember:
Unity is **MORE IMPORTANT** than any Fiqh Issue
DON'T BREAK THE UNITY!

Summary

In this Hour we have completed Surah Kafiroon, Alhumdulillah! Let's continue pondering over what we have learnt so far in our salah. Remember this Surah is a protection from shirk. Never fall in to the sin of shirk: this sin Allah will never forgive unless you repent. Therefore this Surah is very important.

For grammar we studied another Past Tense pattern. Practice these patterns. You need to be familiar with them.

So far we have learnt 85 words which occur in the Quran 17,510 times. Alhumdulillah!

Workshop

The quiz questions and the exercises are provided to further your understanding. Don't worry if you can't answer all of the questions in the quiz. Try your best to answer as many as you can. See Appendix A to check your answers.

Quiz 10

1. How should we deal with differences with regards to tawheed issues?
2. How should we deal with differences with regards to fiqh issues?
3. Why is Surah Kafiroon a very important Surah?
4. What are some of the virtues of this Surah?
5. Form the Past Tense for the following verbs. Don't worry about the meanings of these words. For these words use the pattern (عَلِمَ)

Exercise

Insert the CD-ROM accompanying this book into your drive. Select the appropriate folder and do the quiz for this Hour. You may do the quiz as many times as you like in order to further your understanding.

Hour 11

At the end of this Hour you will have learnt

Surah Kawthar and the Present Tense

In this Hour we will study Surah Kawthar. This is one of the shortest Surahs in the Quran. A review of Surah Kawthar before we study it:

1. It is the seventh from last Surah of the Quran.
2. It was revealed in Makkah.
3. It discusses the blessings and favours given by Allah to Prophet Muhammad (Peace be upon him).
4. It talks about Al-Kawthar (the river in paradise) being given to Prophet Muhammad (Peace be upon him).

Let's make Dua to Allah and let's approach this Hour in the firm belief that Allah will make this Hour easy for us.

The highlights of this hour include:

- Surah Kawthar verses 1-3
- Grammar – the Present Tense
- Advice and guidance

Surah Kawthar Verse 1

In this verse Allah tells us of a blessing given to Prophet Muhammad (Peace be upon him).

Table 11.1.1

الْكَوْثَرَ	أَعْطَيْنَاكَ	إِنَّا
Al-Kawthar	We have granted you	Indeed, We

There are two new words in this verse.

Table 11.1.2

إِنَّا
Indeed, We
إِنَّا   Means "Indeed, We". See Table 9.3.7 which shows "indeed He".

Table 11.1.3

New Word	أَعْطَيْنَاكَ
We have granted you	
أَعْطَيْنَاكَ (أَعْطَى) Means "to give", "to grant". (نَا) means "We". (كَ) means "you".	

Table 11.1.4

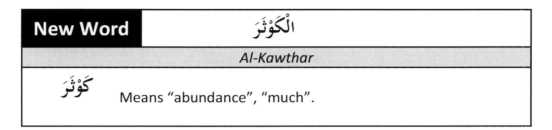

New Word	الْكَوْثَرَ
	Al-Kawthar
كَوْثَرَ	Means "abundance", "much".

Lessons derived from this verse

Do you know how dangerous innovations are?

Allah is referring to a river in paradise when He mentions "Al-Kawthar" in this verse. This is one of the great blessings given to Prophet Muhammad (Peace be upon him). In a Hadith, Prophet Muhammad (Peace be upon him) describes this river. It is a river whose banks are of gold and its riverbed is pearls. Its water is whiter than milk and sweeter than honey. Those who innovate in religion will not be permitted to drink. A beautiful description of this river, but the one who innovates in religion will be deprived from its blessings.

BEWARE OF INNOVATION! It is the path of Shaitan.

Surah Kawthar Verse 2

In this verse Allah instructs Prophet Muhammad (Peace be upon him) to thank Him for His blessings by praying and sacrificing to Allah.

Table 11.2.1

وَانْحَرْ	لِرَبِّكَ	فَصَلِّ
and sacrifice	*for your Lord*	*So pray*

There are two new words in this verse.

Table 11.2.2

New Word	فَصَلِّ
	So pray
فَ	Means "So". It is a prefix. See Table 9.3.2.
صَلِّ	Means "pray". This is an imperative tense form. Meaning it is a command given to Prophet Muhammad (Peace be upon him). We will cover this tense in a later grammar lesson.

Table 11.2.3

	لِرَبِّكَ
	for your Lord
لِ	Means "for". See the Hour 5 grammar lesson on Prepositions.
رَبِّكَ	Means "your Lord". (كَ) means "your". See Possessive Adjectives in the Hour 3 grammar lesson.

Table 11.2.4

New Word	وَانْحَرْ
	and sacrifice
وَانْحَرْ	Means "and sacrifice". This is an imperative tense form. Meaning it is a command given to Prophet Muhammad (Peace be upon him).

Think of (يَوْمُ النَّحَر) "the day of sacrifice". This will help you remember the meaning of this word.

Lessons derived from this verse

Are you grateful to Allah?

Allah is telling Prophet Muhammad (Peace be upon him) that, since "We have given to you Al-Kawthar in the hereafter and in this world," then offer your prayers and sacrifices sincerely and only to your Lord. Reflect for a moment on how much Allah has given to us. Just think about the air that we breathe every moment. We should also show our gratitude to Allah by praying ONLY to Him and sacrificing ONLY for Him.

Salah and Sacrifice are the two greatest acts of worship.
No wonder Shaitan distracts us from our salah and our mind keeps on wandering.
In Sha Allah with this course your mind will not wander.

Surah Kawthar Verse 3

In this verse Allah is warning those who are enemies of Prophet Muhammad (Peace be upon him) and his teachings.

Table 11.3.1

الْأَبْتَرُ	هُوَ	إِنَّ شَانِئَكَ
the one cut off	*he (is)*	*Indeed your enemy*

There are two new words in this verse.

Table 11.3.2

New Word	إِنَّ شَانِئَكَ
Indeed your enemy	
إِنَّ	Means "indeed". See Table 9.3.7.
شَانِئَكَ	Means "your enemy" (شَانِئ) comes from the *masdar* (شَنَأٌ) which means "to hate". Here it means "the one who hates you" i.e. your enemy.

Table 11.3.3

هُوَ
he is
هُوَ Means "he". See Pronouns in the Hour 1 grammar lesson.

Table 11.3.4

New Word	الْأَبْتَرُ
	the one cut off
أَبْتَرُ	Means "the one cut off". It comes from the *masdar* (بَتَرَ) which means "to cut off".

Lessons derived from this verse

Do not hate any of the Teachings of Islam

This verse does not apply only to those who are enemies of Prophet Muhammad (Peace be upon him). It also applies to those who are enemies to the message he brought with him, i.e. the guidance, the truth and the teachings. So: we may not be an enemy of Prophet Muhammad (Peace be upon him,) but we need to ask ourselves, do we really love the teachings that he came with? Do we love the *hijab*, the beard, and so forth?

Practice what you have learned

الْكَوْثَرَ	أَعْطَيْنَاكَ	إِنَّا
Al-Kawthar	We have granted you	Indeed, We

وَانْحَرْ	لِرَبِّكَ	فَصَلِّ
and sacrifice	for your Lord	So pray

الْأَبْتَرُ	هُوَ	إِنَّ شَانِئَكَ
the one cut off	he (is)	Indeed your enemy

Don't forget to ponder over the meaning during your next Salah. Pause after every verse, imagine the response from Allah, and try to build humility and love for Allah in your Salah.

Revision of vocabulary words studied

Meaning	Arabic Word
We have granted you	أَعْطَيْنَاكَ
Kawthar	كَوْثَرَ
So pray	فَصَلِّ
sacrifice	اَنْحَرْ
your enemy	شَانِئَكَ
one cut off	أَبْتَرُ

Phew! Alhumdulillah!

We have completed Surah Kawthar. Without Allah's help it would not have been possible, so let's say Alhumdulillah! Let's start to ponder over what we have learnt so far in our salah, and let's increase our gratitude towards Allah by offering prayers and sacrifice. Remember to understand it, ponder over it, live it, and also spread it.

Take a Break!

In the next section you are going to learn Arabic Grammar.

Grammar – the Present Tense

Only three tenses In Arabic

In the grammar lesson in Hour 9, we said that there are three tenses in Arabic: the Past, the Present and the Imperative Tenses. We have so far completed the Past Tense, and you should be able to form the Past Tense easily, using any of the three patterns.

Now we will look at the Present Tense. In English we say, he writes, he is writing, he reads, he is reading and so on. Now that you know how to form the Past Tense, forming the Present Tense isn't as difficult.

Different Patterns of Present Tense

Just like the three patterns for Past Tense, similarly there are three common patterns for Present Tense formation. Remember the pattern may change if the number of letters in the Root Word increases. We will start with the three patterns for Present Tense formation when using Root Words of three letters.

Table 11.4.1

Present Tense Patterns		
يَفْتَحُ	يَجْلِسُ	يَنْصُرُ

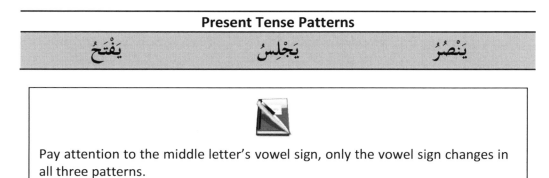

Pay attention to the middle letter's vowel sign, only the vowel sign changes in all three patterns.

Present Tense Form

In this lesson we will form the Present Tense using the first pattern. Table 11.4.2 shows you the Present Tense form for the masculine gender using the pattern (يَنْصُرُ). Study these Present Tense forms by paying close attention to the prefixes of the Present Tense forms. This will make it easy for you to study because you just need to remember the prefixes in forming the Present Tense. Don't confuse them with the Past Tense, where we were focusing on the suffixes.

Table 11.4.2

Present Tense Pattern: يَنْصُرُ		Gender: Masculine
Indicative Letter	**Present Tense Form**	**Meaning**
ي	يَكْتُبُ	He writes (Singular)
	يَكْتُبَانِ	They write (Dual)
	يَكْتُبُونَ	They write (Plural)
ت	تَكْتُبُ	You write (Singular)
	تَكْتُبَانِ	You write (Dual)
	تَكْتُبُونَ	You write (Plural)

Table 11.4.3

Present Tense Pattern: يَنْصُرُ		Gender: Feminine
Indicative Letter	**Present Tense Form**	**Meaning**
ت	تَكْتُبُ	She writes (Singular)
	تَكْتُبَانِ	They write (Dual)
ي	يَكْتُبْنَ	They write (Plural)
ت	تَكْتُبِينَ	You write (Singular)
	تَكْتُبَانِ	You write (Dual)
	تَكْتُبْنَ	You write (Plural)

Table 11.4.4

Present Tense Pattern: يَنْصُرُ		Gender: Both (Masculine and Feminine)
Indicative Letter	**Present Tense Form**	**Meaning**
أ	أَكْتُبُ	I write
ن	نَكْتُبُ	We write

SIGNS TO SHOW THAT A WORD IS A PRESENT TENSE
All verbs in the Present Tense start with one of the following letters
(أ، ي، ت، ن) known as the indicative letters for the Present Tense.

Study the examples above, paying close attention to the indicative letters, and see if you can come up with a few examples of your own from the vocabulary you have learnt so far. If you cannot remember any, you may go back, and see if you can find any words to use to form Present Tense Verbs.

Advice and Guidance from the Author

Is your worship of Allah a burden on your shoulders, or is it due to your love for Him?

When we say we love Allah and His teachings, our actions must show our love for Allah. Our actions are our evidence of our love for Allah. If we just say it and our actions do not show it, then our religion just becomes nice words, and no one is interested in nice words.

When we claim any quality that we have, it has to be demonstrated. If I say I am the best writer, you will say, show me. If I say I am the best teacher, you will say, show me. Similarly when we say we love Allah, we need to show that we love Allah and our actions must testify to this.

When you love someone you do what pleases them, and your greatest joy is pleasing the one whom you love. If you love your spouse, your greatest joy will be pleasing your spouse. At the same time there is honour (*tashreef*) in serving the one you love. And only when this love has gone or is weakened does serving that person become a burden (*takleef*). It goes from *tashreef* only into *takleef*; from honour to a burden. Unfortunately, for some of us, worship of Allah has become a burden, *takleef*. We don't worship Him because we love Him. We only worship Him to take duty off our shoulders and get it out of our way.

True obedience to Allah will only come when you love Allah

Aisha (Radiyallahu Anha) says that "The first verses to be revealed were not about Halal and Haram. If the first verses to be revealed were about not consuming alcohol, the people would have said, we will never give up alcohol." (Hadith) The first verses to be revealed were about who Allah is, and loving Allah. Later on when the verses about Halal and Haram came, the companions embraced them immediately due to their love for Allah.

When the verses were revealed prohibiting alcohol, barrels of alcohol were emptied in the streets of Madinah never to be filled up again. When verses came about *hijab*, the companions said "We were tearing pieces of cloth to cover ourselves up." This obedience can only come when you have love for Allah.

No Love = No obedience to Allah
No Love = Our worship to Allah is a burden
Love Present = Complete obedience to Allah
Love Present = You will feel honoured worshipping Allah.

Love Allah first and then by knowing who Allah is you will love Him more. The more you know Him the more you will love Him. In Sha Allah this course will help you in knowing who Allah is by understanding the message of Allah, the Quran.

Summary

In this Hour we have completed Surah Kawthar, Alhumdulillah. Let's continue pondering what we have learnt so far in our salah. Remember to be engaged in the two acts most beloved by Allah: Salah and Sacrifice. Also remember to perform all acts of worship for Allah alone and no one else.

For grammar we studied the Present Tense. Practice forming the Present Tense; I can assure you that with Allah's help you will get used to the process.

So far we have learnt 91 words that occur in the Quran 17,527 times. Alhumdulillah!

Workshop

The quiz questions and the exercises are provided to further your understanding. Don't worry if you can't answer all of the questions in the quiz. Try your best to answer as many as you can. See Appendix A to check your answers.

Quiz 11

1. What is kawthar?
2. What is the description of the river in paradise?
3. Who will not get to drink from this river?
4. How can I love Allah?
5. Form the Present Tense of the following verbs. Don't worry about

   their meanings. These words use the pattern (يَنْصُرُ)

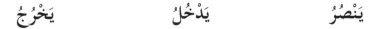

يَخْرُجُ   يَدْخُلُ   يَنْصُرُ

Exercise

Insert the CD-ROM accompanying this book into your drive. Select the appropriate folder and do the quiz for this hour. You may do the quiz as many times as you like in order to further your understanding.

Hour **12**

At the end of this Hour you will have learnt

103 New Words 17,859 Total Words	Our Aim 200 Words Our Aim 25,000 Words

Surah Ma'un and the Present Tense

In this Hour we will study Surah Ma'un. A bit of review of this Surah before studying it:

1. It is the eighth from the last Surah of the Quran
2. It was revealed in Makkah
3. It is called Ma'un because Allah condemned those who refuse to perform neighbourly deeds.

The highlights of this hour include:

- Surah Ma'un verses 1-7
- Grammar – the Present Tense
- Advice and guidance

Surah Ma'un Verse 1

In this verse Allah is asking us a question: who is the one who denies the Day of Judgment.

Table 12.1.1

بِالدِّينِ	يُكَذِّبُ	الَّذِي	أَرَأَيْتَ
the judgment?	denies	the one who	Have you seen

There is only one new word in this verse.

Table 12.1.2

أَرَأَيْتَ	
Have you seen	
أَ	Means "have". It is used to ask questions.
رَأَيْتَ	Means "you saw". See Table 9.2.2.

Table 12.1.3

الَّذِي	
the one who	
الَّذِي	Means "who" See Relative Pronouns in the Hour 8 grammar lesson.

Table 12.1.4

New Word	يُكَذِّبُ
	denies
يُكَذِّبُ	Means "he denies". It comes from the *masdar* (تَكْذِيْب) which means "to deny".

Table 12.1.5

بِالدِّينِ
the judgment?
دِين Means "judgment". See Table 3.1.4.

Lessons derived from this verse

Who is the one who denies the Day of Judgment

Allah asks this question, and answers it in the following verses of this Surah.

Just proclaiming that you believe in the Day of Judgment is NOT sufficient. Your actions must demonstrate that you believe in it.

Surah Ma'un Verse 2

This verse gives the first characteristic of the person who denies the Day of Judgment.

Table 12.2.1

الْيَتِيمَ	يَدُعُّ	الَّذِي	فَذَلِكَ
the orphan	repulses	(is) the one who	Then that

There are two new words in this verse.

Table 12.2.2

فَذَلِكَ	
Then that	
فَ	Means "Then". It is a prefix. See Table 9.3.2.
ذَلِك	Means "that". See Demonstrative Pronouns in the Hour 7 grammar lesson.

Table 12.2.3

الَّذِي	
(is) the one who	
الَّذِي	Means "who". See the Hour 8 grammar lesson on relative nouns.

Table 12.2.4

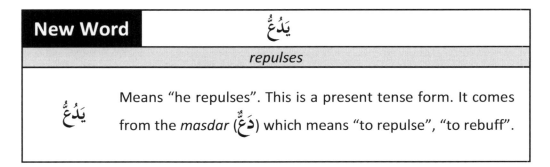

New Word	يَدُعُّ
repulses	
يَدُعُّ	Means "he repulses". This is a present tense form. It comes from the *masdar* (دَعٌّ) which means "to repulse", "to rebuff".

Table 12.2.5

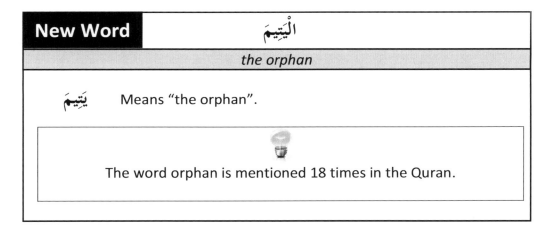

New Word	الْيَتِيمَ
the orphan	
يَتِيمَ	Means "the orphan".

> The word orphan is mentioned 18 times in the Quran.

Lessons derived from this verse

Do you know how important taking care of Orphans is?

In the Quran Allah mentions orphans and taking care of them eighteen times. Can you imagine how important it is to take care of orphans? Allah is saying that the one who denies the Day of Judgment is he who oppresses the orphan and does not give him his just due. He does not feed him, nor is he kind to him.

We need to ask ourselves, do we take care of orphans? Or do we look down upon them and not care for them?

Prophet Muhammad (Peace be upon him) said, "The one who cares for an orphan and myself will be together in paradise like this," and he held his two fingers together. (Bukhari)

Always take care of the orphans.

Surah Ma'un Verse 3

In this verse Allah gives the second characteristic of the one who denies the Day of Judgment.

Table 12.3.1

الْمِسْكِينِ	طَعَامِ	عَلَى	وَلَا يَحُضُّ
the poor.	feeding	on	and not urges

There are three new words in this verse.

Table 12.3.2

New Word	يَحُضُّ
and not urges	
يَحُضُّ	Means "he urges". This is a present tense form. It comes from the *masdar* (حَضَّ) which means "to urge", "to encourage".

Table 12.3.3

عَلَى	
on	
عَلَى	Means "on". See the Hour 6 grammar lesson on prepositions.

Table 12.3.4

New Word	طَعَام
feeding	
طَعَام	Means "feeding", as a noun it means "food".

Table 12.3.5

New Word	الْمِسْكِين
the poor.	
الْمِسْكِين	Means "the poor".

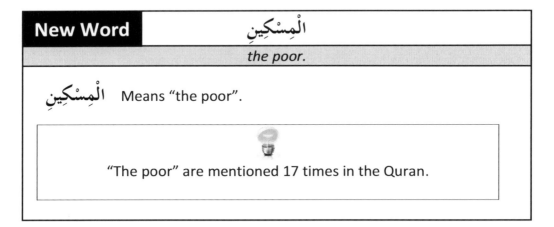

"The poor" are mentioned 17 times in the Quran.

Lessons derived from this verse

Do we feed the poor or do we make excuses?

When we see a poor person, do we feed them, do we give to them from what Allah has given to us? Or do we say, "I don't think you are poor," or "I don't believe you that you are poor, so I will not give you anything from my wealth."

To investigate is NOT our business

Remember that investigating is not our business. Many times a person came to Prophet Muhammad (Peace be upon him) and said "I don't have food, I am poor." Prophet Muhammad (Peace be upon him) went inside, and whatever he had he gave it to the person. He did not ask, or have doubts about him, and say to himself, "I don't think he is poor."

What the poor person does with your money is irrelevant

Once a man was walking down the street, and a mother carrying her baby approached him and said, "My baby is dying. I need some food," so he gave her $1000. Later on, when he went home he heard on the news that the woman carrying the baby was fooling people, saying her baby is dying. He said Alhumdulillah when he heard this. His family asked him: "Why are you saying Alhumdulillah? You have been fooled!" He said, "The baby is not dying any more. My aim was to save the baby, and the baby is saved!"

When a person is in need, always give a helping hand. Never Refuse!

Surah Ma'un Verse 4

In these next two verses Allah curses those who are neglectful of their Salah.

Table 12.4.1

لِلْمُصَلِّينَ	فَوَيْلٌ
to those who pray	So woe

There is one new word in this verse.

Table 12.4.2

New Word	فَوَيْلٌ
	So woe
فَ	Means "So". It is a prefix. See Table 9.3.2.
وَيْلٌ	Means "woe", "destruction".

Table 12.4.3

لِلْمُصَلِّينَ
to those who pray
مُصَلِّينَ	Means "those who are offering salah". This is the plural form for (مُصَلٍّ) which means "one who is offering salah".

Surah Ma'un Verse 5

This verse is cursing those who are neglectful of their Salah.

Table 12.5.1

سَاهُونَ	صَلَاتِهِمْ	هُمْ عَنْ	الَّذِينَ
neglectful	their prayers	(they) are with	those who

There is only one new word in this verse.

Table 12.5.2

الَّذِينَ
those who

الَّذِينَ	Means "who". See Relative Pronouns in the Hour 8 grammar lesson.

Table 12.5.3

هُمْ عَنْ
(they) are with

هُمْ	Means "they". See the Hour 1 grammar lesson on Pronouns.
عَنْ	Means "with". See the Hour 5 grammar lesson on Prepositions.

Table 12.5.4

صَلَاتِهِمْ
their prayers

صَلَاة	Means "prayers".

Table 12.5.5

New Word	سَاهُونَ
neglectful;	

سَاهُونَ	Means "neglectful". It comes from the *masdar* (سَهْوٌ) which means "negligence", "mistake".

You know when we make a mistake in Salah, we do (سَجْدَة سَهو),
the prostration of negligence. This will help you remember the meaning of this word.

Lessons derived from this verse

Time to Think!

We need to ask ourselves these questions:

- Do we offer salah five times a day?
- If so, do we offer them on time?
- If so, are we sincere when we offer them?
- Is your mind wandering and thinking about the *dunya*? In Sha Allah you should now have a lot more *khushu* and sincerity than you did before this course.

Better **LATE** than **NEVER**!

In this verse Allah curses those who do good deeds and show them off to others.

Table 12.6.1

يُرَاءُونَ	الَّذِينَ هُمْ
show off	*Those who*

There is only one new word in this verse.

Table 12.6.2

الَّذِينَ هُمْ	
Those who	
الَّذِينَ	Means "who" See the Hour 8 grammar lesson on Relative Nouns.
هُمْ	Means "they" See the Hour 1 grammar lesson on Pronouns.

Table 12.6.3

New Word	يُرَاءُونَ
	show off
يُرَاءُونَ	Means "they show off". It comes from the *masdar* (مُرَاءَاةٌ) which means "to show off".

Lessons derived from this verse

After every verse, imagine Allah is talking to you!

Allah is saying, woe to people who show off their good deeds. We need to ask ourselves, do we boast about what we do? In every single verse, Allah is talking to you. Don't think "This verse is not for me: Allah is talking about other people who do evil deeds." No! Allah is talking to you. Ask yourself, ponder these verses, and change yourself.

> Don't think "I am perfect." You can **NEVER** be perfect. There is always room for improvement.

Surah Ma'un Verse 7

In this verse Allah curses those who are not good to their neighbours.

Table 12.7.1

الْمَاعُونَ	وَيَمْنَعُونَ
(neighbourly) needs.	and refuse

There are two new words in this verse.

Table 12.7.2

New Word	وَيَمْنَعُونَ
	and refuse
يَمْنَعُونَ	Means "they refuse" It comes from the *masdar* (مَنْعٌ) which means "to refuse", "to prevent".

Table 12.7.3

New Word	الْمَاعُونَ
(neighbourly) needs.	
مَاعُونَ	Means "the small things, such as small kindness and gifts, like sugar, salt, needle etc."

Lessons derived from this verse

Are you selective in being good to your neighbours?

Allah is saying woe to people who refuse to provide for their neighbours' needs. We need to ask ourselves, how do we behave to our neighbours? Do we differentiate between muslims and non-muslims? Are we selective in showing our kindness to them? For example: "I will only be good to them if they are good to me"?

Love for everyone what you love for yourself

Prophet Muhammad (Peace be upon him) said, "You cannot be a believer until you love for your brother what you love for yourself." (Muslim)

Imam Nawawi commenting on this Hadith says that the brotherhood mentioned here is not the brotherhood of faith, but the brotherhood of humanity. Which means you cannot be a believer until you love for your brother in humanity what you love for yourself.

Practice what you have learned

أَرَأَيْتَ	الَّذِي	يُكَذِّبُ	بِالدِّينِ
Have you seen	the one who	denies	the judgment?

فَذَلِكَ	الَّذِي	يَدُعُّ	الْيَتِيمَ
Then that	(is) the one who	repulses	the orphan

وَلَا يَحُضُّ	عَلَى	طَعَامِ	الْمِسْكِينِ
and not urges	on	feeding	the poor.

فَوَيْلٌ	لِلْمُصَلِّينَ
So woe	to those who pray

الَّذِينَ	هُمْ عَنْ	صَلَاتِهِمْ	سَاهُونَ
those who	(they) are with	their prayers	neglectful;

الَّذِينَ هُمْ	يُرَاءُونَ
Those who	show off

وَيَمْنَعُونَ	الْمَاعُونَ
and refuse	(neighbourly) needs.

Don't forget to ponder over the meaning in your next Salah. Pause after every verse, imagine the response from Allah, and try to build humility and love for Allah in your Salah.

Revision of vocabulary words studied

Meaning	Arabic Word
denies	يُكَذِّبُ
he repulses	يَدُعُّ
orphan	يَتِيمَ
he urges	يَحُضُّ
feeding / food	طَعَامِ
poor	مِسْكِينِ
woe	وَيْلٌ
neglectful	سَاهُونَ
show off	يُرَاءُونَ
they refuse	يَمْنَعُونَ
neighborly needs	مَاعُونَ

Phew! Alhumdulillah!

We have completed Surah Ma'un. Without Allah's help it would not have been possible, so let's say Alhumdulillah!. Let's ponder what we have learnt so far in our salah, and let's take care of orphans, and the poor. Let's do good deeds for the sake of Allah and not to show them off, and let's be good and kind to our neighbours. Remember to understand the message from this surah, ponder over it, implement it and also spread it.

Take a Break!

Grammar – the Present Tense

Recap:

In Hour 11 we learnt one formation process for the Present Tense. We said that there are three patterns, and we used the first one (يَنْصُرُ). In this Hour we will look at the second pattern which is (يَجْلِسُ).

Table 12.8.1

Present Tense Pattern: يَجْلِسُ		Gender: Masculine
Indicative Letter	**Present Tense Form**	**Meaning**
ي	يَجْلِسُ	He sits (Singular)
	يَجْلِسَانِ	They sit (Dual)
	يَجْلِسُونَ	They sit (Plural)
ت	تَجْلِسُ	You sit (Singular)
	تَجْلِسَانِ	You sit (Dual)
	تَجْلِسُونَ	You sit (Plural)

Table 12.8.2

Present Tense Pattern: يَجْلِسُ		Gender: Feminine
Indicative Letter	**Present Tense Form**	**Meaning**
ت	تَجْلِسُ	She sits (Singular)
	تَجْلِسَانِ	They sit (Dual)
ي	يَجْلِسْنَ	They sit (Plural)
	تَجْلِسِينَ	You sit (Singular)
ت	تَجْلِسَانِ	You sit (Dual)
	تَجْلِسْنَ	You sit (Plural)

Table 12.8.3

Present Tense Pattern: يَجْلِسُ		Gender: Both (Masculine and Feminine)
Indicative Letter	**Present Tense Form**	**Meaning**
أ	أَجْلِسُ	I sit
ن	نَجْلِسُ	We sit

SIGNS TO SHOW THAT A WORD IS A PRESENT TENSE

All Present Tense verbs start with one of the following letters, (أ، ي،

ت، ن) known as the indicative letters for the Present Tense.

Study these Present Tense Verbs, paying close attention to the indicative letters, and see if you can come up with some examples of your own from the vocabulary you have learnt so far. If you cannot think of any, you may go back and see if you can find any words to use to practice forming the Present Tense.

Advice and Guidance from the Author

Excellent Akhlaq (morals) and less Ibadah (worship), or less Akhlaq and a lot of Ibadah, which one is better?

If you have excellent akhlaq and minimum ibadah, then your abundance of akhlaq will make up for the deficiency in your ibadah.

However, if you have an abundance of ibadah and no akhlaq, then your abundance of ibadah will not make up for the deficiency in your akhlaq.

A person praying five times a day can still be in hell

A person came to Prophet Muhammad (Peace be upon him) and said, "Oh Prophet of Allah, there is this woman who prays day and night, but she is not good with her neighbours", The Prophet (Peace be upon him) said, "She is in hell". Then the person said, "There is another woman who only prays her minimum salah, five times a day, but she is excellent with her neighbours." The Prophet (Peace be upon him) said, "She is in paradise".

DON'T be selective among your neighbours. Be good all the time and with everyone.

Be good in your own homes first

Sometimes we are so concerned about what is happening in other parts of the world, and we feel for our brothers and sisters living elsewhere, but in our own homes, we are occasionally guilty of injustice towards our own family. We want to be just with, and be good to, our Muslim brothers and sisters, but we forget our own family.

Think **GLOBALLY** act **LOCALLY**
It becomes a problem when we think **GLOBALLY**
but don't act **LOCALLY**

Summary

In this hour we have completed Surah Ma'un, Alhumdulillah! Let's continue pondering what we have learnt so far in our salah. Remember to be good, take care of the orphans, the poor and the needy and be good to your neighbours.

For grammar we studied the Present Tense. Try to master these forms: by now you should be able to easily form the Present Tense.

So far we have learnt 103 words that occur in the Quran 17,859 times. Alhumdulillah!

Workshop

The quiz questions and the exercises are provided to further your understanding. Don't worry if you can't answer all of the questions in the quiz. Try your best to answer as many as you can. See Appendix A to check your answers.

Quiz 12

1. What is the reward for taking care of orphans?
2. Who are the people who deny the Day of Judgment?
3. Whom has Allah cursed in this Surah?
4. Form the Present Tense for the following verbs. Don't worry about the meanings: these words use the pattern (يَجْلِسُ)

يَنْعِمُ   يَحْسِبُ   يَضْرِبُ

Exercise

Insert the CD-ROM accompanying this book into your drive. Select the appropriate folder and do the quiz for this hour. You may do the quiz as many times as you like in order to further your understanding.

Hour 13

At the end of this Hour you will have learnt

112 New Words 17,995 Total Words	Our Aim 200 Words Our Aim 25,000 Words

Surah Quraish and the Imperative Tense

In this Hour we will study Surah Quraish. A bit of review of this Surah before studying it:

1. It is the ninth from the last Surah of the Quran
2. It was revealed in Makkah
3. It reminds the Quraish tribe of Allah's favours to them
4. It also talks about the physical needs Allah met for them.

Let's make Dua to Allah and let's approach this Hour in the firm belief that Allah will make this Hour easy for us.

The highlights of this hour include:

- Surah Quraish verses 1-4
- Grammar – the Imperative Tense
- Advice and guidance

Surah Quraish Verse 1

In this verse Allah relates some of the favours He granted the Quraish tribe.

Table 13.1.1

قُرَيْشٍ	لِإِيلَافِ
(of the) Quraish,	*For (the) covenants*

There are two new words in this verse.

Table 13.1.2

New Word	لِإِيلَافِ
For (the) covenants	
لِ	Means "for". See the Hour 5 grammar lesson on Prepositions.
إِيلَافِ	Means "covenants". A pact or promise, often with religious connotations. To stick to something and be devoted to it with a sense of familiarity.

Table 13.1.3

New Word	قُرَيْشٍ
(of the) Quraish,	
قُرَيْشٍ	Means "Quraish". The dominant tribe of Makkah.

Surah Quraish Verse 2

In this verse Allah continues listing His favours to the Quraish.

Table 13.2.1

وَالصَّيْفِ	الشِّتَاءِ	رِحْلَةَ	إِيلَافِهِمْ
and summer.	(in) winter	(covering) journeys	their covenants

There are three new words in this verse.

Table 13.2.2

إِيلَافِهِمْ
their covenants
إِيلَافِ   Means "covenants". See Table 13.1.2 above.

Table 13.2.3

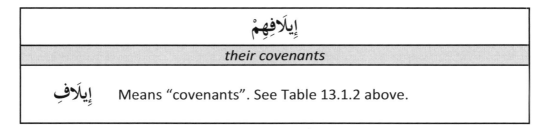

New Word	رِحْلَةَ
(covering) journeys	
رِحْلَةَ Means "journey", "trip".	

Table 13.2.4

New Word	الشِّتَاءِ
(in) winter	
شِتَاءِ Means "winter". 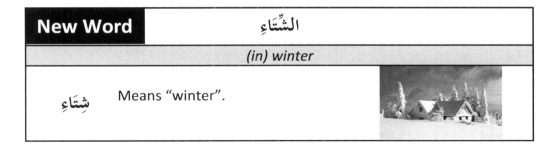	

Table 13.2.5

New Word	وَالصَّيْفِ
and summer.	
صَيْفِ Means "summer". 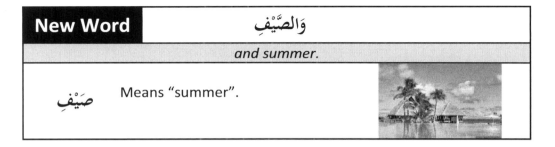	

Lessons derived from this verse

Don't be ungrateful to your Lord

The Quraish tribe was able to trade during summer and winter without any difficulties, so Allah is reminding the Quraish of His favours granted to them. We also need to remind ourselves of Allah's favours to us and be grateful for His favours and blessings upon us.

Don't let Shaitan make you ungrateful to your Lord.

Surah Quraish Verse 3

In this verse Allah instructs the Quraish to worship Him.

Table 13.3.1

الْبَيْتِ	هَذَا	رَبَّ	فَلْيَعْبُدُوا
house,	(of) this	(the) Lord	So let them worship

There is one new word in this verse.

Table 13.3.2

فَلْيَعْبُدُوا	
So let them worship	
فَ	Means "So". See Table 9.3.2 for this prefix.
يَعْبُدُوا	Means "they worship". This is a Plural Present Tense form. See Table 3.2.3.

Table 13.3.3

رَبَّ	
(the) Lord	
رَبَّ	Means "Lord".

Table 13.3.4

هَذَا
(of) this
هَذَا   Means "this". See the Hour 7 grammar lesson on Demonstrative Pronouns.

Table 13.3.5

New Word	الْبَيْتِ
	house,

بَيْتِ   Means "house".

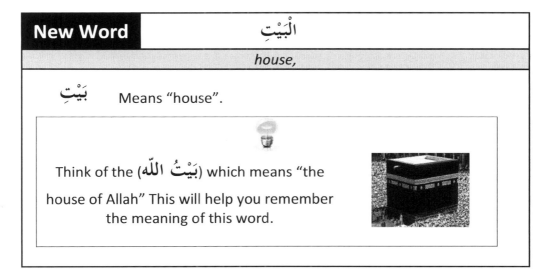

Think of the (بَيْتُ اللّه) which means "the house of Allah" This will help you remember the meaning of this word.

Lessons derived from this verse

Do you really worship Allah alone?

Worship should be to Allah alone and no one else. Prophet Muhammad (Peace be upon him) said, "A time will come when people will make their priests their Lords." So the companions asked "How?" He replied, "When the priests make Halal or Haram you obey them. This obedience to them is worshipping them." That's the reason that blind belief is neither expected nor accepted in Islam. Allah has given every human being intellect for us to use it and not let someone else tell us what to do.

IN ISLAM BLIND BELIEF IS NEITHER EXPECTED NOR ACCEPTED.
Use the intellect Allah has given you.
Don't let someone else do the thinking for you, you are giving so much power to someone else.

<u>DON'T LET SOMEONE ELSE DO THE THINKING FOR YOU!</u>

Surah Quraish Verse 4a

In this verse Allah mentions the two most important things that life revolves around, which are food and safety.

Table 13.4.1

جُوع	مِنْ	أَطْعَمَهُمْ	الَّذِي
hunger	*against*	*fed them*	*Who*

There is only one new word in this verse.

Table 13.4.2

الَّذِي
Who
الَّذِي Means "Who". See the Hour 8 of grammar lesson on Relative Pronouns.

Table 13.4.3

أَطْعَمَهُمْ	
fed them	
أَطْعَمَ	Means "he fed". See Table 12.3.4. The root word is the same (طعم).
هُمْ	Means "them".

Table 13.4.4

مِنْ	
against	
مِنْ	Means "against". See the Hour 5 grammar lesson on Prepositions.

Table 13.4.5

New Word	جُوعٍ
hunger,	
جُوعٍ	Means "hunger".

Surah Quraish Verse 4b

This is the second part of the verse.

Table 13.4.6

مِنْ خَوْفٍ	وَآمَنَهُمْ
from fear.	*and gave them security*

There are two new words in this verse.

Table 13.4.7

New Word	وَآمَنَهُمْ
	and gave them security
آمَنَ	Means "He gave security".
هُمْ	Means "them".

Table 13.4.8

New Word	مِنْ خَوْفٍ
	from fear.
مِنْ	Means "from". See the grammar lesson in Hour 5 for prepositions.
خَوْفٍ	Means "fear".

Lessons derived from this verse

Do you know the two greatest needs of a human being?

The two greatest physical needs of a human being are:

1. Food
2. Safety.

So Allah is saying "Worship the Lord who has taken care of these two great physical needs." He has given you food and He has given you safety. Imagine living in a place of hunger and danger. The question is, when Allah has given us food and safety then what must be our response?

According to an article in "The Guardian", dated 10th January 2013, it says almost half of the world's food is thrown away.

So we need to be grateful to Allah, not just saying it with our voices, but also showing by our actions that we are grateful to Allah that every day He feeds our stomachs with food.

Thirty million people a year
DIE of HUNGER

Practice what you have learned

لِإِيلَافِ	قُرَيْشٍ
For (the) covenants	(of the) Quraish,

إِيلَافِهِمْ	رِحْلَةَ	الشِّتَاءِ	وَالصَّيْفِ
their covenants	(covering) journeys	(in) winter	and summer.

فَلْيَعْبُدُوا	رَبَّ	هَذَا	الْبَيْتِ
So let them worship	(the) Lord	(of) this	house,

الَّذِي	أَطْعَمَهُمْ	مِنْ	جُوعٍ
Who	fed them	against	hunger,

وَآمَنَهُمْ	مِنْ خَوْفٍ
and gave them security	from fear.

Don't forget to ponder over the meaning in your next Salah. Pause after every verse, imagine the response from Allah, and try to build humility and love for Allah in your Salah.

Revision of Vocabulary words studied

Meaning	Arabic Word
covenants	إِيلَافِ
Quraish	قُرَيْشٍ
journey	رِحْلَةَ
winter	شِتَاءِ
summer	صَيْفِ
house	بَيْتِ
hunger	جُوعٍ
he gave security	آمَنَ
fear	خَوْفٍ

Phew! Alhumdulillah!

We have completed Surah Quraish. Without Allah's help it would not have been possible, so let's say Alhumdulillah! Let's start to ponder what we have learnt so far in our salah, let's be grateful to Allah for providing us with food and safety. Understand the message from this Surah, ponder over it, implement it and also spread it.

Take a Break!

In the next section, you are going to learn Imperative Tense for Arabic Grammar.

Grammar – the Imperative Tense

Only three tenses In Arabic

In the Hour 9 grammar lesson we said that there are three tenses in Arabic: The Past, Present, and Imperative Tenses. We have so far completed the study of the Past and Present Tenses. You should now be able to form these tenses without any difficulties. You can always go back and do revision as and when needed.

The Imperative Tense

This Hour we will look at the Imperative Tense, the process of formation and the various patterns. For example in English we have commands such as, write, read, eat, sleep, sit etc. Forming the Imperative Tense isn't as difficult as forming the Past and Present Tenses.

The Imperative Tense is formed by taking the Present Tense form, deleting the prefix, adding the letter (إٕ) or (إِ) at the beginning, and finally adding the vowel *sukoon* at the end.

 *Sukoon* is one of the Arabic vowels. It is placed over a letter when no sound should be pronounced after the letter.

It really isn't difficult! Figure 13.1 demonstrates how easy it is to form the Imperative Tense.

Figure 13.1

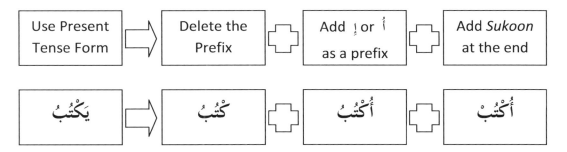

When to use إِ or أُ as a prefix?

If the middle letter of the Present Tense form is (ـُ) then you will use (أُ). In the other two cases as in (ـَ) and (ـِ), you will use (إِ). Study the two examples in Figure 13.2 and pay close attention to the middle letter and the prefix.

Figure 13.2 Change of prefix

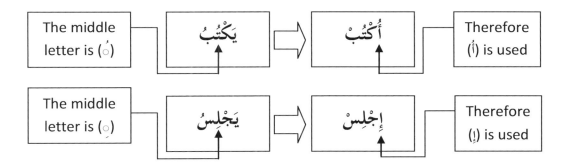

There are three patterns for forming the Imperative Tense using this rule.

Table 13.5.1

Imperative Tense Patterns		
إِفْتَحْ	إِجْلِسْ	أُكْتُبْ

Now you know the rule and the patterns as to how to form the Imperative Tense, let us apply it. Table 13.5.2 shows you the Imperative Tense form for the masculine gender using the first pattern which is (أُكْتُبْ). Study these forms and you will see how the above rule is applied.

Table 13.5.2

Imperative Tense Pattern: أُكْتُبْ	Gender: Masculine
Imperative Tense Form	**Meaning**
أُكْتُبْ	Write (Singular)
أُكْتُبَا	Write (Dual)
أُكْتُبُوْا	Write (Plural)

Table 13.5.3

Imperative Tense Pattern: أُكْتُبْ	Gender: Feminine
Imperative Tense Form	**Meaning**
أُكْتُبِيْ	Write (Singular)
أُكْتُبَا	Write (Dual)

You also delete the (نْ) from the Present Tense form when changing it to the Imperative Tense, except in (Feminine Plural) where you keep it.

Study these Imperative Tense verbs, and see if you can come up with a few examples of your own from the vocabulary you have learnt so far. If you cannot remember any, you may go back and see if you can find any words to use as further practice in forming the Imperative Tense.

Advice and Guidance from the Author

How can you gain the entire world?

In a Hadith the Prophet Muhammad (Peace be upon him) said, "Whosoever wakes safe in his bed, healthy in his body, while he has enough to sustain him for his day and night, then it is as if he has gained the entire world."

We focus so much on what we don't have, that we forget to enjoy what we DO have.

Let's enjoy what Allah has given to us, instead of worrying about the things that we don't have.

Summary

In this Hour we have completed Surah Quraish, Alhumdulillah! Let's continue pondering over what we have learnt so far in our salah. Remember to be grateful to Allah for everything He has given to you.

You must demonstrate your gratitude with your actions, otherwise your gratitude is nothing but nice words, and nice words mean nothing, we all want to see action.

So far we have learnt 112 words that occur in the Quran 17,995 times. Alhumdulillah!

Workshop

The quiz questions and the exercises are provided to further your understanding. Don't worry if you can't answer all of the questions in the quiz. Try your best to answer as many as you can. See Appendix A to check your answers.

Quiz 13

1. What are the two greatest physical needs of a human being?
2. How can someone gain the entire world?
3. How should we be grateful to Allah?
4. What are the steps in the process of forming the Imperative Tense?
5. Form the Imperative Tense for the following verbs. Don't worry about the meanings of these words.

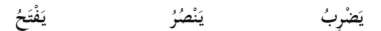

يَفْتَحُ   يَنْصُرُ   يَضْرِبُ

Exercise

Insert the CD-ROM accompanying this book into your drive. Select the appropriate folder and do the quiz for this Hour. You may do the quiz as many times as you like in order to further your understanding.

13

Hour 14

At the end of this Hour you will have learnt

126 New Words **18,684 Total Words**	**Our Aim 200 Words** **Our Aim 25,000 Words**

Surah Fil and Negation

In this Hour we will study Surah Fil. A bit of review of this Surah before studying it:

1. It is the tenth from the last Surah of the Quran.
2. It was revealed in Makkah.
3. It talks about how Allah destroyed the people of Elephant, who were stronger and wealthier than the Quraish tribe.
4. It also talks about Allah destroying these people as they were on their way to destroy the *ka'abah.*

The highlights of this Hour include:

- Surah Quraish verses 1-5
- Grammar – Negation
- Advice and guidance

Surah Fil Verse 1

In this verse Allah is relating something that happened to the people of Elephant.

Table 14.1.1

الْفِيلِ	بِأَصْحَابِ	رَبُّكَ	فَعَلَ	كَيْفَ	تَرَ	أَلَمْ
(of the) elephant?	with (the) companions	your Lord	dealt	how	you seen	Have not

There are several new words in this verse. We will go through this verse one word at a time.

Table 14.1.2

أَلَمْ	
Have not	
أَ	Means "have". It is used to ask questions. See Table 12.1.2.
لَمْ	Means "not". See Table 7.3.2.

Table 14.1.3

تَرَ	
you seen	
تَرَ	Means "you seen". See Table 9.2.2. This is a Present Tense form.

Table 14.1.4

New Word	كَيْفَ
how	
كَيْفَ	Means "how". It is used for asking questions. For example, (كَيْفَ حَال) which means "how are you?".

Table 14.1.5

New Word	فَعَلَ
dealt	
فَعَلَ	Means "he did", "he dealt".

Table 14.1.6

رَبُّكَ	
your Lord	
رَبُّكَ	Means "your Lord".

Table 14.1.7

New Word	بِأَصْحَابِ
with (the) companions	
بِ	Means "with". See the Hour 5 grammar lesson on prepositions.

أَصْحَاب	Means "companions". This is the plural form of (صَاحِب) which means "companion".

Think of the word (صحابة) which refers to the companions of Prophet Muhammad (Peace be upon him). This will help you remember the meaning of this word.

Table 14.1.8

New Word	الْفِيلِ
	(of the) Elephant?
فِيل	Means "Elephant".

Lessons derived from this verse

Allah is asking us but we did not respond!

Allah is asking us the question, "Haven't you seen?" Allah wants us to ponder over this story. We read this Surah many times and Allah is asking us a question, but there is no reply from us. Let us ponder over - and take a lesson from - this Surah. What is the lesson? Lets continue.

14

Surah Fil Verse 2

In this verse Allah mentions that He destroyed the plan of the people of Elephant, which was to destroy the house of Allah.

Table 14.2.1

تَضْلِيلٍ	فِي	كَيْدَهُمْ	يَجْعَلْ	أَلَمْ
astray?	in	their plan	He make	Did not

There are two new words in this verse.

Table 14.2.2

أَلَمْ
Did not
أَلَمْ   Means "Did not".

Table 14.2.3

New Word	يَجْعَلْ
He make	
يَجْعَلْ	Means "He make". This is the Present Tense Form. This word occurs in the Quran 150 times. It comes from the masdar (جعل) which means "to make".

Table 14.2.4

New Word	كَيْدَهُمْ
their plan	
كَيْدَ	Means "plan".

Table 14.2.5

فِي
in
فِي	Means "in". See the Hour 6 grammar lesson on Prepositions. [In English we would use the word 'go' here.]

Table 14.2.6

New Word	تَضْلِيلٍ
astray?	
تَضْلِيلٍ	Means "to mislead", "to misguide". This is also the *masdar* form.

Lessons Derived from This Verse

Planning ahead is one characteristic of a believer

Whatever Allah plans, it's the best plan for us. Allah says in the Quran that "He is the best planner." (Quran 3:54). This does not mean that we as Muslims do not plan ahead. The Prophet (Peace be upon him) said, "There is no intelligence like planning," (Hadith). Intelligence is all about planning. Remember the following four steps:

1. Plan to the best of your ability
2. Make Dua to Allah
3. Leave it in the hands of Allah
4. Be optimistic.

Being optimistic is the best characteristic (Hadith)

If you fail to **PLAN** – You plan to **FAIL**

Surah Fil Verse 3

In this verse Allah tells us how he destroyed their plan. Read on to see what happened and how He destroyed them.

Table 14.3.1

أَبَابِيلَ	طَيْرًا	عَلَيْهِمْ	وَأَرْسَلَ
(in) flocks	*birds*	*upon them*	*And He sent*

There are three new words in this verse.

Table 14.3.2

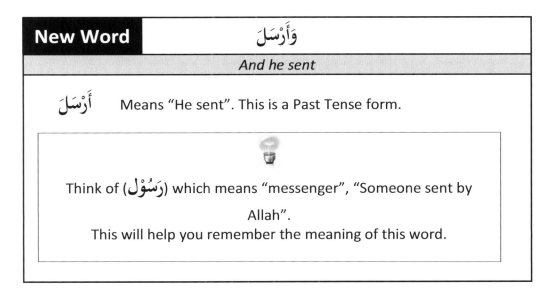

New Word	وَأَرْسَلَ
	And he sent

أَرْسَلَ   Means "He sent". This is a Past Tense form.

> Think of (رَسُوْل) which means "messenger", "Someone sent by Allah".
> This will help you remember the meaning of this word.

Table 14.3.3

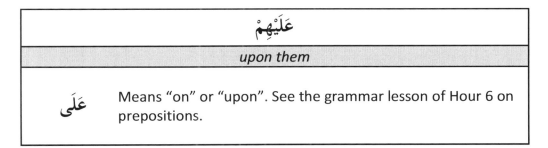

عَلَيْهِمْ
upon them

عَلَى   Means "on" or "upon". See the grammar lesson of Hour 6 on prepositions.

Table 14.3.4

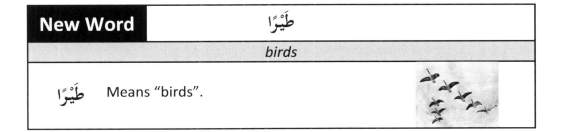

New Word	طَيْرًا
	birds

طَيْرًا   Means "birds".

14

Table 14.3.5

New Word	أَبَابِيلَ
(in) flocks	
أَبَابِيلَ Means "flocks".	

Surah Fil Verse 4

In this verse Allah continues to describe the punishment and their destruction.

Table 14.4.1

سِجِّيلٍ	مِنْ	بِحِجَارَةٍ	تَرْمِيهِمْ
baked clay	of	with stones	throwing upon them

There are three new words in this verse.

Table 14.4.2

New Word	تَرْمِيهِمْ
throwing upon them	
تَرْمِي	Means "she throws" It comes from the *masdar* (رَمْيٌ) which means "to throw".

248

Table 14.4.3

New Word	بِحِجَارَةٍ
	with stones

بِ	Means "with". See the grammar lesson in Hour 5 on Prepositions.
حِجَارَةٍ	Means "stones". This is the plural form for (حَجَرٌ) which means "stone". 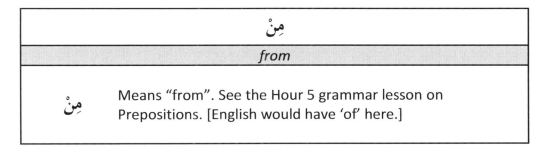

Table 14.4.4

مِنْ
from

مِنْ	Means "from". See the Hour 5 grammar lesson on Prepositions. [English would have 'of' here.]

Table 14.4.5

New Word	سِجِّيلٍ
	baked clay

سِجِّيلٍ	Means "baked clay".

Surah Fil Verse 5

In this verse Allah tells us of the end of the people of Elephant.

Table 14.5.1 Verse 5

مَأْكُولٍ	كَعَصْفٍ	فَجَعَلَهُمْ
eaten up.	like (an empty field of) stalks	then He made them

There are two new words in this verse.

Table 14.5.2

فَجَعَلَهُمْ	
then He made them	
فَ	Means "So". See Table 9.3.2. It is a prefix. [English would use "then" here.]
جَعَلَ	Means "He made". This is the Past Tense Form. See Table 14.2.3.

Table 14.5.3

New Word	كَعَصْفٍ
like (an empty field of) stalks	
كَ	Means "like", when it behaves as a prefix with a noun as in this verse.
عَصْفٍ	Means "empty field of stalks and straw".

250

Table 14.5.4

New Word	مَأْكُولٍ
	eaten-up

مَأْكُولٍ	Means "eaten up". It comes from the *masdar* (أَكْلٌ) which means "to eat". This is a Passive Participle Verb form. We will cover this subject in the grammar lesson of Hour 19.

Lessons derived from this verse

Allah is giving you a chance.

In these last few verses Allah is talking about how He destroyed the people of Elephant, who were on their way to destroy the ka'abah. We need to ask ourselves "How much do we disobey Allah?" If Allah wants, He can punish anyone, anytime. However Allah says in the Quran, that He "gives respite until an appointed term". (Quran 35:45) So before that appointed term comes, change yourselves.

No one knows when their term will come to an end!
We all know our DOB (Date of Birth) but no one knows their DOD (Date of Death).

Practice what you have learned

أَلَمْ	تَرَ	كَيْفَ	فَعَلَ	رَبُّكَ	بِأَصْحَابِ	الْفِيلِ
Have not	you seen	how	dealt	your Lord	with (the) companions	(of the) Elephant?

أَلَمْ	يَجْعَلْ	كَيْدَهُمْ	فِي	تَضْلِيلٍ
Did not	He make	their plan	in	astray?

وَأَرْسَلَ	عَلَيْهِمْ	طَيْرًا	أَبَابِيلَ
And He sent	upon them	birds	(in) flocks

تَرْمِيهِمْ	بِحِجَارَةٍ	مِنْ	سِجِّيلٍ
throwing upon them	with stones	of	baked clay

فَجَعَلَهُمْ	كَعَصْفٍ	مَأْكُولٍ
then He made them	like (an empty field of) stalks	eaten up.

Don't forget to ponder over the meaning in your next Salah. Pause after every verse, imagine the response from Allah, and try to build humility and love for Allah in your Salah.

Revision of Vocabulary words studied

Meaning	Arabic Word
how	كَيْفَ
he did	فَعَلَ
companions	أَصْحَابِ
elephant	فِيلِ
he make	يَجْعَلْ
plan	كَيْدَ
he sent	أَرْسَلَ
birds	طَيْرًا
flocks	أَبَابِيلَ
she throws	تَرْمِي
stones	حِجَارَةٍ
baked clay	سِجِّيلٍ
like	كَ
empty field of stalks and straw	عَصْفٍ
eaten-up	مَأْكُولٍ

Phew! Alhumdulillah!

We have completed Surah Fil. Without Allah's help it would not have been possible, so let's say Alhumdulillah! Let's start to ponder over what we have learnt so far in our salah, let's ask Allah to save us from the punishment in this world and the hereafter. Remember to understand the message from this surah, ponder over it, implement it and also spread it.

Take a Break!

In the next section you are going to learn Arabic Grammar. You will learn Negation in today's grammar lesson.

Grammar – Negation

So far in our previous grammar lessons, we have learnt the three tenses, Past, Present and Imperative. In this lesson you will learn how to form negatation in Arabic Grammar. For example in English we say, don't write, don't read, don't eat, and so forth.

Negation is formed by taking the Present Tense form, adding (لاَ) as a prefix, and adding the vowel *sukoon* at the end.

Don't be confused! Figure 14.1 shows how easy the process is.

Figure 14.1

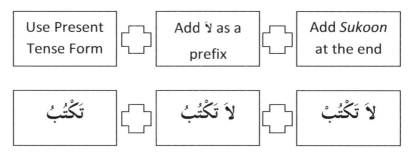

It is always the Present Tense Verb form that you need to use, that will be the basis of forming negation. For example, (تَكْتُبُ) will become (لَا تَكْتُبْ), (تَجْلِسُ) will become (لاَ تَجْلِسْ) and so on. The pattern required by the Present Tense does not change, you simply add (لاَ) as prefix, and *sukoon* at the end.

Table 14.6.1 shows you the Negated verbs for masculine gender using this rule. Study these verbs and you will see how this rule is applied when forming Negated verbs.

Table 14.6.1

Negated Verbs	Gender: *Masculine*
	Meaning
لاَتَكْتُبْ	Do not write (Singular)
لاَتَكْتُبَا	Do not write (Dual)
لاَتَكْتُبُوْا	Do not write (Plural)

Table 14.6.2 shows you the Negated verbs for feminine gender using this rule.

Table 14.6.2

Negated Verbs	Gender: *Feminine*
	Meaning
لاَتَكْتُبِيْ	Do not write (Singular)
لاَتَكْتُبَا	Do not write (Dual)
لاَتَكْتُبْنَ	Do not write (Plural)

You also delete the (نَ) from the Present Tense form when changing it to

Negated verbs, except in (Feminine Plural) where you keep the (نَ).

Study these Negated verbs, and see if you can come up with a few examples of your own from the vocabulary you have learnt so far. If you cannot remember any, you may go back and see if you can find any words to use as further practice in forming Negations.

Advice and Guidance from the Author

Bad habits are like a comfortable bed – easy to get in to but difficult to get out of.

We all make mistakes in our lives, in the sense that no one is perfect. The question is not about making a mistake, it is what do you do when you make one? Do you remain where you are, or do you make a change? And it is better to make a change rather than remain where you are.

However, a big problem arises when our mistakes turn into bad habits. And they say that "bad habits are like a comfortable bed, very easy to get in to, but very difficult to get out of". So we do not want our mistakes and sins turning into bad habits.

Do you know the best Dua you can ask from Allah?

A person came to Prophet Muhammad (Peace be upon him) and asked, "What is the best Dua that you can teach me?" He replied: "Ask Allah for good in this world and in the hereafter." The next day, the person came again and asked the same question. The Prophet (Peace be upon him) replied: "Ask Allah for good in this world and in the hereafter." The third day, the person came again and asked the same question. The Prophet (Peace be upon him) replied "Ask Allah for good in this world and in the hereafter, because if you are given the goodness of this world and the hereafter you will be successful". (Hadith)

14

Summary

In this Hour we have completed Surah Fil, Alhumdulillah! Let's continue pondering over what we have learnt so far in our salah. Remember to change any bad habits you have.

For grammar we studied Negated verbs. Try to master how to form these by studying them and you will easily become familiar with constructing Negated verbs.

So far we have learnt 126 words that occur in the Quran 18,684 times. Alhumdulillah!

Workshop

The quiz questions and the exercises are provided to further your understanding. Don't worry if you can't answer all of the questions in the quiz. Try your best to answer as many as you can. See Appendix A to check your answers.

Quiz 14

1. What does Islam have to say about planning?
2. What is the best *dua* you can make?
3. What are the steps to form Negated Verbs?
4. Form Negated Verbs from the following verbs. Don't worry about the meanings of these words.

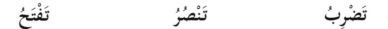

تَفْتَحُ   تَنْصُرُ   تَضْرِبُ

Exercise

Insert the CD-ROM accompanying this book in your drive. Select the appropriate folder and do the quiz for this Hour. You may do the quiz as many times as you like in order to further your understanding.

PART IV

First two *rukus* from Surah Baqrah

Hour

Hour 15

At the end of this Hour you will have learnt

137 New Words	**Our Aim 200 Words**
19,944 Total Words	**Our Aim 25,000 Words**

Surah Baqrah Verses 1-3 and Superlatives

So far, you have completed Surah Fatihah, the first chapter of the Quran, and the last ten chapters. In this Hour we will begin to study Surah Baqrah. By the end of Hour 24, we will complete the first two *rukus* of Surah Baqrah. A bit of review of this Surah before studying it.

1. It is the second Surah of the Quran
2. It is one of the first Surahs to be revealed in Madinah
3. It is the longest Surah of the Quran
4. This Surah has the longest verse in the Quran, Verse: 282
5. It is the Surah in which the last verse of the Quran was revealed, Verse: 281
6. Shaitan will not enter a house in which Surah Baqrah has been recited (Hadith)
7. This Surah contains a thousand new incidents, a thousand commands and a thousand prohibitions.

Let's make Dua to Allah and let's approach this Hour in the firm belief that Allah will make this Hour easy for us.

The highlights of this Hour include:

- Surah Baqrah verses 1-3
- Grammar – Superlatives
- Advice and guidance

Surah Baqrah Verse 1

This surah begins with three individual letters.

Table 15.1.1

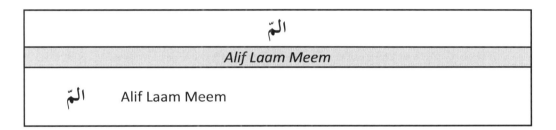

الٓمّ
Alif Laam Meem
الٓمّ   Alif Laam Meem

Lessons derived from this Verse

Meaning of Alif Laam Meem

Some scholars say these are the names of Allah, some say these are names of some of the Surahs of the Quran. The best opinion from all the scholars is that it testifies to the miraculousness of the Quran; that Allah is saying that with these letters, these are your letters, try to produce a Quran like this. This opinion is preferred by many scholars, because every time Allah mentions these letters Allah immediately states the greatness of the Quran. However, only Allah knows the correct meaning.

15

Some ignorant people say some of the words in the Quran don't mean anything, such as these letters. Such people are making a major mistake. They do carry a specific meaning. The correct meaning only Allah knows.

The Quran is a miracle but it has not changed our lives: why?

Allah illustrates in several places in the Quran that this book is a miracle. Why has it not yet changed our life? The reason is that we have not understood the Quran. This course will In Sha Allah help you to understand the Quran and change your life.

The number one thing that guarantees positive change in your life is to read the Quran with understanding.

Surah Baqrah Verse 2

In this verse Allah states the greatness of the Quran, and that it is a guide for believers.

Table 15.2.1

لِلْمُتَّقِينَ	هُدًى	فِيهِ	لَا رَيْبَ	الْكِتَابُ	ذَلِكَ
for (the) God fearing.	a guidance	in it	no doubt	the book	That (is)

There are three new words in this verse.

Table 15.2.2

ذَلِكَ
That (is)
ذَلِكَ   Means "That". See the Hour 7 grammar lesson on Demonstrative Pronouns.   (ذلك) is used for a distant object, but the Quran is here, so why didn't Allah use (هذا)?   Because the word (ذلك) does not necessary point to something distant; it can also be used to point to something high in status. The Qur'an is very high and exalted in its status, and in that sense it is "far."

Table 15.2.3

New Word	الْكِتَابُ
	the book
كِتَابُ Means "book". In this verse, it is referring to the Glorious Quran.	

15

263

Table 15.2.4

New Word	لَا رَيْبَ
	no doubt
لَا	Means "no".
رَيْبَ	Means "doubt".

Table 15.2.5

فِيهِ
in it
فِي   Means "in". See the Hour 6 grammar lesson on Prepositions.

Table 15.2.6

هُدًى
a guidance
هُدًى   Means "guidance". See Table 4.1.2.

Table 15.2.7

New Word	لِلْمُتَّقِينَ
	for (the) God fearing.
لِ	Means "for". See the Hour 5 grammar lesson on

مُتَّقِينَ	Means "God fearing people". It comes from the *masdar* (اِتِّقَاءٌ) which means "to beware of".

Prepositions.

Lessons derived from this verse

Have you ever wondered what is meant by "fearing Allah"?

When Allah tells us to fear Him, it does not mean to fear Him the way we fear a human being, or a policeman or an animal and so forth. That is not the kind of fear expected by Allah. Remember, Allah is the Most Gracious, the Most Merciful, so to have a fear of Allah the same as the way we fear His creation is not doing justice to Allah's attributes of the Most Gracious the Most Merciful.

When we fear Allah, it is the fear which comes out of love for Allah. If there is no love for Allah we cannot fear Him. For example, suppose you love someone in this world, for instance your spouse, and they tell you that if you don't do so and so thing, they won't want to speak to you. Now, because of your love for that person, you will do that thing they have told you to do. They did not scare you, but because of your love for that person, the fear came to you that if you didn't do this thing they would not speak to you. So it's the fear that comes out of love.

Don't try to **FEAR** Allah – **LOVE** Allah - and fear will come naturally.

15

Surah Baqrah Verse 3a

In this verse Allah describes the characteristics of a believer.

Table 15.3.1

الصَّلَاةَ	وَيُقِيمُونَ	بِالْغَيْبِ	يُؤْمِنُونَ	الَّذِينَ
the prayer	and establish	in the unseen	believe	Those who

There are three new words in this verse.

Table 15.3.2

الَّذِينَ	
Those who	
الَّذِينَ	Means "Those". See the Hour 8 grammar lesson on Relative Pronouns.

Table 15.3.3

New Word	يُؤْمِنُونَ
believe	
يُؤْمِنُونَ	Means "they believe". It comes from the *masdar* (إيْمَان) which means "to believe".
Imaan includes, to say with your tongue, to show with your actions and to believe in your heart. All three are important for belief.	

Table 15.3.4

New Word	بِالْغَيْبِ
	in the unseen
بِ	Means "in". See the Hour 6 grammar lesson on prepositions.
غَيْبِ	Means "unseen". For example, the Hereafter, Paradise, Hell and so forth.

Table 15.3.5

New Word	وَيُقِيمُونَ
	and establish
يُقِيمُونَ	Means "they establish". It comes from the *masdar* (إِقَامَة) which means "to make (something) stand straight".

Table 15.3.6

الصَّلَاةَ
the prayer
صَلَاةَ — Means "prayer". See Table 12.5.4.

Surah Baqrah Verse 3b

This verse continues the previous verse.

Table 15.3.7

يُنْفِقُونَ	رَزَقْنَاهُمْ	وَمِمَّا
they spend	we have provided them	and from what

There are two new words in this verse.

Table 15.3.8

وَمِمَّا
and from what

مِمَّا   Means "from what".

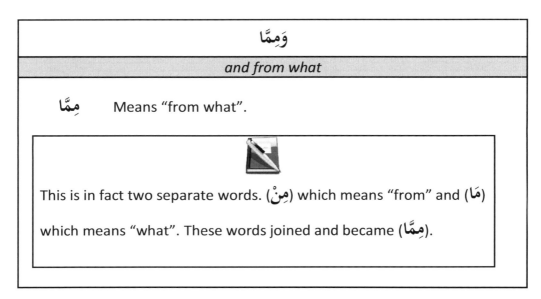

This is in fact two separate words. (مِنْ) which means "from" and (مَا) which means "what". These words joined and became (مِمَّا).

Table 15.3.9

New Word	رَزَقْنَاهُمْ
	we have provided them

رَزَقْنَا   Means "we have provided". It comes from the root word (رزق) which means "sustenance".

Table 15.3.10

New Word	يُنْفِقُونَ
	they spend.
يُنْفِقُونَ	Means "they spend". It comes from the root word (نفق) which means "to run out". And because when you spend, your wealth goes away and runs out the root words are the same.

Lessons derived from this verse

Do you know the characteristics of God-fearing people?

In this verse Allah is describing the characteristics of those who fear Him. The first is to believe in the unseen, that is the Hereafter, Heaven, Hell and so forth. The second is to establish regular prayers, and the third is to spend your wealth in the path of Allah.

Missing any of these steps is not acceptable

Islam is a set of beliefs, these beliefs must be demonstrated in actions, and these actions are rituals. These rituals must impact the character of the individual, and the *character* of the individual is expressed in the *actions* of that individual.

15

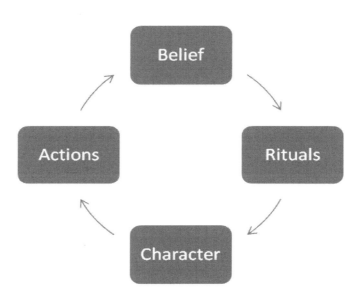

None of the links in the chain above can be missing. That's why Allah and Prophet Muhammad (Peace be upon him) would always refer to Islam to any of these four steps, Belief, Rituals, Character and Actions.

Without action, our religion is nothing but a philosophy and nice words, and no one is interested in nice words, we all want to see action.

Practice what you have learned

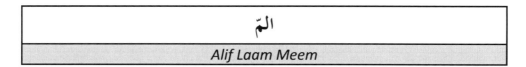

الٓمّ
Alif Laam Meem

لِلْمُتَّقِينَ	هُدًى	فِيهِ	لَا رَيْبَ	الْكِتَابُ	ذَلِكَ
for (the) God fearing.	*a guidance*	*in it*	*no doubt*	*the book*	*This (is)*

الصَّلَاةَ	وَيُقِيمُونَ	بِالْغَيْبِ	يُؤْمِنُونَ	الَّذِينَ
the prayer	and establish	in the unseen	believe	Those who

يُنْفِقُونَ	رَزَقْنَاهُمْ	وَمِمَّا
they spend.	we have provided them	and from what

Don't forget to ponder over the meaning in your next Salah. Pause after every verse, imagine the response from Allah, and try to build humility and love for Allah in your Salah.

Revision of Vocabulary words studied

Meaning	Arabic Word
book	كِتَابٌ
doubt	رَيْبَ
guidance	هُدًى
God fearing people	مُتَّقِينَ
they believe	يُؤْمِنُونَ
unseen	غَيْبِ
they establish	يُقِيمُونَ
we provided	رَزَقْنَا
they spend	يُنْفِقُونَ

15

Phew! Alhumdulillah!

We have completed the first three verses of Surah Baqrah. Without Allah's help it would not have been possible, so let's say Alhumdulillah! Let's start to ponder over what we have learnt so far in our salah, let's ask Allah to guide us from His book and to make us in to people who love Him and fear Him. Remember to understand the message from these verses, ponder over them, implement them and also spread them.

Take a Break!

In the next section, you are going to learn Arabic Grammar. For todays lesson you will learn Superlatives.

Grammar – Superlatives

In this lesson you will learn how to form Superlatives in Arabic Grammar. For example in English we say, bigg*est*, small*est*, tall*est*, *most* beautiful etc. So superlatives in Arabic are similar to "est" or "most" in English.

Different Patterns of Superlatives

In Arabic there are two different patterns. In English, the Superlatives are the same for both masculine and feminine genders, but in Arabic they differ.

Table 15.4.1

Superlative Patterns		
	Masculine	Feminine
Singular	أَفْعَلُ	فُعْلَى
Plural	أَفَاعِل	فُعْلَيَات

Now you know the patterns for Superlatives, we will give you some examples which will help you and give you better understanding. Table 15.4.2 illustrates the process using the word (أَكْبَر) which means "the greatest".

Table 15.4.2

Superlative Patterns		
	Masculine	Feminine
Singular	أَكْبَر	كُبْرَى
Plural	أَكَابِر	كُبْرَيَات

15

Table 15.4.3 illustrates the process using the word (اَحْسَن) which means "the most beautiful".

Table 15.4.3

Superlative Patterns		
	Masculine	Feminine
Singular	أَحْسَن	حُسْنَى
Plural	أَحَاسِن	حُسْنَيَات

Exceptions in certain words

You should now be familiar with forming Superlatives. However there are exceptions. There are nouns which look like superlatives. The basic rule is that a noun which has the meaning of a colour, any defect in the human body, or a sickness, may look like a superlative form, but it is not. Table 15.4.4 illustrates some of these nouns.

Table 15.4.4

Colour		
أَبْيَض	أَسْوَد	أَحْمَر
white	black	red
Sickness or Defect in the human body		
أَعْمَى	أَصَمّ	أَبْكَم
blind	deaf	dumb

As you can see since these denote colours, defects in the human body or illnesses they are not regarded as Superlative verbs.

Study these Superlative patterns, and see if you can come up with a few examples of your own from the vocabulary you have learnt so far. If you cannot remember any, you may go back, and see if you can find any words to use as further practice in forming Superlatives.

Advice and Guidance from the Author

Best book of guidance

The best book of guidance is the book of Allah, the Quran. Since this book is a book of guidance, we can only be guided if we understand it. This is the aim of this course, to help you understand the Quran and so be guided.

Is salah a burden on your shoulders?

Allah is saying that for those who establish regular prayers this is a book of guidance. The question is, do we establish our prayers because it is a burden on our shoulders? or to get it out of the way? To be honest, that is what most of us do. We only pray salah to get it out of the way. In Sha Allah with this course, when you start to understand the Quran, your salah will no longer be a burden on you, it will become an honour for you to worship Allah.

If you understand the message of Allah which you read in your salah, this will change your salah from *takleef* (a burden) into *tashreef* (an honour).

15

Summary

In this hour we have completed the first three verses of Surah Baqrah, Alhumdulillah! Let's continue pondering over what we have learnt so far in our salah.

For grammar we studied how to form Superlatives. Try to master how to form these by practicing them and you will become familiar with the process.

So far we have learnt 137 words that come in the Quran 19,944 times. Alhumdulillah!

Workshop

The quiz questions and the exercises are provided to further your understanding. Don't worry if you can't answer all of the questions in the quiz. Try your best to answer as many as you can. See Appendix A to check your answers.

Quiz 15

1. What are the four steps related to Imaan?
2. What is the best book of guidance?
3. How can you change your salah from a burden into an honour?
4. Make Superlative forms for the following verbs. Don't worry about the meanings for these words. The first form of Masculine Singular is already done for you.

اَجْمَل   اَصْغَر   اَنْصَر

Exercise

Insert the CD-ROM accompanying this book in your drive. Select the appropriate folder and do the quiz for this hour. You may do the quiz as many times as you like in order to further your understanding.

15

Hour **16**

At the end of this Hour you will have learnt

142 New Words **20,401 Total Words**	**Our Aim 200 Words** **Our Aim 25,000** **Words**

Surah Baqrah Verses 4-5 and Comparatives

In this Hour we will continue with Surah Baqrah and study verses 4-5. In these verses Allah is describing the qualities of those people who are following guidance, and those who are successful in this world and in the hereafter.

The highlights of this Hour include:

- Surah Baqrah verses 4-5
- Grammar – Comparatives
- Advice and guidance

Surah Baqrah Verse 4a

In this verse Allah continues to describe the qualities of those people who are God fearing.

Table 16.1.1

إِلَيْكَ	أُنْزِلَ	بِمَا	يُؤْمِنُونَ	وَالَّذِينَ
to you	(is) sent down	in what	believe	And those who

There is only one new word in this verse, all the rest are repeated words.

Table 16.1.2

وَالَّذِينَ
And those who
الَّذِينَ   Means "those". See the Hour 8 grammar lesson on Relative Pronouns.

Table 16.1.3

يُؤْمِنُونَ
believe
يُؤْمِنُونَ   Means "they believe". See Table 15.3.3.

Table 16.1.4

بِمَا
in what
بِ   Means "in". See the Hour 6 grammar lesson on Prepositions.
مَا   Means "what". See Table 6.2.3.

Table 16.1.5

New Word	أُنْزِلَ
(is) sent down	
أُنْزِلَ	Means "sent down". It comes from the root word (نزل) which means "to descend", "to come down". This is a Passive verb, which we will study in a future Grammar lesson.

Table 16.1.6

إِلَيْكَ
to you
إِلَى   Means "to". See the Hour 6 grammar lesson on Prepositions.

Surah Baqrah Verse 4b

This is a continuation of the previous verse.

Table 16.1.7

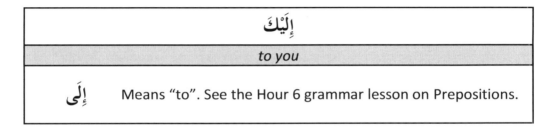

مِنْ قَبْلِكَ	أُنْزِلَ	وَمَا
(from) before you	was sent down	and what

There is only one new word in this verse.

Table 16.1.8

وَمَا
and what
مَا   Means "what". See Table 6.2.3.

Table 16.1.9

أُنْزِلَ
was sent down
أُنْزِلَ   Means "sent down". See Table 16.1.5.

Table 16.1.10

New Word	مِنْ قَبْلِكَ
	(from) before you

مِنْ	Means "from". See the Hour 5 grammar lesson on Prepositions.
قَبْلِ	Means "before".
كَ	Means "you". This is a Possessive Adjective and we have already studied this in our grammar lesson of hour 3.

Surah Baqrah Verse 4c

This is a continuation of the previous verse.

Table 16.1.11

يُوقِنُونَ	هُمْ	وَبِالْآخِرَةِ
firmly believe.	they	and in the hereafter

There are two new words in this verse.

Table 16.1.12

New Word	وَبِالْآخِرَةِ
	and in the hereafter
بِ	Means "in". See the Hour 6 grammar lesson on Prepositions.
آخِرَةِ	Means "hereafter".

Table 16.1.13

هُمْ
they
هُمْ   Means "they". See the Hour 1 grammar lesson on Pronouns.

Table 16.1.14

New Word	يُوقِنُونَ
	firmly believe

> يُوقِنُونَ Means "(they) firmly believe". It comes from the *masdar* (إِيْقَان) which means "to firmly believe".

Lessons derived from this verse

Qualities of God-fearing People

In this verse Allah is describing the characteristics of God-fearing people. One of the characteristics of those who fear Allah is to believe in everything that was sent down to Prophet Muhammad (Peace be upon him). This includes the Quran and the sayings of Prophet Muhammad (Peace be upon him). What does it mean to believe in them? Just saying it aloud is NOT sufficient. Our actions MUST demonstrate that we believe in the Prophet Muhammad (Peace be upon him).

We **MUST** believe in the previous revelations. This does not mean we believe in the current Bible. We believe in the previous revelation, i.e. the revelation given to Prophet Jesus (Peace be upon him), and **NOT** the current Bible.

Another quality of God fearing people is to believe in the hereafter. Believing in the hereafter does not merely mean to say it aloud. Again your actions MUST show that you believe in the hereafter, by preparing for it.

True belief in the hereafter is displayed by preparing for it.
It **MUST** be demonstrated by your actions.

16

Surah Baqrah Verse 5a

In this verse Allah says that the people who have the characteristics given in the previous verses are on guidance.

Table 16.2.1

رَبِّهِمْ	مِنْ	هُدًى	عَلَى	أُولَئِكَ
their Lord	from	guidance	on	Those (are)

There is only one new word in this verse.

Table 16.2.2

New Word	أُولَئِكَ
	Those (are)
أُولَئِكَ	Means "those". See the Hour 7 grammar lesson on Demonstrative Pronouns.

Table 16.2.3

عَلَى
on
عَلَى   Means "on". See the Hour 6 grammar lesson on Prepositions.

Table 16.2.4

هُدًى	
guidance	
هُدًى	Means "guidance". See Table 4.1.2.

Table 16.2.5

مِنْ	
from	
مِنْ	Means "from". See the Hour 5 grammar lesson on Prepositions.

Table 16.2.6

رَبِّهِمْ	
their Lord	
رَبِّهِمْ	Means "their Lord". (هِمْ) is the Possessive Adjective. See the Hour 3 grammar lesson.

Surah Baqrah Verse 5b

This is a continuation of the previous verse.

16

Table 16.2.7

الْمُفْلِحُونَ	هُمْ	وَأُولَئِكَ
(are) the successful ones.	they	and those

There is only one new word in this verse.

Table 16.2.8

وَأُولَئِكَ
and those
أُولَئِكَ   Means "those". See the Hour 7 grammar lesson on Demonstrative Pronouns.

Table 16.2.9

هُمْ
they
هُمْ   Means "they". See the Hour 1 grammar lesson on Pronouns.

Table 16.2.10

New Word	الْمُفْلِحُونَ
	(are) the successful ones
مُفْلِحُونَ	Means "those who are successful". It comes from the *masdar* (إفْلَاح) which means "to be successful". This is an Active Participle verb, which we will study in future

grammar lessons.

In azan the caller says (حَيَّ عَلَى الْفَلاَح) which means "come to success". This will help you remember the meaning of this word.

Lessons derived from this verse

Characteristics of guided and successful people

The Quran mentions these characteristics of those who are guided and successful:

- be conscious of Allah (have taqwa)
- believe in the unseen
- establish the salah
- spend from what Allah has provided to/for you
- believe in what was revealed to the Prophet Muhammad (Peace be upon him)
- believe in what was revealed before him (all previous scriptures) and
- have complete and certain conviction in the Hereafter.

Ask yourself which of these characteristics is missing from your life, and start to implement all of them from today.

How do you make a change in your life?

Psychologists say that if you want to make a change in your life, or you want to make something a habit, then do that thing for twenty one days. If you repeat an action for twenty one days, it becomes a habit. If you want to stop

16

smoking, do not smoke for twenty one days, and if you can do that, then you can stop smoking for the rest of your life.

Success here does not ONLY mean success in the hereafter, it means success in this world too.

Practice what you have learned

وَالَّذِينَ	يُؤْمِنُونَ	بِمَا	أُنْزِلَ	إِلَيْكَ
And those who	believe	in what	(is) sent down	to you

وَمَا	أُنْزِلَ	مِنْ قَبْلِكَ
and what	was sent down	before you

وَبِالْآخِرَةِ	هُمْ	يُوقِنُونَ
and in the hereafter	they	firmly believe.

أُولَئِكَ	عَلَى	هُدًى	مِنْ	رَبِّهِمْ
Those (are)	on	guidance	from	their Lord

وَأُولَئِكَ	هُمْ	الْمُفْلِحُونَ
and those	they	(are) the successful ones.

288

Don't forget to ponder over the meaning in your next Salah. Pause after every verse, imagine the response from Allah, and try to build humility and love for Allah in your Salah.

Revision of Vocabulary words studied

Meaning	Arabic Word
was sent down	أُنْزِلَ
before you	قَبْلِكَ
hereafter	آخِرَة
they firmly believe	يُوقِنُونَ
those	أُولَئِكَ
successful ones	مُفْلِحُونَ

Phew! Alhumdulillah!

We have completed verses 4-5 of Surah Baqrah. Without Allah's help it would not have been possible, so let's say Alhumdulillah! Let's start to ponder over what we have learnt so far in our salah. Let's ask Allah to make us into people who have been guided by Allah and into those who are successful in this world and in the hereafter. Ameen. Remember to understand the message from these verses, ponder over it, implement it and also spread it.

Take a Break!

16

In the next section, you are going to learn Arabic Grammar. For todays lesson you will learn Comparatives.

Grammar – Comparatives

In English we say, big*er than*, small*er than*, tall*er than*, *more* beautiful *than* and so forth. So Comparatives in Arabic are similar to "-er than" or "more – than" in English.

In order to form comparatives, use the process illustrated in figure 16.1. The rule is to use the Superlative form followed by the preposition (مِنْ).

Figure 16.1

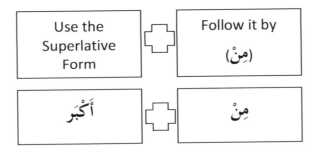

Now you know how simple it is to form Comparatives in Arabic grammar.

Table 16.3.1

Comparative Examples		
	Comparative form	**Meaning**
Masculine/Singular	أَكْبَر مِنْ	Bigger than
Feminine/Singular	كُبْرَى مِنْ	Bigger than
Masculine/Singular	أَصْغَر مِنْ	Smaller than
Feminine/Singular	صُغْرَى مِنْ	Smaller than

Study these Comparative examples, and see if you can come up with a few examples of your own from the vocabulary you have learnt so far. If you cannot remember any, you may go back and see if you can find any words to use as further practice in forming Comparatives.

Advice and Guidance from the Author

Do you think you can live the life you want and at the time of death you will recite the kalimah?

Allah says in these verses that true success is for those who firmly believe in the hereafter. The question is, do your actions demonstrate that you believe in the hereafter?

We are so indulged in this worldly life, satisfying our desires with the pleasures of this world, and we think that when death comes we will recite lailaha illal llah and that's it, we will be ok.

Do you know that at the time of death, your tongue will not speak, it is whatever is in your heart that will speak. If you have love for this world in your heart, then that will speak. If your heart is full of hatred, grudges against others, and jealousy and so on then that will speak. But if your heart is full of Love for Allah, then and ONLY then the tongue will be given permission to say lailaha illal llah.

Path of Shaitan: Enjoy your life exactly the way you want and at the time of death just recite the kalimah.
Path of Allah: Have love for Me throughout your life, and I will grant you kalimah and a blessed ending.

What are the best deeds to prepare for the hereafter?

The best deeds to do for the hereafter are those deeds which benefit people. As Allah says in the Quran "while that which benefits people remains on the earth" (Quran 13:17). Also in the hadith the Prophet (Peace be upon him) said that "Three things will benefit a person when he dies; the knowledge which he spread, continuous charity, and the pious offspring he left behind". (Hadith)

All of these three things stated by Prophet Muhammad (Peace be upon him) benefit people.

Do those deeds that will benefit people. You will be rewarded so long as people benefit from it.

Summary

In this Hour we have completed verses 4-5 from Surah Baqrah, Alhumdulillah! Let's continue pondering what we have learnt so far in our salah. Remember to prepare yourself for the hereafter.

For grammar we studied how to form Comparatives. Try to master how to form these by studying them and they will easily become familiar.

So far we have learnt 142 words that come in the Quran 20,401 times. Alhumdulillah!

Workshop

The quiz questions and the exercises are provided to further your understanding. Don't worry if you can't answer all of the questions in the quiz. Try your best to answer as many as you can. See Appendix A to check your answers.

Quiz 16

1. What are the characteristics of those who are guided by Allah and successful?
2. How can a person make a change in his life?
3. What are the best deeds for the hereafter?
4. Make comparative forms for the following words. Don't worry about the meanings of these words.

أَرْخَص   أَجْمَل   اَحْسَن

Exercise

Insert the CD-ROM accompanying this book in your drive. Select the appropriate folder and do the quiz for this Hour. You may do the quiz as many times as you like in order to further your understanding.

16

Hour 17

At the end of this Hour you will have learnt

Surah Baqrah Verses 6-7 and Active Participles

In this Hour we will continue with Surah Baqrah and study verses 6-7. In these verses Allah is talking about those people whose hearts and hearing Allah has sealed. Therefore whether you warn them or you do not, it does not make a difference to them.

Let's make Dua to Allah and let's approach this Hour in the firm belief that Allah will make this Hour easy for us.

The highlights of this Hour include:

- Surah Baqrah verses 6-7
- Grammar – Active Participles
- Advice and guidance

Surah Baqrah Verse 6a

In this verse Allah is talking about people for whom it makes no difference whether you warn them or not.

Table 17.1.1

عَلَيْهِمْ	سَوَاء	كَفَرُوا	الَّذِينَ	إِنَّ
on them,	(it) is (the) same	disbelieved	those who	Indeed

There is only one new word in this verse.

Table 17.1.2

إِنَّ
Indeed
إِنَّ   Means "Indeed". See Table 9.3.7.

Table 17.1.3

الَّذِينَ
those who
الَّذِينَ   Means "those". See the Hour 8 grammar lesson on Relative Pronouns.

Table 17.1.4

كَفَرُوا
disbelieved
كَفَرُوا   Means "they disbelieved". See Table 10.1.4.

Table 17.1.5

New Word	سَوَاءٌ
(it) is (the) same	
سَوَاءٌ Means "it is equal", "it is the same".	

Table 17.1.6

عَلَيْهِمْ
on them
عَلَيْهِمْ   Means "on them". (عَلَى) See the Hour 6 grammar lesson on Prepositions. [English would say "to them"].

Surah Baqrah Verse 6b

This is a continuation of the previous verse.

Table 17.1.7

لَا يُؤْمِنُونَ	تُنْذِرْهُمْ	لَمْ	أَمْ	أَأَنْذَرْتَهُم
not they believe.	*you warn them*	*not*	*or*	*whether you warn them*

There are two new words in this verse.

Table 17.1.8

New Word	أَأَنْذَرْتَهُم
	whether you warn them
أَ	This letter is used for asking questions, but the meaning changes depending on the context. It can mean "do?" "are?" "is?". Here it means "Whether". We will cover this in more detail in future grammar lessons.
أَنْذَرْتَ	Means "you warn". It comes from the *masdar* (إِنْذَار) which means "to warn", "warning". This is a Present Tense.

Table 17.1.9

New Word	أَمْ
	or
أَمْ	Means "or".

This word normally comes after the (أَ) just like it is used at the beginning of this sentence. The meaning of it is "or" [meaning: whether (this) or (that)].

Table 17.1.10

لَمْ
not
لَمْ   Means "not". See Table 7.3.2.

Table 17.1.11

تُنْذِرْهُمْ
you warn them
تُنْذِرْ   Means "you warn". See Table 17.1.8.

Table 17.1.12

لَا يُؤْمِنُونَ
not they believe.

لَا	Means "not".
يُؤْمِنُونَ	Means "they believe". See Table 15.3.3.

Lessons derived from this verse

Do not stop delivering Allah's message

Prophet Muhammad (Peace be upon him) was very eager to have people believe in him and in the message that he brought from Allah, but many people did not believe. Yet this did not stop Prophet Muhammad (Peace be upon him) from continuing to deliver Allah's message.

So, when you deliver Allah's message to anyone - whether Muslim or Not Yet Muslim - and they don't accept it or believe it, this should not stop you from persevering in delivering Allah's message.

Does this verse change our lives?

In many verses Allah describes His punishments, yet this makes no difference in our lives. "Yes," we say, "we believe in His punishments", but if what you believe does not impact how you behave, then what you believe is not really important.

Surah Baqrah Verse 7a

In this verse Allah is describing the people who will not change having heard Allah's message.

Table 17.2.1

سَمْعِهِمْ	وَعَلَى	قُلُوبِهِمْ	عَلَى	خَتَمَ اللَّهُ
their hearing	and on	their hearts	on	Allah has set a seal

There are three new words in this part of the verse.

Table 17.2.2

New Word	خَتَمَ اللّٰهُ
	Allah has set a seal

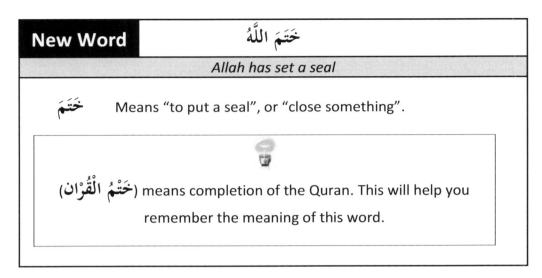

خَتَمَ   Means "to put a seal", or "close something".

(خَتْمُ الْقُرْان) means completion of the Quran. This will help you remember the meaning of this word.

Table 17.2.3

عَلَى
on

عَلَى   Means "on". See the Hour 6 grammar lesson on Prepositions.

Table 17.2.4

New Word	قُلُوبِهِمْ
	their hearts

قُلُوبِ   Means "hearts". This is the plural form of (قَلْب) which means "heart".

Table 17.2.5

وَعَلَى
and on
عَلَى   Means "on". See the Hour 6 grammar lesson on Prepositions.

Table 17.2.6

New Word	سَمْعِهِمْ
	their hearing
سَمْع Means "hearing".	

Surah Baqrah Verse 7b

This is a continuation of the previous verse.

Table 17.2.7

عَظِيم	عَذَاب	وَلَهُم	غِشَاوَةٌ	أَبْصَارِهِمْ	وَعَلَى
great.	(is) a punishment	and for them	(is) a veil	their eyes	and on

There are four new words in this verse.

Table 17.2.8

وَعَلَى
and on
عَلَى   Means "on". See the Hour 6 grammar lesson on Prepositions.

Table 17.2.9

New Word	أَبْصَارِهِمْ
	their eyes
أَبْصَار Means "eyes". This is the plural form of (بَصَر) which means "eye".	

Table 17.2.10

New Word	غِشَاوَةٌ
	(is) a veil
غِشَاوَةٌ Means "veil".	

Table 17.2.11

وَلَهُم
and for them
لَهُم   Means "for them". The letter (ل) is a preposition: see the Hour 5 grammar lesson.

Table 17.2.12

New Word	عَذَاب
(is) a punishment	
عَذَاب Means "punishment".	

Table 17.2.13

New Word	عَظِيم
great	

عَظِيم   Means "great", "big".

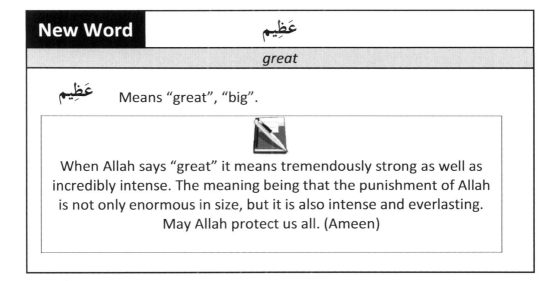

When Allah says "great" it means tremendously strong as well as incredibly intense. The meaning being that the punishment of Allah is not only enormous in size, but it is also intense and everlasting. May Allah protect us all. (Ameen)

Lessons derived from this verse

Has Allah sealed your heart and hearing?

In the Hadith the Prophet (Peace be upon him) said: 'When a person commits a sin, a black dot is engraved on their heart, as he continues to sin, the dots increase until their heart is covered. This is the stain that Allah says "Nay! But on their hearts is the stain which they used to earn." ' (Quran 83:14) (Hadith).

When Shaitan controls a person and he obeys Shaitan, Allah seals that person's heart, hearing, and sight. As a result he can neither see the guidance, nor hear it; neither comprehend nor understand the message.

Don't ever let Shaitan control you.

Practice what you have learned

Let us practice what you have learned so far. Practice will make it perfect. As it is beautifully said, "Practice makes it perfect."

عَلَيْهِمْ	سَوَاء	كَفَرُوا	الَّذِينَ	إِنّ
on them,	(it) is the same	disbelieved	those who	Indeed

لَا يُؤْمِنُونَ	تُنْذِرْهُمْ	لَمْ	أَمْ	أَأَنْذَرْتَهُم
not they believe	you warn them	not	or	whether you warn them

سَمْعِهِمْ	وَعَلَى	قُلُوبِهِمْ	عَلَى	خَتَمَ اللَّهُ
their hearing	and on	their hearts	on	Allah has set a seal

عَظِيم	عَذَاب	وَلَهُم	غِشَاوَةٌ	أَبْصَارِهِمْ	وَعَلَى
great.	(is) a punishment	and for them	(is) a veil	their eyes	and on

Don't forget to ponder over the meaning in your next Salah. Pause after every verse, imagine the response from Allah, and try to build humility and love for Allah in your Salah.

Revision of vocabulary words studied

Meaning	Arabic Word
same	سَوَاء
you warn	أَنْذَرْتَ
or	أَمْ
he set a seal	خَتَمَ
hearts	قُلُوبِ
hearing	سَمْعِ
eyes	أَبْصَارِ
veil	غِشَاوَةٌ
punishment	عَذَاب
great	عَظِيم

Phew! Alhumdulillah!

We have completed verses 6-7 of Surah Baqrah. Without Allah's help it would not have been possible, so let's say Alhumdulillah! Let's start to ponder over what we have learnt so far in our salah, let's ask Allah to open our hearts if they are sealed, and to make our hearts firm in His religion. Remember to understand the message from this surah, ponder over it, implement it and also spread it.

Take a Break!

Grammar – Active Participles

In English we say, writer, reciter, worshipper and so forth, so the Active Participle in Arabic is similar to "-er" in English.

Different Patterns of Active Participles

In Arabic there are two different patterns because, unlike English, the Active Participles have to conform to feminine and masculine genders.

Table 17.3.1

Active Participle Patterns	
Masculine	Feminine
فَاعِلٌ	فَاعِلَةٌ

Now you know the patterns for Active Participles, we will give you some more examples which will help you and give you a better understanding.

Table 17.3.2

Active Participle Examples			
Masculine		Feminine	
writer	كَاتِبٌ	writer	كَاتِبَةٌ
worshipper	عَابِدٌ	worshipper	عَابِدَةٌ
reciter	قَارِئٌ	reciter	قَارِئَةٌ

Study these Active Participle examples and how to form them, and see if you can come up with a few examples of your own from the vocabulary you have learnt so far. If you cannot remember any, you may go back and see if you can find any words to use as further practice in forming Active Participles.

Advice and guidance from the Author

How can I remove the seal from my heart and hearing?

If Allah has put a seal on your heart, then the way to remove this is through repentance. Prophet Muhammad (Peace be upon him) would repent to Allah a hundred times a day, even though his heart was not sealed by Allah. So how much do you think we should ask Allah for forgiveness?

There are two things that put a seal on a persons heart.
Sins and negligence from remembering Allah. (Imam Ibn Qayyim)

The heart keeps on changing

The heart constantly changes, which is why the Prophet Muhammad (Peace be upon him) said that a person can be a believer during the day yet by evening he could be a non-believer. Similarly a person can be a non-believer during the day and by evening he can be a believer. So the heart can change at any time. That is why the Prophet Muhammad (Peace be upon him) would make this Dua to Allah:

(يَا مُقَلِّبَ الْقُلُوبِ ثَبِّتْ قَلْبِي عَلَى دِينِكَ)

Which means "O Allah, Changer of the hearts, make my heart firm upon your religion". Let's make this Dua too, and let's fill our hearts with the love of Allah instead of the love of this dunya.

> Dunya will **ALWAYS** let you down,
> but ALLAH will **NEVER LET YOU DOWN!**

Unfortunately, often we run to the one who always lets us down, i.e. dunya, instead of running to the One who **NEVER** lets us down, i.e. Allah.

Summary

In this Hour we have completed verses 6 and7 from Surah Baqrah, Alhumdulillah! Let's continue pondering over what we have learnt so far in our salah. Remember: do not allow Shaitan to control you.

For grammar we studied Active Participles. Try to master how to form these by studying them and you will become familiar with the process.

So far we have learnt 151 words that occur in the Quran 20,994 times. Alhumdulillah!

Workshop

The quiz questions and the exercises are provided to further your understanding. Don't worry if you can't answer all of the questions in the quiz. Try your best to answer as many as you can. See Appendix A to check your answers.

Quiz 17

1. What is the Dua we should make to Allah for our hearts to remain in the religion of Islam?
2. What happens when Allah puts a seal on a person's heart?
3. What are the two patterns you have learnt for Active Participles?

4. Form Active Participles for the following verbs in both Masculine and Feminine genders. Don't worry about the meanings of these words.

فتح نصر ضرب

Exercise

Insert the CD-ROM accompanying this book in your drive. Select the appropriate folder and do the quiz for this Hour. You may do the quiz as many times as you like in order to further your understanding.

Hour **18**

At the end of this Hour you will have learnt

Surah Baqrah Verses 8-9 and different patterns of Active Participles

In this Hour we will continue with Surah Baqrah and study verses 8-9. In these verses Allah is talking about people who *say* that they believe in Allah and in the hereafter, but are not true believers.

Let's make Dua to Allah and let's approach this Hour in the firm belief that Allah will make this Hour easy for us.

The highlights of this Hour include:

- Surah Baqrah verses 8-9
- Grammar – Different Patterns of Active Participles
- Advice and guidance

Surah Baqrah Verse 8a

In this verse Allah is talking about people who say "We believe in Allah," but they are not really believers.

Table 18.1.1

يَقُولُ	مَنْ	النَّاسِ	وَمِن
say:	(are some) who	the people	And of

There are no new words in this verse, all words are repeated.

Table 18.1.2

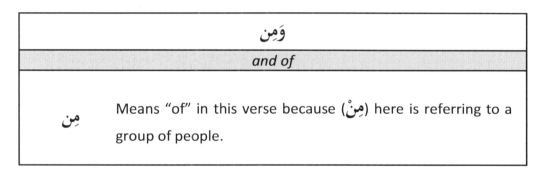

وَمِن	
and of	
مِن	Means "of" in this verse because (مِنْ) here is referring to a group of people.

Table 18.1.3

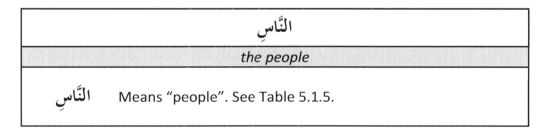

النَّاسِ	
the people	
النَّاسِ	Means "people". See Table 5.1.5.

Table 18.1.4

مَنْ
(are some) who
مَنْ   Means "who".

One of the first questions we will be asked immediately after we are buried is (مَنْ رَبُّك) which means "Who is your Lord?"

Table 18.1.5

يَقُولُ
say
يَقُولُ   Means "he says". It comes from the same *masdar* as (قُلْ), see Table 5.1.2.

Surah Baqrah Verse 8b

This is a continuation of the previous verse.

Table 18.1.6

الْآخِرِ	وَبِالْيَوْمِ	بِاللَّهِ	آمَنَّا
last	*and in the day*	*in Allah*	*We believe*

There are no new words in this verse, all words are repeated.

Table 18.1.7

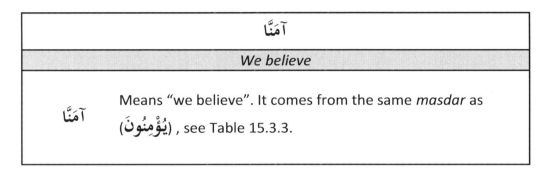

آمَنَّا
We believe
آمَنَّا   Means "we believe". It comes from the same *masdar* as (يُؤْمِنُونَ) , see Table 15.3.3.

Table 18.1.8

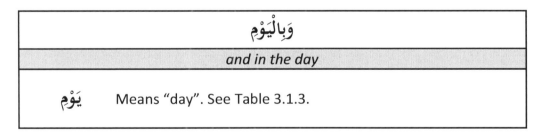

بِاللَّهِ
in Allah
بِ   Means "in". See the Hour 5 grammar lesson on Prepositions.

Table 18.1.9

وَبِالْيَوْم
and in the day
يَوْم   Means "day". See Table 3.1.3.

Table 18.1.10

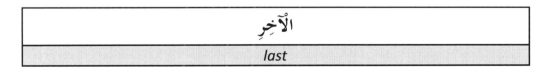

الْآخِرِ
last

<table>
<tr><td>آخِرِ</td><td>Means "last". In the context of this verse it is referring to "the hereafter". (آخِرَةٍ), "hereafter", see Table 16.1.12.</td></tr>
</table>

آخِرِ	Means "last". In the context of this verse it is referring to "the hereafter". (آخِرَةٍ), "hereafter", see Table 16.1.12.

Surah Baqrah Verse 8c

This is a continuation of the previous verse.

Table 18.1.11

بِمُؤْمِنِينَ	هُمْ	وَمَا
believers (really).	they are	but not

There are no new words in this verse, all words are repeated.

Table 18.1.12

وَمَا	
but not	
مَا	This word has two meanings, "not" and "what". In this context it means "not". See Table 6.2.3.

Table 18.1.13

هُمْ	
they are	
هُمْ	Means "they". See the Hour 1 grammar lesson on Pronouns.

Table 18.1.14

بِمُؤْمِنِينَ
believers (really).
مُؤْمِنِينَ   Means "believers". See Table 15.3.3. This is an Active Participle verb of plural form. We will study this pattern later in this hour.

Lessons derived from this Verse

Three points for Imaan that you MUST know

Allah says in this verse that there are people who say "We believe in Allah," but they are not true believers. Just saying that you believe in Allah and in the hereafter is not sufficient. There are three parts to Imaan:

1. It must be demonstrated in your speech
2. It must be believed in your heart
3. It must be demonstrated "by your limbs" i.e. through actions.

None of these three points can be missing at any time. If any one of these links is missing from the chain, there is a problem with your Imaan, and you need to do something about it. So ask yourself: are any of these missing in me? or, can I improve any of them?

You can **NEVER** be perfect; there is always room for improvement.

Surah Baqrah Verse 9a

In this verse Allah is describing the actions of some of the people who deceive Allah and believers.

Table 18.2.1

آمَنُوا	وَالَّذِينَ	يُخَادِعُونَ اللَّهَ
believe	and those who	They deceive Allah

There is only one new word in this verse.

Table 18.2.2

New Word	يُخَادِعُونَ اللَّهَ
	They deceive Allah
يُخَادِعُونَ	Means "They deceive". It comes from the *masdar* (خَدْعٌ) which means "to conceal reality".

Table 18.2.3

وَالَّذِينَ
and those who
الَّذِينَ   Means "those". See the Hour 8 grammar lesson on Relative Pronouns.

Table 18.2.4

آمَنُوا
believe
آمَنُوا — Means "believe". See Table 15.3.3. This is the Past Tense plural form of the verb.

Surah Baqrah Verse 9b

This is a continuation of the previous verse.

Table 18.2.5

يَشْعُرُونَ	وَمَا	أَنْفُسَهُمْ	إِلَّا	وَمَا يَخْدَعُونَ
they realize (it)	and not	themselves	except	and not they deceive

There are three new words in this verse.

Table 18.2.6

وَمَا يَخْدَعُونَ
and not they deceive
مَا — This word has two meanings. "not" and "what". In this sentence it means "not". See Table 6.2.3.
يَخْدَعُونَ — Means "they deceive". See Table 18.2.2. This is the Present Tense Plural form of the verb.

Table 18.2.7

New Word	إِلَّا
except	
إِلَّا	Means "except". This is used in Arabic for excluding or separating out some-one or some-thing.

Table 18.2.8

New Word	أَنْفُسَهُمْ
themselves	
أَنْفُس	Means "selves". This is the plural form of (نَفْس) which means "self".

Table 18.2.9

وَمَا
and not

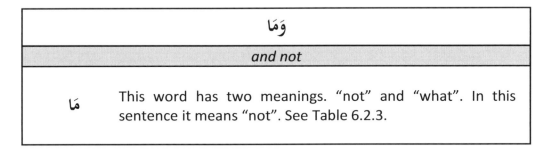

مَا	This word has two meanings. "not" and "what". In this sentence it means "not". See Table 6.2.3.

Table 18.2.10

New Word	يَشْعُرُونَ
they realize (it).	

<table>
<tr><td>يَشْعُرُونَ</td><td>Means "they realize". It comes from the root word (شَعَر) which means "to know the reality", "to realize".</td></tr>
</table>

Lessons derived from this Verse

Do you think you are deceiving Allah?

Hypocrites show belief outwardly, saying that they believe in Allah and in the hereafter while concealing disbelief. They think that they are deceiving and misleading Allah, but Allah is All-Knowing and you cannot escape from Him. He is fully aware of everything that we do, and what we have in our hearts. We learn something very important from this verse: that what you say you must mean, and what you mean you must say.

MEAN what you say and **SAY** what you mean.

Practice what you have learned

يَقُولُ	مَنْ	النَّاسِ	وَمِن
say:	*(are some) who*	*the people*	*And of*

الْآخِرِ	وَبِالْيَوْمِ	بِاللَّهِ	آمَنَّا
last	*and in the day*	*in Allah*	*We believe*

بِمُؤْمِنِينَ	هُم	وَمَا
believers (really).	they are	but not

آمَنُوا	وَالَّذِينَ	يُخَادِعُونَ اللَّهَ
believe	and those who	They deceive Allah

يَشْعُرُونَ	وَمَا	أَنْفُسَهُم	إِلَّا	وَمَا يَخْدَعُونَ
they realize (it).	and not	themselves	except	and not they deceive

Don't forget to ponder over the meaning in your next Salah. Pause after every verse, imagine the response from Allah, and try to build humility and love for Allah in your Salah.

Revision of vocabulary words studied

Meaning	Arabic Word
last	آخِرِ
They deceive	يُخَادِعُونَ
except	إِلَّا
selves	أَنْفُسَ
they realize	يَشْعُرُونَ

Phew! Alhumdulillah!

We have completed verses 8-9 of Surah Baqrah. Without Allah's help it would not have been possible, so let's say Alhumdulillah! Let's start to ponder over what we have learnt so far in our salah and let's be true believers of Allah. Remember to understand the message from these verses, ponder over them, implement them and also spread them.

Take a Break!

In the next section, you are going to learn Arabic Grammar. For todays lesson you will learn somemore patterns for Active Participles.

Grammar – more Patterns for Active Participles

In the previous Hour you learnt two patterns for Active Participles. Remember, you can always go back and revise if you think you need to. However there are many different forms of Active Participles that are used in the Quran and in the Arabic language.

In today's grammar lesson you will study another four Active Participles that are commonly used.

Table 18.3.1

Active Participles – Four commonly used patterns			
Different Patterns	مُفْعِلْ	فَعَّال	فَعُوْل	فَعِيْلٌ
Examples	مُسْلِمْ	غَفَّار	غَفُوْر	سَمِيْع
	مُؤْمِنْ	وَهَّاب	شَكُوْر	بَصِيْر
	مُفْسِدْ	رَزَّاق	كَفُوْر	عَلِيْم
	مُحْسِنْ	فَتَّاح	رَؤُوْف	رَحِيْم

These patterns of Active Participles are used for intensiveness in their meanings. For example, All hearing, All knowing and so on.

Study these patterns for Active Participles, and see if you can come up with a few examples of your own from the vocabulary you have learnt so far. If you cannot remember any, you may go back and see if you can find any words to use as further practice in forming these patterns.

Advice and guidance from the Author

Don't deceive anyone

We must be honest with Allah as well as with His creation. We may sometimes be able to deceive His creations, but we can **NEVER** deceive Allah.

Be Honest! Don't deceive anyone!

Action is compulsory for our Imaan to be complete

Many Muslims say with their tongues that they believe in Allah and in the hereafter, and they believe it in their hearts. However, many Muslims fail in the third category and that is taking action. Our actions demonstrate whether we do or do not believe in Allah and in the hereafter.

Do we love for others what we love for ourselves?

In the Hadith the Prophet (Peace be upon him) said: "You cannot be a believer until you love for your brother what you love for yourself," (Hadith). Do we love for our brothers what we love for ourselves?

Imam Nawawi (Rahmatullahi Alayi) comments on this Hadith and says that the brotherhood mentioned in this Hadith is not the brotherhood of faith, it is the brotherhood of humanity. That means you cannot be a believer until you love for your brother in humanity what you love for yourself.

People are to be loved and things are to be used.
Problems arise when things are loved and people are used.

Make love easy and hate difficult

In the Hadith the Prophet (Peace be upon him) said: "You shall never enter paradise until you have faith and you shall never have faith until you have love for one another." (Hadith)

Nowadays we have to teach people how to love one another. Love has become difficult and hate has become easy. Everyone is hating one another, instead of loving one another. Let's make love easy and hate difficult.

When we are talking to others, let us try to use pleasant words. When we are talking to others, we have a collection of words in our vocabulary for hating others, but we have very few words to express our love to (or for) someone. We need to change this and add nice words to our vocabularies.

Summary

In this hour we have completed verses 8-9 from Surah Baqrah, Alhumdulillah! Let's continue pondering what we have learnt so far in our salah.

For grammar we studied Different Patterns of Active Participle. Try to master forming these by studying them and you will soon become familiar with the processes.

So far we have learnt 155 words that come in the Quran 22,324 times. Alhumdulillah!

Workshop

The quiz questions and the exercises are provided to further your understanding. Don't worry if you can't answer all of the questions in the quiz. Try your best to answer as many as you can. See Appendix A to check your answers.

Quiz 18

1. What are the three points which make up Imaan?
2. Give one of the characteristic of a hypocrite.
3. What are the different patterns of Active Participles you have learnt?
4. Form Active Participles for the following verbs. Use the patterns given under each verb.

مُفْعِلْ	فَعَّال	فَعُوْل	فَعِيْل
قسط	جبر	ودد	قدر
نعم	قهر	صبر	عظم

Exercise

Insert the CD-ROM accompanying this book into your drive. Select the appropriate folder and do the quiz for this Hour. You may do the quiz as many times as you like in order to further your understanding.

Hour **19**

At the end of this Hour you will have learnt

160 New Words	Our Aim 200 Words
22,444 Total Words	Our Aim 25,000 Words

Surah Baqrah Verses 10-11 and Passive Participles

In this Hour we will continue with Surah Baqrah and study verses 10-11. In these verses Allah is saying that those who deceive Allah and the believers have a disease in their hearts, and He is warning them of painful punishment because of their lies against Allah.

Let's make Dua to Allah and let's approach this Hour in the firm belief that Allah will make this Hour easy for us

The highlights of this Hour include:

- Surah Baqrah verses 10-11
- Grammar – Passive Participles
- Advice and guidance

Surah Baqrah Verse 10a

In this verse Allah tells us that there is a sickness in the hearts of people who deceive Him.

Table 19.1.1

فِي	قُلُوبِهِمْ	مَرَضٌ	فَزَادَهُمُ	اللَّهُ	مَرَضًا
In	their hearts	(is) a disease	so increased them	Allah	(in) disease

There are two new words in this verse.

Table 19.1.2

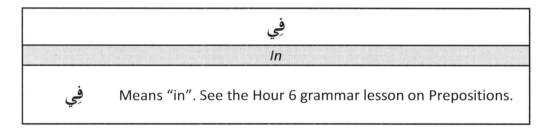

فِي	
In	
فِي	Means "in". See the Hour 6 grammar lesson on Prepositions.

Table 19.1.3

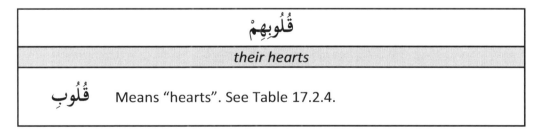

قُلُوبِهِمْ	
their hearts	
قُلُوبِ	Means "hearts". See Table 17.2.4.

Table 19.1.4

New Word	مَرَضٌ
(is) a disease	

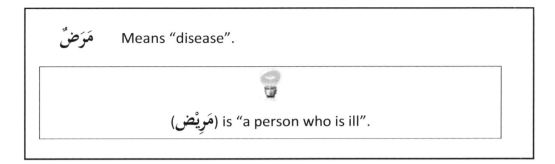

مَرَضٌ Means "disease".

(مَرِيْض) is "a person who is ill".

Table 19.1.5

New Word	فَزَادَهُمُ
	so increased them
فَ	Means "so". It is a prefix. See Table 9.3.2.
زَاد	Means "he increased".
هُمُ	Means "them". See the Hour 3 grammar lesson on Possessive Adjectives.

Table 19.1.6

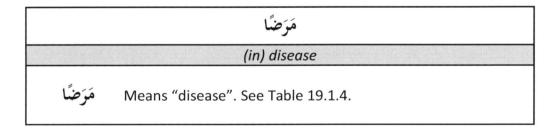

مَرَضًا
(in) disease
مَرَضًا Means "disease". See Table 19.1.4.

Surah Baqrah Verse 10b

This is a continuation of the previous verse.

Table 19.1.7

يَكْذِبُون	كَانُوا	بِمَا	أَلِيمٌ	عَذَابٌ	وَلَهُمْ
(they) lie	they used to	because	painful	(is) a punishment	and for them

There are four new words in this verse.

Table 19.1.8

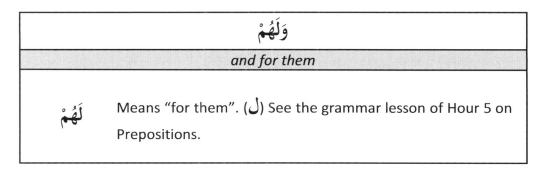

وَلَهُمْ	
and for them	
لَهُمْ	Means "for them". (ل) See the grammar lesson of Hour 5 on Prepositions.

Table 19.1.9

عَذَابٌ	
(is) a punishment	
عَذَابٌ	Means "punishment". See Table 17.2.12.

Table 19.1.10

New Word	أَلِيمٌ
painful	
أَلِيمٌ	Means "painful". It comes from the root word (ءلم)

which means "pain".

(أَلِيْم) doesn't only mean pain. It means it will cause pain again and again.

Table 19.1.11

New Word	بِمَا
because	
بِمَا	Means "because".

Table 19.1.12

New Word	كَانُوا
they used to	
كَانُوا	Means "they used to". See note below.

Table 19.1.13

New Word	يَكْذِبُون
(they) lie	
يَكْذِبُون	Means "they lie". It comes from the root word (كذب) which means "to lie".

When there is (كَانَ) or (كَانُوْا) before a Present Tense verb, as in this verse, it gives the meaning of doing an action continuously. Meaning, they always lie.

Lessons derived from this Verse

Do you have any of these characteristics?

Allah tells us that people who deceive Him and His believers have a sickness in their hearts. This is not a physical disease, it is doubting Allah and Islam, which is a disease in faith.

Hypocrites have two characteristics. The first is that they lie and the second that they deny the unseen. Allah told the Prophet Muhammad (Peace be upon him) the names of some of the hypocrites, and then He described the characteristics of hypocrites: that they lie and they deny the unseen.

Three signs of a hypocrite

In a Hadith the Prophet Muhammad (Peace be upon him) said "The hypocrite has three signs: when he speaks, he lies; when he is trusted, he proves dishonest; and when he promises, he breaks his promise." (Hadith)

We need to ask ourselves, are we doing any of these three things? If we are not, Alhumdulillah! If we <u>are</u>, let's remove these bad habits immediately.

Remove bad actions from your life **BEFORE** they turn in to **BAD HABITS**.

Surah Baqrah Verse 11a

In this verse Allah tells us that these people would spread corruption in the land and they would justify it by saying they are reformers.

Table 19.2.1

الْأَرْضِ	فِي	لَا تُفْسِدُوا	قِيلَ لَهُمْ	وَإِذَا
the earth"	in	"Do not spread corruption	it is said to them	And when

There are two new words in this verse.

Table 19.2.2

وَإِذَا
And when
إِذَا   Means "when". See Table 6.3.4.

Table 19.2.3

قِيلَ لَهُمْ
it is said to them
قِيلَ   Means "it is said". It comes from the same *masdar* as the word (قُلْ) which we studied in Table 5.1.2. This (قِيلَ) is the Passive form.
لَهُمْ   Means "to them". (ل) Means "to" or "for". See the Hour 5 grammar lesson on Prepositions.

Table 19.2.4

New Word	لَا تُفْسِدُوا
"Do not spread corruption	
تُفْسِدُوا	Means "you spread corruption". This is the Present Plural form of the verb. It comes from the *masdar* (إِفْسَاد) which means "to spread corruption".

Table 19.2.5

فِي
in
فِي Means "in". See the Hour 6 grammar lesson on Prepositions.

Table 19.2.6

New Word	الْأَرْضِ
the earth"	
أَرْضِ Means "earth".	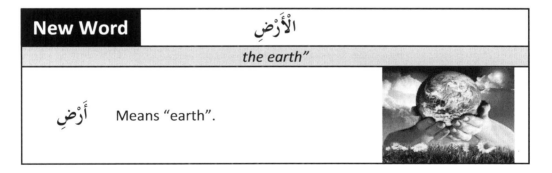

Surah Baqrah Verse 11b

This is a continuation of the previous verse.

Table 19.2.7

مُصْلِحُونَ	نَحْنُ	إِنَّمَا	قَالُوا
reformers	we (are)	only	they say

There are two new words in this verse.

Table 19.2.8

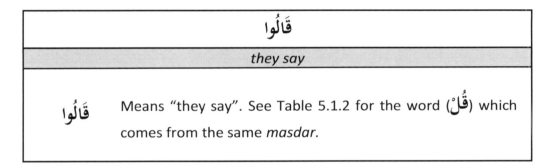

قَالُوا
they say

قَالُوا	Means "they say". See Table 5.1.2 for the word (قُلْ) which comes from the same *masdar*.

Table 19.2.9

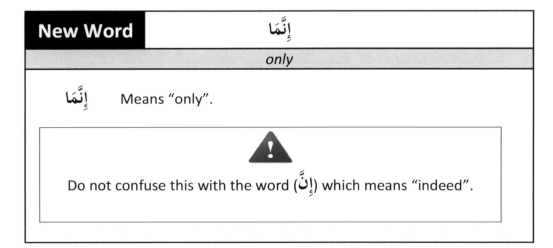

New Word	إِنَّمَا
	only

إِنَّمَا	Means "only".

> ⚠️
>
> Do not confuse this with the word (إِنَّ) which means "indeed".

Table 19.2.10

نَحْنُ
we (are)
نَحْنُ   Means "we". See the Hour 1 grammar lesson on Pronouns.

Table 19.2.11

New Word	مُصْلِحُونَ
	reformers
مُصْلِحُونَ Means "reformers". It comes from the *masdar* (إِصْلَاح) which means "to reform".	

Lessons derived from this Verse

Improvement: a good characteristic of a believer

A believer is expected to rectify and reform themselves and those around them. Rectifying means to make things right and make up for bad actions and situations. Reforming means to increase good actions and eliminate evil ones. In the Quran a believer is referred to someone who is actively engaged in the betterment and progress of himself and those around him.

Improvement is expected in three different areas of a believer's life:

1. Rooting bad habits out of yourself: we all have bad habits so we need to begin rectifying and reforming ourselves first.
2. We continue to rectify and reform our spouses and children and those around us. Ask yourself: "What is the change I want to see in

the world?" Then see if you can make this change first in your own home.

3. At the same time, we continue to rectify and reform our community, the people living around us, and see what changes we can make there.

Practice what you have learned

في	قُلُوبِهِمْ	مَرَضٌ	فَزَادَهُمُ	اللَّهُ	مَرَضًا
In	their hearts	(is) a disease	so increased them	Allah	(in) disease

وَلَهُمْ	عَذَابٌ	أَلِيمٌ	بِمَا	كَانُوا	يَكْذِبُون
and for them	(is) a punishment	painful	because	they used to	(they) lie

وَإِذَا	قِيلَ لَهُمْ	لَا تُفْسِدُوا	فِي	الْأَرْضِ
And when	it is said to them	"Do not spread corruption	in	the earth"

قَالُوا	إِنَّمَا	نَحْنُ	مُصْلِحُونَ
they say	only	we (are)	reformers

Don't forget to ponder over the meaning in your next Salah. Pause after every verse, imagine the response from Allah, and try to build humility and love for Allah in your Salah.

Revision of Vocabulary words studied

Meaning	Arabic Word
disease	مَرَضٌ
he increased	زَادَ
painful	أَلِيمٌ
because	بِمَا
they used to	كَانُوا
they lie	يَكْذِبُون
Do not spread corruption	لَا تُفْسِدُوا
earth	أَرْضِ
only	إِنَّمَا
reformers	مُصْلِحُونَ

Phew! Alhumdulillah!

We have completed verses 10-11 of Surah Baqrah. Without Allah's help it would not have been possible, so let's say Alhumdulillah! Let's start to ponder over what we have learnt so far in our salah, let's ask Allah to make us people who are involved in reforming and rectifying. Remember to understand the message from these verses, ponder over them, implement them and also spread them.

Take a Break!

In the next section, you are going to learn Arabic Grammar. For todays lesson you will learn Passive Participles.

Grammar – Passive Participles

Passive Participles are used when the action for which the verb stands for is performed. For example, written, eaten, listened and so forth. So in English, a word that ends in –ed is a passive participle.

In English, the Passive Participles do not change for gender. In Arabic the patterns are different: one for masculine and another for feminine.

Table 19.3.1

Passive Participle Pattern	
Masculine	Feminine
مَفْعُوْلٌ	مَفْعُوْلَةٌ

Now you have seen the patterns, here are some examples which will help you have a better understanding.

Table 19.3.2

Active Participle Examples			
Masculine		Feminine	
written	مَكْتُوْب	written	مَكْتُوْبَةٌ
eaten	مَأْكُوْل	eaten	مَأْكُوْلَةٌ
read	مَقْرُوْئ	read	مَقْرُوْئَةٌ

Study these Passive Participle examples, and see if you can come up with a few examples of your own from the vocabulary you have learnt so far. If you cannot remember any, you may go back and see if you can find any words to use as further practice in forming Passive Participles.

Advice and guidance from the Author

Two things that can destroy a person's life

Fear and grief are two things that can destroy a person's life. Fear of the future, of what will happen tomorrow, can be devastating. Grief, being sorry about what happened yesterday, that you forget to live today. Grief steals your peace of mind. Both of these two emotions are the most common things that shatter a person's life.

However, in the Quran, Allah promises that a person who is actively engaged in rectifying and reforming their lives and those of the people around them "Shall have no fear, and nor shall they grieve." So if you want to protect yourself from fear and grief, engage yourself in reforming (doing things better) and rectifying (improving bad things).

We need Muslims to be Reformers. There is no point looking at faults and cursing them: that won't solve the problem. Instead ask yourself what can I do to remove this fault?

The problem is not making a mistake; the problem is what you do after you make a mistake.
Do you remain where you are?
Or do you do something about it?

Summary

In this hour we have completed verses 10-11 from Surah Baqrah, Alhumdulillah! Let's continue pondering what we have learnt so far in our salah. Remember to engage yourself in reforming and rectifying starting with yourself.

For grammar we studied Passive Participles. Try to master how to form these by studying them and you will become familiar with the process.

So far we have learnt 160 words that occur in the Quran 22,444 times. Alhumdulillah!

Workshop

The quiz questions and the exercises are provided to further your understanding. Don't worry if you can't answer all of the questions in the quiz. Try your best to answer as many as you can. See Appendix A to check your answers.

Quiz 19

1. What are the three signs of a hypocrite?
2. What is the difference between rectifying and reforming?
3. What are the two things that can destroy a person's life?
4. What are the two patterns you have learnt for Passive Participle formation?
5. Form Passive Participles for the following verbs, both the Masculine and Feminine genders. Don't worry about the meanings of these words.

فتح   نصر   ضرب

Exercise

Insert the CD-ROM accompanying this book in your drive. Select the appropriate folder and do the quiz for this Hour. You may do the quiz as many times as you like in order to further your understanding.

Hour **20**

At the end of this Hour you will have learnt

Surah Baqrah Verses 12-13 and Nouns of Place

In this Hour we will continue with Surah Baqrah and study verses 12-13. In these verses Allah replies to these people that they are not reformers: in fact they are the ones who spread corruption in the land.

Let's make Dua to Allah and let's approach this Hour in the firm belief that Allah will make this Hour easy for us.

The highlights of this Hour include:

- Surah Baqrah verses 12-13
- Grammar – Nouns of Place
- Advice and guidance

Surah Baqrah Verse 12

In this verse Allah is responding to those who try to justify their spreading of corruption in the land by saying that they are reformers.

Table 20.1.1

لَا يَشْعُرُونَ	وَلَكِنْ	هُمُ الْمُفْسِدُونَ	إِنَّهُمْ	أَلَا
not they realize	but	(are) the ones who spread corruption	indeed they	Beware

There are two new words in this verse.

Table 20.1.2

New Word	أَلَا
	Beware
أَلَا	Means "Beware". This word is used to alert the listener.

Table 20.1.3

إِنَّهُمْ
indeed they
إِنَّ	Means "indeed". See Table 9.3.7.
هُمْ	Means "they". See the Hour 3 grammar lesson on Possessive Adjectives.

Table 20.1.4

هُمُ الْمُفْسِدُونَ	
(are) the ones who spread corruption	
هُمُ	Means "they". See the Hour 3 grammar lesson on Possessive Adjectives..
مُفْسِدُونَ	Means "those who spread corruption". It comes from the same *masdar* as the word (تُفْسِدُوْا) - see Table 19.2.4. In this verse (مُفْسِدُونَ) is an Active Participle Plural verb.

Table 20.1.5

New Word	وَلَكِنْ
but	
وَلَكِنْ	Means "but".

Table 20.1.6

لَا يَشْعُرُونَ	
not they realize	
لَا	Means "not".
يَشْعُرُونَ	Means "they realize". See Table 18.2.10.

Lessons derived from this Verse

Never commit a sin and then justify it

These people were disobeying Allah by spreading the corruption, and they tried to justify it by saying, "We are only reformers." We need to ask ourselves a very important question: how often do we disobey Allah and then try to justify our actions? Disobeying Allah is dangerous in itself, but to justify it is even more dangerous.

Don't commit a sin and then justify it – you won't be given the ability to **REPENT.**

Surah Baqrah Verse 13a

In this verse Allah tells us of another response from deceivers. When they are told"Believe the way the companions believed", they respond "Should we believe the way these fools believed?".

Table 20.2.1

النَّاسُ	آمَنَ	كَمَا	آمِنُوا	لَهُمْ	قِيلَ	وَإِذَا
the people	believe"	as	"Believe	to them	it is said	and when

There is one new word in this verse.

Table 20.2.2

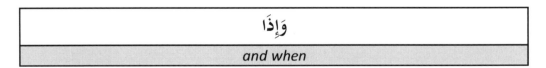

وَإِذَا
and when

إِذَا	Means "when". See Table 6.3.4.

Table 20.2.3

قِيلَ
it is said
قِيلَ   Means "it is said". It comes from the same *masdar* as the word (قُلْ), see Table 5.1.2. Here this word (قِيلَ) is in the Passive form.

Table 20.2.4

لَهُمْ
to them
لَهُمْ   Means "to them". (ل) Means "to" or "for". See the Hour 5 grammar lesson on Prepositions.

Table 20.2.5

آمِنُوا
"Believe
آمِنُوا   Means "you believe". It comes from the same *masdar* as (يُؤْمِنُونَ), see Table 15.3.3. Here (آمِنُوا) is in the Imperative (command) form.

Table 20.2.6

New Word	كَمَا
	as
كَمَا	Means "as", "like".

Table 20.2.7

آمَنَ
believe
آمَنَ   Means "he believed". It comes from the same *masdar* as (يُؤْمِنُونَ), see Table 15.3.3 of hour 15. Here (آمَنَ) is in the Past Tense form.

Table 20.2.8

النَّاسُ
the people
النَّاسِ   Means "people". See Table 5.1.5.

Surah Baqrah Verse 13b

This is a continuation of the previous verse.

Table 20.2.9

السُّفَهَاءُ	آمَنَ	كَمَا	اَنُؤْمِنُ	قَالُوا
the fools	believe?"	as	"Shall we believe	they say

There is only one new word in this verse.

Table 20.2.10

قَالُوا
they say

قَالُوا	Means "they say". It comes from the same *masdar* as the word (قُلْ), see Table 5.1.2.

Table 20.2.11

اَنُؤْمِنُ
"Shall we believe

اَ	Means "shall?". It is used for asking questions.
نُؤْمِنُ	Means "we believe". It comes from the same *masdar* as (يُؤْمِنُونَ), see Table 15.3.3. Here this word (نُؤْمِنُ) is in the Present Tense form.

Table 20.2.12

كَمَا	
as	
كَمَا	Means "as", "like". See Table 20.2.6.

Table 20.2.13

آمَنَ	
believe?"	
آمَنَ	Means "he believed". It comes from the same *masdar* as (يُؤْمِنُونَ), see Table 15.3.3. Here this word (آمَنَ) is in the Past Tense form.

Table 20.2.14

New Word	السُّفَهَاءُ
the fools	
سُفَهَاءُ	Means "fools". It comes from the *masdar* (سَفَاهَة) which means "foolishness".

Surah Baqrah Verse 13c

This is a continuation of the previous verse.

Table 20.2.15

لَا يَعْلَمُونَ	وَلَكِنْ	هُمُ السُّفَهَاءُ	إِنَّهُمْ	أَلَا
not they know.	but	(are) the fools	indeed they	Beware:

There is only one new word in this verse.

Table 20.2.16

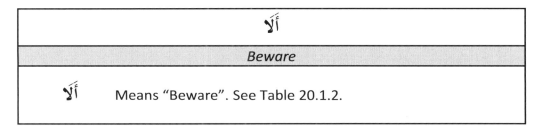

أَلَا		
Beware		
أَلَا	Means "Beware". See Table 20.1.2.	

Table 20.2.17

إِنَّهُمْ	
indeed they	
إِنَّ	Means "indeed". See Table 9.3.7.
هُمْ	Means "they". See the Hour 3 grammar lesson on Possessive Adjectives.

Table 20.2.18

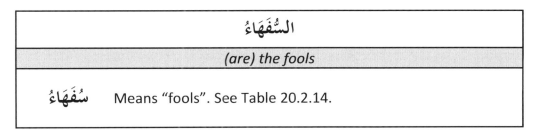

السُّفَهَاءُ	
(are) the fools	
سُفَهَاءُ	Means "fools". See Table 20.2.14.

Table 20.2.19

وَلَكِنْ
but
وَلَكِنْ   Means "but". See Table 20.1.5.

Table 20.2.20

New Word	لَا يَعْلَمُونَ
	not they know.

لَا	Means "not".
يَعْلَمُونَ	Means "they know". It comes from the root word (علم), which means "knowledge".

An (عَالِم) is "someone who has knowledge".

Lessons derived from this Verse

Respect the companions

Allah is saying when the devious were told to believe like the companions, they said, shall we believe as the fools believe? They were arrogant and belittled the companions. We must respect all the companions all the time unconditionally. Whenever we mention their names, we must say "Allah is pleased with them". There are three points to remember when we talk about respecting the companions:

- Love them and respect them from your heart
- Love them and respect them with your tongue
- Love them and respect them by following them.

Don't belittle others

Don't belittle anyone, because when we do this we only end up crushing another's soul, crushing another's spirit, and we become the architects of the demise of one another. This is not acceptable behaviour in a believer.

NEVER belittle another human being.
REMEMBER: They are human beings who have been honoured by Allah.

Practice what you have learned

لَا يَشْعُرُونَ	وَلَكِنْ	هُمُ الْمُفْسِدُونَ	إِنَّهُمْ	أَلَا
not they realize	*but*	*(are) the ones who spread corruption*	*indeed they*	*Beware*

النَّاسُ	آمَنَ	كَمَا	آمِنُوا	لَهُمْ	قِيلَ	وَإِذَا
the people	believe"	as	"Believe	to them	it is said	and when

السُّفَهَاءُ	آمَنَ	كَمَا	أَنُؤْمِنُ	قَالُوا
the fools	believe?"	as	"Shall we believe	they say

لَا يَعْلَمُونَ	وَلَكِنْ	هُمُ السُّفَهَاءُ	إِنَّهُمْ	أَلَا
not they know.	but	(are) the fools	indeed they	Beware:

Don't forget to ponder over the meaning in your next Salah. Stop after every verse, imagine the response from Allah, and try to build humility and love for Allah in your Salah.

Revision of vocabulary words studied

Meaning	Arabic Word
beware	أَلَا
fools	سُفَهَاءُ
they know	يَعْلَمُونَ

Phew! Alhumdulillah!

We have completed verses 12-13 of Surah Baqrah. Without Allah's help it would not have been possible, so let's say Alhumdulillah! Let's start to ponder over what we have learnt so far in our salah, love and follow the Prophet (Peace be upon him) and his companions. Let's not belittle anyone - whether our own family, our spouses, the people who we interact with every day, or the community. Remember to understand the message in these verses, ponder over it, implement it and also spread it.

Take a Break!

In the next section, you are going to learn Arabic Grammar. For todays lesson you will learn Nouns of Place.

20

Grammar – Nouns of Place

In this lesson you will learn how to form Nouns of Place in Arabic Grammar. For example in English we say, a place of worship: a mosque; a place of studying: a school; a place to eat: a restaurant, and so forth. These Nouns of Place are formed from the verb describing the action at a particular place.

Different Pattern of Place Nouns

When you are forming Nouns of Places, there are two patterns that you can use. These patterns don't differ according to gender like in the case of Active and Passive participle. In forming nouns of places the patterns are dictated by the vowels on the middle letter. Table 20.3.1 illustrates these two patterns.

Table 20.3.1

Nouns of Places Patterns	
مَفْعِلٌ	مَفْعَلٌ

When do I use which pattern?

The rule for choosing the pattern is that you need to change the verb into its present tense form, and if the middle letter is (ﹻ) you use the pattern (مَفْعِلٌ) otherwise you use the pattern (مَفْعَلٌ). Study the two examples below which show the two patterns. Don't be confused! Figure 20.1 demonstrates when to use which pattern for Nouns of Places.

Figure 20.1

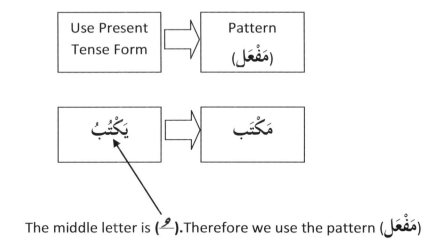

The middle letter is (ـُ). Therefore we use the pattern (مَفْعَل)

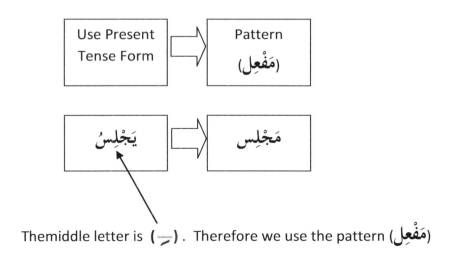

Themiddle letter is (ـِ) . Therefore we use the pattern (مَفْعِل)

Now you have seen the patterns for Nouns of Place and when to use them, here are some examples which will help to give you a better understanding.

Table 20.3.2

Nouns of Place Examples			
مَفْعَل		مَفْعِل	
A place to work (Office)	مَكْتَبٌ	A place of sitting (Gathering)	مَجْلِس
A place to eat (Restaurant)	مَطْعَمٌ	A place of prostration (Mosque)	مَسْجِد
A place to enter (Entrance)	مَدْخَلٌ	A place of sunset	مَغْرِب

Study these Nouns of Place examples and how to form them, and see if you can come up with a few examples of your own from the vocabulary you have learnt so far. If you cannot remember any, you may go back, and see if you can find any words to use as further practice in forming Nouns of Place.

Advice and guidance from the Author

Did you know that no one is perfect?

We must never justify our mistakes, or else we won't be given the ability to repent. Instead, as soon as you make a mistake, try to rectify it. Man is moulded by faults, once we recognize that fault and we are engaged in rectifying and reforming the mistake that we just made, the chances are that we are better people *after* the fault than we were before. I am not inviting or recommending anyone to go and sin or make mistakes: the point I am making is that making a mistake, having a fault, is not the end of the world. But having that fault can lead to us being better people than we were before. So the question is not whether you made a mistake or not: it is what did you do after you made the mistake?

Path of Allah: If you make a mistake turn to Allah and return to good deeds.
Path of Shaitan: Make a mistake and justify it.

Summary

In this Hour we have completed verses 12-13 from Surah Baqrah, Alhumdulillah! Let's continue pondering what we have learnt so far in our salah. Remember, making a mistake is not the end of the world. So *do* rectify your mistakes and always follow up your mistakes with good deeds.

For grammar we studied Nouns of Place. Try to master how to form these by studying them and you will soon become familiar with the process.

So far we have learnt 162 words that occur in the Quran 22,964 times. Alhumdulillah!

Workshop

The quiz questions and the exercises are provided to further your understanding. Don't worry if you can't answer all of the questions in the quiz. Try your best to answer as many as you can. See Appendix A to check your answers.

Quiz 20

1. What happens when you try to justify your sins and mistakes?
2. What are the three points you have learnt for respecting the companions?
3. What are the two patterns you have learnt for forming Nouns of Place?
4. When do you use them?

5. Form Nouns of Place for the following verbs. Use both patterns. Don't worry about the meanings of these words.

Exercise

Insert the CD-ROM accompanying this book in your drive. Select the appropriate folder and do the quiz for this Hour. You may do the quiz as many times as you like in order to further your understanding.

Hour **21**

At the end of this Hour you will have learnt

173 New Words	**Our Aim 200 Words**
23,117 Total Words	**Our Aim 25,000 Words**

Surah Baqrah Verses 14-15 and Interrogative Particles

In this Hour we will continue with Surah Baqrah and study verses 14-15. In these verses Allah is talking about how the hypocrites behave when they meet with the believers, and how that behaviour changes when they are alone. He also tells us the punishment for the hypocrites.

Let's make Dua to Allah and let's approach this Hour in the firm belief that Allah will make this Hour easy for us.

The highlights of this Hour include:

- Surah Baqrah verses 14-15
- Grammar – Interrogative Particles
- Advice and guidance

Surah Baqrah Verse 14a

In this verse Allah is talking about the behaviour of the hypocrites when they meet believers.

Table 21.1.1

آمَنَّا	قَالُوا	آمَنُوا	الَّذِينَ	لَقُوا	وَإِذَا
"We believe"	they say	believe	(with) those who	they meet	And when

There is only one new word in this verse.

Table 21.1.2

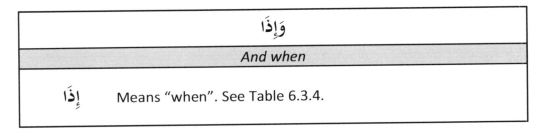

وَإِذَا
And when
إِذَا   Means "when". See Table 6.3.4.

Table 21.1.3

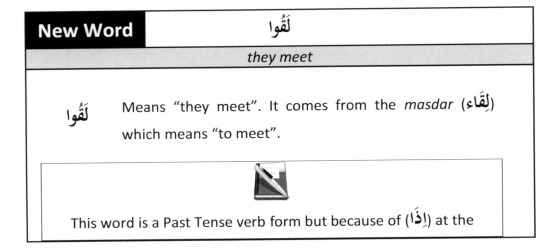

New Word	لَقُوا
	they meet

لَقُوا   Means "they meet". It comes from the *masdar* (لِقَاء) which means "to meet".

This word is a Past Tense verb form but because of (إِذَا) at the beginning of this verse, the meaning of it changes to the Present Tense.

Table 21.1.4

الَّذِينَ
(with) those who
الَّذِينَ   Means "those". See the Hour 8 grammar lesson on Relative Pronouns.

Table 21.1.5

آمَنُوا
believe
آمَنُوا   Means "you believed". It comes from the same *masdar* as (يُؤْمِنُونَ), see Table 15.3.3. In this verse the word (آمَنُوا) is in the Past Tense form.

Table 21.1.6

قَالُوا
They say
قَالُوا   Means "they say". It comes from the same *masdar* as the word (قُلْ), see Table 5.1.2.

21

Table 21.1.7

آمَنَّا
"We believe."
آمَنَّا   Means "we believe". It comes from the same *masdar* as (يُؤْمِنُونَ), see Table 15.3.3. In this verse (آمَنَّا) is in the Past Tense form.

Surah Baqrah Verse 14b

This is a continuation of the previous verse.

Table 21.1.8

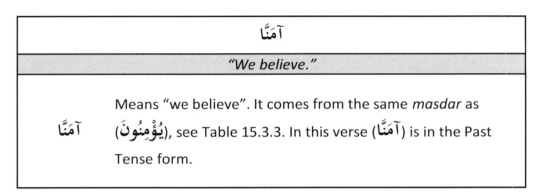

مَعَكُمْ	إِنَّا	قَالُوا	شَيَاطِينِهِمْ	إِلَى	خَلَوْا	وَإِذَا
(are) with you	"Indeed we	they say,	their shaitans	with	they are alone	and when

There is only one new word in this verse.

Table 21.1.9

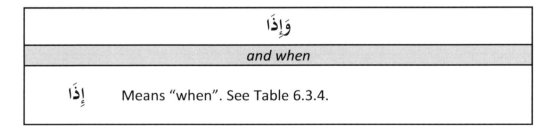

وَإِذَا
and when
إِذَا   Means "when". See Table 6.3.4.

Table 21.1.10

New Word	خَلَوْا
they are alone	
خَلَوْا	Means "they are alone". It comes from the *masdar* (خَلْوَة) which means "privacy".

Table 21.1.11

إِلَى
with
إِلَى	Means "to". See Hour 6 grammar lesson on Prepositions. [In English we would use "with".]

Table 21.1.12

شَيَاطِينِهِمْ
their shaitans
شَيَاطِين	Means "shaitans". This is the Plural of (شَيْطَان) which means "shaitan". See Table 2.1.4.

Table 21.1.13

قَالُوا
they say,

قَالُوا	Means "they say". It comes from the same *masdar* as the word (قُلْ), see Table 5.1.2.

Table 21.1.14

إِنَّا
"Indeed we
إِنَّا — Means "Indeed we". See Table 11.1.2.

Table 21.1.15

مَعَكُمْ
(are) with you
مَعَ — Means "with". See the Hour 5 grammar lesson on Prepositions.

Surah Baqrah Verse 14c

This is a continuation of the previous verse.

Table 21.1.16

مُسْتَهْزِئُون	نَحْنُ	إِنَّمَا
mocking."	*we (were)*	*only*

There is only one new word in this verse.

Table 21.1.17

إِنَّمَا
only
إِنَّمَا   Means "only". See Table 19.2.9.

Table 21.1.18

نَحْنُ
we (were)
نَحْنُ   Means "we". See the Hour 1 grammar lesson on Pronouns.

Table 21.1.19

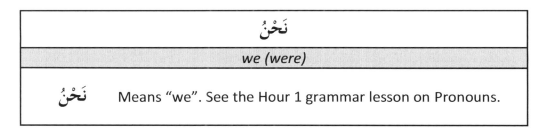

New Word	مُسْتَهْزِئُون
	mocking"

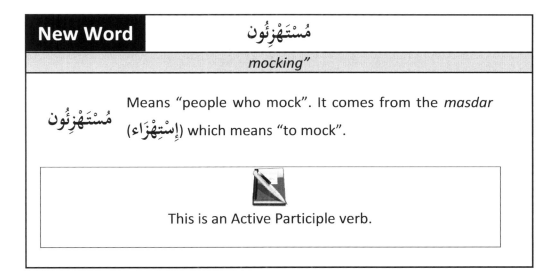

مُسْتَهْزِئُون   Means "people who mock". It comes from the *masdar* (إِسْتِهْزَاء) which means "to mock".

This is an Active Participle verb.

Lessons derived from this Verse

Allah knows what is in your heart

The hypocrites tried to deceive the believers, by pretending that they were believers. They didn't realize that Allah knows what is in everyone's heart. Allah knows what you hide, so be aware of this at all times.

Beware of devils – they will take you away from this course

When the hypocrites were alone with their shaitans, their devils, they would say "We are with you." The devils that the Quran is referring to are their leaders and masters. Remember there are devils amongst both the jinn kind and the human kind. Stay away from both kinds of devils.

These shaitans are always trying to take us away from Allah and His remembrance; they don't want us to perform deeds that will get us closer to Allah. Courses like this, that teach us the Quran, bring a person closer to Allah. The devils will try their best to take you away from anything that increases your knowledge of the Quran.

Devils will not leave you alone until you leave this world.
They will try to take you away from the Quran and courses like this that teach the Quran.

Surah Baqrah Verse 15a

In this verse Allah is saying that He mocks these hypocrites in return. which suits his majesty.

Table 21.2.1

بِهِمْ	يَسْتَهْزِئُ	اللَّهُ
at them	*mocks*	*Allah*

There are no new words in this verse.

Table 21.2.2

اللَّهُ
Allah
اللَّهُ   Means "Allah".

Table 21.2.3

يَسْتَهْزِئُ
mocks
يَسْتَهْزِئُ   Means "he mocks". See Table 21.1.19.

Table 21.2.4

بِهِمْ
at them
بِ   Means "in". This is a Preposition and we have already studied this in our grammar lesson of hour 6. [In English we would use "at".]

Surah Baqrah Verse 15b

This is a continuation of the previous verse.

Table 21.2.5

يَعْمَهُونَ	طُغْيَانِهِمْ	فِي	وَيَمُدُّهُمْ
they wander blindly	their transgression	in	and prolongs them

There are three new words in this verse.

Table 21.2.6

New Word	وَيَمُدُّهُمْ
	and prolongs them
يَمُدُّ	Means "he prolongs". It comes from the *masdar* (مَدَّ) which means "to prolong", "to extend".

Table 21.2.7

فِي
in
فِي   Means "in". See the Hour 6 grammar lesson on Prepositions.

Table 21.2.8

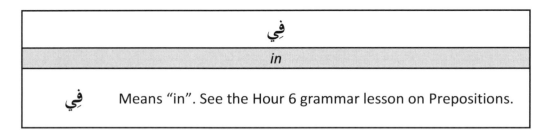

New Word	طُغْيَانِهِمْ

their transgression
طُغْيَانِ Means "transgression".

Table 21.2.9

New Word	يَعْمَهُونَ
they wander blindly	
يَعْمَهُونَ	Means "they wander blindly". It comes from the *masdar* (عَمَهٌ) which means "blindness of the heart".

Lessons derived from this Verse

When your time is up, it's up!

Allah mocks the hypocrites by postponing their punishment. This is not done to be good to them. It is postponed so that they may continue in – and perhaps increase in – sinfulness. We have learnt that Allah gives them chances for a period of time. But once your time is up, it's up. No more chances.

When your time is up, it's up!

Practice what you have Learned

آمَنَّا	قَالُوا	آمَنُوا	الَّذِينَ	لَقُوا	وَإِذَا
"We believe"	they say	believe	(with) those who	they meet	And when

مَعَكُمْ	إِنَّا	قَالُوا	شَيَاطِينِهِمْ	إِلَى	خَلَوْا	وَإِذَا
(are) with you	"Indeed we	they say,	their shaitans	with	they are alone	and when

مُسْتَهْزِئُون	نَحْنُ	إِنَّمَا
mocking"	we (were)	only

بِهِمْ	يَسْتَهْزِئُ	اللَّهُ
at them	mocks	Allah

يَعْمَهُونَ	طُغْيَانِهِمْ	فِي	وَيَمُدُّهُمْ
they wander blindly	their transgression	in	and prolongs them

Don't forget to ponder over the meaning in your next Salah. Pause after every verse, imagine the response from Allah, and try to build humility and love for Allah in your Salah.

Revision of vocabulary words studied

Meaning	Arabic Word
they meet	لَقُوا
they are alone	خَلَوْا
people who are mocking	مُسْتَهْزِئُون
he prolongs	يَمُدُّ
transgression	طُغْيَان
they wander blindly	يَعْمَهُونَ

Phew! Alhumdulillah!

We have completed verses 14-15 of Surah Baqrah. Without Allah's help it would not have been possible, so let's say Alhumdulillah! Let's start to ponder over what we have learnt so far in our salah. Let's ask Allah to fill our hearts with the love of Allah and His message the Glorious Quran. Remember to understand the message from these verses, ponder over them, implement upon them and also spread them.

Take a Break!

In the next section, you are going to learn Arabic Grammar. You will learn Interrogative Particles.

21

Grammar – Interrogative Particles

Interrogative Particles are used to ask questions. For example in English we say, "Is this your book?", "Are you a student?" and so forth. There are many Interrogative Particles used in Arabic, but we will study the most common ones that occur in the Quran.

Table 21.3.1

Interrogative Particles				
Particle	أَ	هَلْ	مَا	مَنْ
Meaning	Is / Are	Is / Are	What	Who

As you will have noticed, we have already studied most of these Interrogative Particles. Here are some examples which will help to give you a better understanding.

Table 21.3.2

Interrogative Particles				
Example	أَهَذَا كِتَاب	هَلْ اَنْتَ طَالِب	مَا دِيْنُكَ	مَنْ رَبُّكَ
Meaning	Is this a book?	Are you a student?	What is your religion?	Who is your Lord?

These are the four most commonly used Interrogative Particles in the Quran. There are of course more, and here are some of them:

Table 21.3.3

	Interrogative Particles				
Particles	أَيٌّ	كَيْفَ	كَمْ	مَتَى	أَيْنَ
Meaning	Which	How	How many / How much	When	Where

Study these Interrogative Particles, and see if you can come up with a few examples of your own from the vocabulary you have learnt so far. If you cannot remember any, you may go back, and see if you can find any words to use as further practice in using Interrogative Particles.

Advice and guidance from the Author

Why do the non-believers enjoy this world?

We see that many non-believers, people who disobey Allah, nonetheless lead a luxurious life. Just because a person lives in luxury, and follows his own desires, does not mean he is successful. He may look successful but real success is in the hereafter. Any person who has success in this world but is not following Allah and his Prophet Muhammad (Peace be upon him), has only a postponement of his punishment so that he may increase in sinfulness. So don't be deceived by worldly success.

Success of *Dunya* does not mean success of *Akhirah*.

Do you know when a believer rests?

Once a person asked Imam Ahmed ibn Hambal (Rahmatullahi Alayhi), "When does a believer rest?" He replied "when his right foot has entered paradise". Until his foot isn't in paradise shaitan will be following him, trying to lead him astray, and he will have to struggle in this world. So a believer does not rest until his foot is in paradise.

A believer rests when his foot enters Paradise.

Summary

In this hour we have completed verses 14-15 from Surah Baqrah, Alhumdulillah! Let's continue pondering what we have learnt so far in our salah. Remember: do not allow Shaitan to control you and take you away from the Quran. He will try to mislead you till the end.

For grammar we studied Interrogative Particles. Try to master these by studying them and you will easily become familiar with them.

So far we have learnt 173 words that occur in the Quran 23,117 times. Alhumdulillah!

Workshop

The quiz questions and the exercises are provided to further your understanding. Don't worry if you can't answer all of the questions in the quiz. Try your best to answer as many as you can. See Appendix A to check your answers.

Quiz 21

1. When does a believer rest?
2. What are the two categories of devils?
3. How can devils misguide you?

4. Use the following Interrogative Particles to construct sentences. Use examples from the words you have learnt so far in this course.

أَ   مَا   كَيْفَ

Exercise

Insert the CD-ROM accompanying this book into your drive. Select the appropriate folder and do the quiz for this Hour. You may do the quiz as many times as you like in order to further your understanding.

21

Hour 22

At the end of this Hour you will have learnt

191 New Words	**Our Aim 200 Words**
23,498 Total Words	**Our Aim 25,000 Words**

Surah Baqrah Verses 16-17 and Interrogative Particles with Prepositions

In this Hour we will continue with Surah Baqrah and study verses 16-17. In the previous verses Allah talked about what hypocrites would say, and how they would behave. In the next few verses Allah explains why they behave like this through parables.

Let's make Dua to Allah and let's approach this Hour in the firm belief that Allah will make this Hour easy for us.

The highlights of this Hour include:

- Surah Baqrah verses 16-17
- Grammar – Interrogative Particles with Prepositions
- Advice and guidance

Surah Baqrah Verse 16

In this verse Allah is saying that the hypocrites have exchanged error for guidance.

Table 22.1.1

بِالْهُدَى	الضَّلَالَةَ	اشْتَرَوُا	الَّذِينَ	أُولَئِكَ
for guidance	error	bought	(are) the ones who	Those

There is only one new word in this verse.

Table 22.1.2

أُولَئِكَ
Those
أُولَئِكَ   Means "those". See the Hour 7 grammar lesson on Demonstrative Pronouns.

Table 22.1.3

الَّذِينَ
(are) the ones who
الَّذِينَ   Means "the ones who". See the Hour 8 grammar lesson on Relative Pronouns.

22

Table 22.1.4

New Word	اشْتَرَوُا
	bought
اشْتَرَوُا	Means "they bought". It comes from the *masdar* (اِشْتِرَاءٌ) which means "to buy".

Table 22.1.5

الضَّلَالَةَ
error
ضَلَالَةَ — Means "error". See Table 4.3.4.

Table 22.1.6

بِالْهُدَى
for guidance
هُدَى — Means "guidance". See Table 4.1.2.

Surah Baqrah Verse 16b

This is a continuation of the previous verse.

Table 22.1.7

مُهْتَدِينَ	كَانُوا	وَمَا	تِجَارَتُهُمْ	رَبِحَتْ	فَمَا
guided ones	they were	and not	(them) their trade	profited	so not

There are two new words in this verse.

Table 22.1.8

فَمَا
so not
فَ   Means "so". It is a prefix. See Table 9.3.2.
مَا   This word has two meanings. "not" and "what". In this sentence it means "not". See Table 6.2.3.

Table 22.1.9

New Word	رَبِحَتْ
	profited
رَبِحَتْ	Means "she profited". It comes from the *masdar* (رَبَحٌ) which means "to profit".

Table 22.1.10

New Word	تِجَارَتُهُمْ

(them) their trade
تِجَارَة   Means "trade", "commerce".

Table 22.1.11

وَمَا
and not
مَا   This word has two meanings. "not" and "what". In this sentence it means "not". See Table 6.2.3.

Table 22.1.12

كَانُوا
they were
كَانُوا   Means "they were". This is the plural form of (كَانَ). See Table 9.3.8.

Table 22.1.13

مُهْتَدِينَ
guided ones
مُهْتَدِينَ   Means "guided ones". This is an Active Participle plural form. It comes from the *masdar* (اِهْتِدَاءٌ) which means "to be rightly guided".

Lessons derived from this Verse

Have you ever wondered why we always want to upgrade?

In this verse Allah is saying that the hypocrites choose to walk a path away from His guidance, for which there is a high price to pay in the hereafter. We have a very important question to ask ourselves here. How many times have we given priority to this world over Allah and the hereafter?

This world has two obvious drawbacks. The first is that it is not perfect and the second is that it will come to an end. That imperfection is why we always want to upgrade to newer and bigger and better, and we are never satisfied with what we have. If someone says "I have everything in this world: the best car, the best house," they are forgetting the second drawback: this world will come to an end and you will not take that house or car with you when you are placed in your grave.

In contrast to this world, Allah says that the Hereafter is *khair* and *abqa*. This means that the hereafter is perfect. There will be no desire in you to upgrade, since you will have the best. Also, Allah says it will last forever.

So Allah asks us in the Quran, why do you give priority to this world? This world is nothing compared to the hereafter.

22

Do **NOT** purchase this World in exchange for the Hereafter.
This World is **IMPERFECT** and **WILL NEVER LAST.**
The hereafter is **PERFECT** and **WILL LAST FOREVER.**

Islam does not stop anyone from enjoying life, because believers enjoy life while keeping in mind that this world is not a permanent place.

Surah Baqrah Verse 17a

In this verse Allah gives us another parable describing the hypocrites.

Table 22.2.1

نَارًا	اسْتَوْقَدَ	الَّذِي	كَمَثَلِ	مَثَلُهُمْ
a fire	kindled	(of) the one who	(is) like (the) example	Their example

There are two new words in this verse.

Table 22.2.2

New Word	مَثَلُهُمْ
	Their example
مَثَل	Means "their example".

Table 22.2.3

كَمَثَلِ
(is) like (the) example
كَ Means "like".

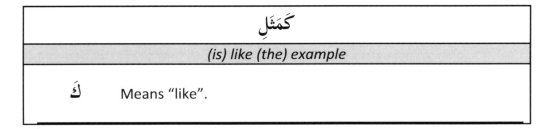

مَثَلِ	Means "the example".

Table 22.2.4

الَّذِي	
(of) the one who	
الَّذِي	Means "who". See the Hour 8 grammar lesson on Relative Pronouns.

Table 22.2.5

New Word	اسْتَوْقَدَ
kindled	
اسْتَوْقَدَ	Means "he kindled", "he lit". It comes from the *masdar* (اِسْتِيْقَادٌ) which means "to kindle".

Table 22.2.6

نَارًا	
a fire	
نَار	Means "fire". See Table 8.3.3.

Surah Baqrah Verse 17b

This is a continuation of the previous verse.

Table 22.2.7

بِنُورِهِمْ	ذَهَبَ اللَّهُ	مَاحَوْلَهُ	أَضَاءَتْ	فَلَمَّا
their light	Allah took away	his surroundings	it lit up	so when

There are five new words in this verse.

Table 22.2.8

New Word	فَلَمَّا
	so when
فَ	Means "so". See Table 9.3.2 for this prefix.
لَمَّا	Means "when".

Table 22.2.9

New Word	أَضَاءَتْ
	it lit up
أَضَاءَتْ	Means "it lit up". It comes from the *masdar* (إِضَاءَةٌ) which means "to illuminate" and "to light up".

Table 22.2.10

New Word	مَاحَوْلَهُ
	his surroundings

| مَا | This word has two meanings. "not" and "what". In this sentence it means "what". We have already covered this word in Table 6.2.3 of Hour 6. |
| حَوْلَ | Means "surroundings". |

Table 22.2.11

New Word	ذَهَبَ اللَّهُ
	Allah took away

| ذَهَبَ | Means "he went". |

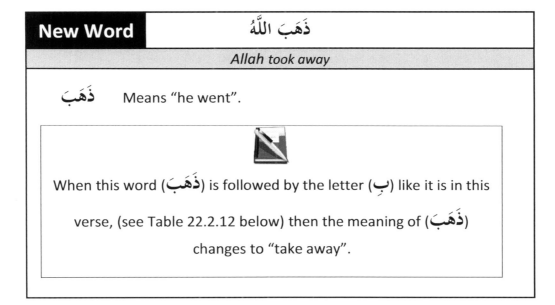

When this word (ذَهَبَ) is followed by the letter (ب) like it is in this verse, (see Table 22.2.12 below) then the meaning of (ذَهَبَ) changes to "take away".

Table 22.2.12

22

New Word	بِنُورِهِمْ
	their light

| بِ | Means "with". See the Hour 5 grammar lesson on Prepositions. |

نُورٍ	Means "light".

Surah Baqrah Verse 17c

This is a continuation of the previous verse.

Table 22.2.13

لَا يُبْصِرُونَ	ظُلُمَاتٍ	فِي	وَتَرَكَهُمْ
(so) they (do) not see.	darkness	in	and left them

There are three new words in this verse.

Table 22.2.14

New Word	وَتَرَكَهُمْ
	and left them
تَرَكَ	Means "he left". It comes from the *masdar* (تَرْك) which means "to leave".

Table 22.2.15

فِي
in
فِي   Means "in". See the Hour 6 grammar lesson on Prepositions.

Table 22.2.16

New Word	ظُلُمَاتٍ
	darkness
ظُلُمَاتٍ	Means "darkness". It is the plural form of (ظُلْمَة) which means "darkness".

Table 22.2.17

New Word	لَا يُبْصِرُونَ
	(so) they (do) not see
لَا	Means "not".
يُبْصِرُونَ	Means "they see". It comes from the *masdar* (إِبْصَار) which means "to see".

Lessons derived from this Verse

Do you know what a believer's weapons are?

In this verse Allah says that He left the hypocrites in darkness. As a result they were unable to find the correct path or travel in the right direction. If you follow the Quran and Hadith (sayings of Prophet Muhammad, Peace be upon him) then Allah will never leave you in darkness. They are your weapons and your defences against the shaitans.

Everyone claims that they follow the Quran and Hadith

Nowadays everyone says they follow the Quran and the Hadith. How do we know whether this claim is true or false? You need to check for yourself in the Quran or Hadith to see whether what you are doing is right. If it matches with the Quran and Hadith then it is right. If it does not then what you are following is not the teaching of the Quran and the Hadith.

Hold tightly on to the Quran and the Hadith and you will **NEVER** be misguided.

Practice what you have Learned

بِالْهُدَى	الضَّلَالَةَ	اشْتَرَوُا	الَّذِينَ	أُولَئِكَ
for guidance	error	bought	(are) the ones who	Those

مُهْتَدِينَ	كَانُوا	وَمَا	تِجَارَتُهُمْ	رَبِحَتْ	فَمَا
guided ones.	they were	and not	(them) their trade	profited	so not

نَارًا	اسْتَوْقَدَ	الَّذِي	كَمَثَلِ	مَثَلُهُمْ
a fire	kindled	(of) the one who	(is) like (the) example	Their example

بِنُورِهِمْ	ذَهَبَ اللَّهُ	مَاحَوْلَهُ	أَضَاءَتْ	فَلَمَّا
their light	Allah took away	his surroundings	it lit up	so when

لَا يُبْصِرُونَ	ظُلُمَاتٍ	فِي	وَتَرَكَهُمْ
(so) they (do) not see.	darkness	in	and left them

Don't forget to ponder over the meaning in your next Salah. Pause after every verse, imagine the response from Allah, and try to build humility and love for Allah in your Salah.

Revision of vocabulary words studied

Meaning	Arabic Word
they bought	اشْتَرَوُا
it profited	رَبِحَتْ
trade	تِجَارَتٍ
example	مَثَل
he kindled	اسْتَوْقَدَ
when	لَمَّا
it lighted	أَضَاءَتْ
surrounding	حَوْل

he took away	ذَهَب بِ
he left	تَرَكَ
darkness	ظُلُمَاتٍ
they see	يُبْصِرُونَ

Phew! Alhumdulillah!

We have completed verses 16-17 of Surah Baqrah. Without Allah's help it would not have been possible, so let's say Alhumdulillah! Let's start to ponder over what we have learnt so far in our salah, let's ask Allah to take us out of darkness into the light of guidance. Remember to understand the message from these verses, ponder over them, implement them and also spread them.

Take a Break!

Grammar – Interrogative Particles with Prepositions

In the previous Hour's grammar lesson you studied Interrogative Particles. You should be familiar with these now, but you may want to quickly look back at that lesson before you start this one, which is about Interrogative Particles joined with Prepositions. They still ask questions, but there is a meaning change when a Preposition is affixed.

Table 21.3.1

Interrogative Particles with Prepositions						
Interrogative Particles with Prepositions	فِيْمَ	لِمَ	مِمَّنْ	لِمَنْ	مِمَّ	بِمَ
Meaning	In what?	For what? (why)	From whom?	For whom	From what?	With what?
Prepositions used	فِيْ	لِ	مِنْ	لِ	مِنْ	بِ
Interrogative Particles used	مَا	مَا	مَن	مَنْ	مَا	مَا

You can see from these examples that when prepositions are affixed to interrogative particles the new word has a different meaning. Study the above Interrogative Particles with Prepositions, and see if you can form sentences using vocabulary you have learnt so far. If you cannot remember any words go back and see if you can find any vocabulary you can use to form sentences using these Interrogative Particles.

Advice and guidance from the Author

What are the characteristics of hypocrites?

The word hypocrite is used for those people who pretend to be believers but are not. A hypocrite is like one who is in total darkness: the darkness of doubts, and the darkness of disbelief. We need to ask ourselves if we have any hypocritical characteristics. Some of these are:

- They make mischief here on earth; they practice corruption.
- They try to deceive Allah and the believers.
- They have doubts about the *deen*.
- They lie constantly.
- They mock the believers.
- They are two-faced: they say one thing to the believers and something else to their friends.

If we don't have any of the above characteristics in us, then all praise is to Allah, but if we have even one of these, we must do something about it.

Hypocrisy is dangerous. Constantly check yourself!

Summary

In this hour we have completed verses 16-17 from Surah Baqrah, Alhumdulillah! Let's continue pondering over what we have learnt so far in our salah. Remember to constantly check yourself for hypocrisy, not because we want to focus on it, but because we want to avoid hypocrisy.

For grammar we studied Interrogative Particles with Prepositions. Try to master these by studying them and you will easily become familiar with them.

So far we have learnt 191 words that occur in the Quran 23,498 times. Alhumdulillah!

Workshop

The quiz questions and the exercises are provided to further your understanding. Don't worry if you can't answer all of the questions in the quiz. Try your best to answer as many as you can. See Appendix A to check your answers.

Quiz 22

1. What are the definitions of this world and the hereafter?
2. How do we know if we are following the Quran and Hadith?
3. What are the characteristics of hypocrisy?
4. What is the meaning of "going into total darkness" in these verses?

Exercise

Insert the CD-ROM accompanying this book into your drive. Select the appropriate folder and do the quiz for this Hour. You may do the quiz as many times as you like in order to further your understanding.

22

Hour 23

At the end of this Hour you will have learnt

205 New Words	**Our Aim 200 Words**	
24,230 Total Words	**Our Aim 25,000 Words**	

Surah Baqrah Verses 18-19 and Passive Verbs

In this Hour we will continue with Surah Baqrah and study verses 18-19. In these verses Allah is giving us another parable describing the hypocrites. Allah describes hypocrites who sometimes know the truth and yet doubt it at other times.

Let's make Dua to Allah and let's approach this Hour in the firm belief that Allah will make this Hour easy for us.

The highlights of this Hour include:

- Surah Baqrah verses 18-19
- Grammar – Passive verbs
- Advice and guidance

Surah Baqrah Verse 18

In this verse Allah is giving a description of the hypocrites.

Table 23.1.1

لَا يَرْجِعُونَ	فَهُمْ	عُمْيٌ	بُكْمٌ	صُمٌّ
(they) will not return	so they	blind	dumb	Deaf

There are four new words in this verse.

Table 23.1.2

New Word	صُمٌّ
Deaf	
صُمٌّ Means "deaf".	

Table 23.1.3

New Word	بُكْمٌ
dumb	
بُكْمٌ Means "dumb", "unable to speak".	

23

Table 23.1.4

New Word	عُمْيٌ
	blind
عُمْيٌ	Means "blind".

Table 23.1.5

فَهُمْ
so they
فَ   Means "so". See Table 9.3.2.

Table 23.1.6

New Word	لَا يَرْجِعُونَ
	(they) will not return.
يَرْجِعُونَ	Means "they will return". It comes from the *masdar* (رُجُوْع) which means "to return".

Lessons derived from this Verse

Are the hypocrites really deaf, dumb, and blind?

Allah is describing people who have received guidance but misused it. As a result Allah took the guidance away from them.

These people are not physically deaf, dumb, and blind, but they are deaf to the truth, unable to speak the truth, and they are blind to the signs and the truth. Allah therefore describes them as deaf, dumb and blind.

There is a big lesson for us here. We have begun studying the Quran, which is a book of guidance from Allah, and if we reject it or misuse it then Allah will take it away from us. So we have a choice. We can study diligently and it will benefit us, or we can misuse it. Let us not be among those who misuse it.

The purpose of the signs of Allah

Every time you look at the creation of Allah, this is a sign to remind you of Him. In the same way that the purpose of a road sign is to direct people in the right direction, similarly the purpose of the signs of Allah is to direct a human being to his creator Allah. When you see the mountains, the trees, the sun, moon, and stars - these are all signs of Allah, they direct us back to Him. Let us not choose to be blind, in enjoying the sight of these signs yet not understanding they take us back to Allah.

We see the signs of Allah day and night, but how often do they really direct us and take us back to Allah?

Surah Baqrah Verse 19a

In this verse Allah is giving another parable of hypocrites.

Table 23.2.1

السَّمَاءِ	مِنَ	كَصَيِّبٍ	أَوْ
the sky	from	like a rainstorm	Or

There are three new words in this verse.

Table 23.2.2

New Word	أَوْ
Or	
أَوْ	Means "or".

Table 23.2.3

New Word	كَصَيِّبٍ
like a rainstorm	
كَ	Means "like". See Table 22.2.3.
صَيِّب	Means "rainstorm".

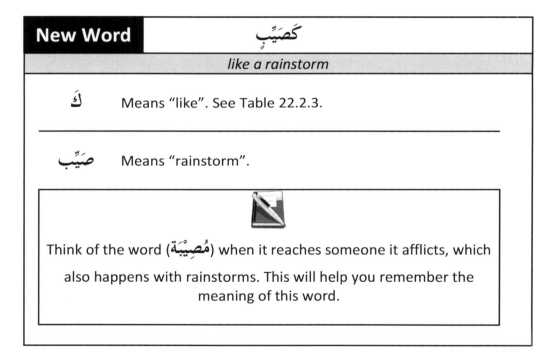

Think of the word (مُصِيْبَة) when it reaches someone it afflicts, which also happens with rainstorms. This will help you remember the meaning of this word.

Table 23.2.4

مِنَ
from

مِنَ	Means "from". See the Hour 5 grammar lesson on Prepositions.

Table 23.2.5

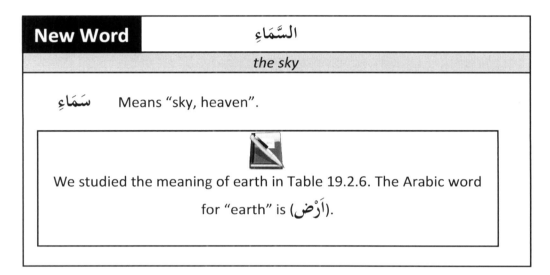

New Word	السَّمَاءِ
	the sky

سَمَاءِ   Means "sky, heaven".

We studied the meaning of earth in Table 19.2.6. The Arabic word for "earth" is (أَرْض).

Surah Baqrah Verse 19b

This is a continuation of the previous verse.

Table 23.2.6

وَبَرْقٌ	وَرَعْدٌ	ظُلُمَاتٌ	فِيهِ
and lightning.	and thunder	darkness	in it (are)

There are two new words in this verse.

Table 23.2.7

فِيهِ

23

in it (are)
فِي   Means "in". See the Hour 6 grammar lesson on Prepositions.

Table 23.2.8

ظُلُمَاتٌ
darkness
ظُلُمَاتٌ   Means "darkness". See Table 22.2.16.

Table 23.2.9

New Word	وَرَعْدٌ
	and thunder
رَعْدٌ Means "thunder".	

Table 23.2.10

New Word	وَبَرْقٌ
	and lightning.
بَرْقٌ Means "lightning".	

Surah Baqrah Verse 19c

This is a continuation of the previous verse.

Table 23.2.11

آذَانِهِمْ	فِي	أَصَابِعَهُمْ	يَجْعَلُونَ
their ears	*in*	*their fingers*	*They put*

There are two new words in this verse.

Table 23.2.12

يَجْعَلُونَ
They put
يَجْعَلُونَ   Means "they put". It comes from the *masdar* (جَعْل) which means "to put". See Table 14.2.3.

Table 23.2.13

New Word	أَصَابِعَهُمْ
	their fingers
أَصَابِعَ Means "fingers". This is the plural form for (إِصْبَع) which means "finger".	

Table 23.2.14

فِي
in
فِي   Means "in". See the Hour 6 grammar lesson on Prepositions.

23

Table 23.2.15

New Word	آذَانِهِمْ
	their ears
آذَانِ	Means "ears". This is the plural form for (أُذُن) which means "ear".

Surah Baqrah Verse 19d

This is a continuation of the previous verse.

Table 23.2.16

الْمَوْتِ	حَذَرَ	الصَّوَاعِقِ	مِنَ
death.	*(in) fear (of)*	*the thunder-claps*	*from*

There are three new words in this verse.

Table 23.2.17

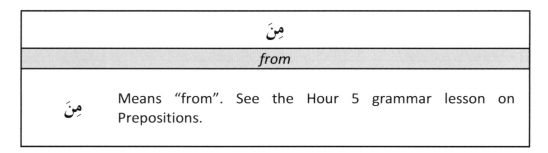

مِنَ
from
مِنَ — Means "from". See the Hour 5 grammar lesson on Prepositions.

Table 23.2.18

New Word	الصَّوَاعِقِ
	the thunder-claps
صَوَاعِقِ	Means "thunder-claps". This is the plural form of (صَاعِقَة) which means "a thunder-clap".

Table 23.2.19

New Word	حَذَرَ
	(in) fear (of)
حَذَرَ	Means "fear".

Table 23.2.20

New Word	الْمَوْتِ
	death.
مَوْت	Means "death".

Surah Baqrah Verse 19e

This is a continuation of the previous verse.

23

Table 23.2.21

بِالْكَافِرِينَ	مُحِيطٌ	وَاللَّهُ
the disbelievers	encompasses	And Allah

There is one new word in this verse.

Table 23.2.22

وَاللَّهُ
And Allah
وَاللَّهُ   Means "And Allah".

Table 23.2.23

New Word	مُحِيطٌ
	encompasses

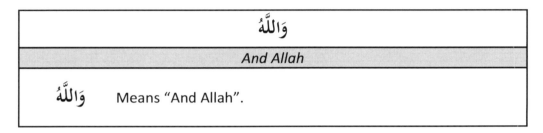

مُحِيطٌ	Means "one who encompasses". This is an Active Participle verb. It comes from the *masdar* (إِحَاطَة) which means "to encompass something".

Table 23.2.24

بِالْكَافِرِينَ
the disbelievers.

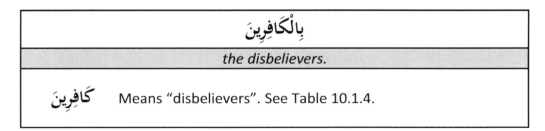

كَافِرِينَ	Means "disbelievers". See Table 10.1.4.

Lessons derived from this Verse

Hypocrites cannot escape

As a person in a heavy rainstorm cannot see the path, hypocrites cannot see the truth. Rain is useful and necessary, but it can be dangerous when accompanied by thunder and lightning. Similarly, the hypocrites professing their Imaan seems like a good thing but in reality it is not. Just as putting their fingers in their ears can't save them from the thunder and lightning, so their claim to believe will not save them either. No matter what these hypocrites do, or how they behave, Allah's decision is final and they cannot escape Him.

Practice what you have Learned

صُمٌّ	بُكْمٌ	عُمْيٌ	فَهُمْ	لَا يَرْجِعُونَ
Deaf	dumb	blind	so they	(they) will not return.

أَوْ	كَصَيِّبٍ	مِنَ	السَّمَاءِ
or	like a rainstorm	from	the sky

فِيهِ	ظُلُمَاتٌ	وَرَعْدٌ	وَبَرْقٌ
in it (are)	darkness	and thunder	and lightning.

يَجْعَلُونَ	أَصَابِعَهُمْ	فِي	آذَانِهِمْ
They put	their fingers	in	their ears

23

الْمَوْتِ	حَذَرَ	الصَّوَاعِقِ	مِنَ
death.	(in) fear (of)	the thunder-claps	from

بِالْكَافِرِينَ	مُحِيطٌ	وَاللَّهُ
the disbelievers.	encompasses	And Allah

Don't forget to ponder over the meaning in your next Salah. Pause after every verse, imagine the response from Allah, and try to build humility and love for Allah in your Salah.

Revision of Vocabulary words studied

Meaning	Arabic Word
deaf	صُمٌّ
dumb	بُكْمٌ
blind	عُمْيٌ
they will return	يَرْجِعُونَ
rainstorm	صَيِّبٌ
sky	سَمَاءٍ
thunder	رَعْدٌ
lightning	بَرْقٌ

fingers	أَصَابِعَ
ears	آذَانِ
thunder-claps	صَوَاعِقِ
fear	حَذَرَ
death	مَوْتِ
encompasses	مُحِيطٌ

Phew! Alhumdulillah!

We have completed verses 18-19 of Surah Baqrah. Without Allah's help it would not have been possible, so let's say Alhumdulillah! Let's start to ponder over what we have learnt so far in our salah, let's ask Allah to guide us with the Quran and, whatever we are studying, may Allah make us of those who benefit from the Quran and not from those who reject it or misuse it. Remember to understand the message from these verses, ponder over them, implement them and also spread them.

Take a Break!

In the next section, you are going to learn Arabic Grammar.You will learn Passive Verbs.

23

Grammar – Passive Verbs

Passive Verbs are used to emphasise the action rather than the actor. Often this is because the action is important but the one who did it is not. For example in English we say, "This work was completed," "My phone was stolen," and so forth. Who completed the work and who stole the phone are not relevant pieces of information.

Patterns for Passive Verbs

In Arabic Passive Verbs have two distinct patterns: one for the Past Tense and the other for the Present Tense.

Table 23.3.1

Passive Verb Patterns	
Past Tense	Present Tense
فُعِلَ	يُفْعَلُ

Here are some examples demonstrating Passive Verb formation.

Table 23.3.2

Active Participle Examples			
Past Tense		Present Tense	
It was written	كُتِبَ	It will be written	يُكْتَبُ
It was taught	دُرِسَ	It will be taught	يُدْرَسُ
It was recited	قُرِئَ	It will be recited	يُقْرَئُ

Study these examples and how to form them. See if you can come up with a few examples of your own from the vocabulary you have learnt so far. If you cannot remember any, you may go back and see if you can find any words to use as further practice in forming Passive Verbs.

Advice and guidance from the Author

You cannot escape Allah – Whatever Allah has planned for you, that will happen

In the same way that the hypocrites cannot escape, no one else can escape from Allah and what He has decided and planned for us. Therefore don't worry when calamities befall you, because worrying will not help. People spend so much time worrying about the future and being sorry about what happened yesterday, that they forget to live today. The Quran says, "Your affairs have already been decided in heaven", so why worry?

There is always a solution to problems, and even if there is no solution to your problem, then worrying will not help, so again why worry?

When you start to worry about the future, you end up driving away the peace and happiness from your home.

Do you want to know what the strongest thing created by Allah is?

A person asked Ali (Radiyallu Anhu) this question. He spread out all ten fingers and said ten things.
1. He said the mountains exist for years and years so they must be the strongest thing made by Allah.

2. Then he said the mountains can be cut by a metal tool, so metal must be stronger than the mountains.

3. But the metal can be melted with fire, so the fire must be stronger than metal.

4. But the fire can be put out by water, so the water must be stronger than fire.

5. But the water is controlled by the clouds, so the clouds must be stronger than water.

6. But the cloud is moved by winds, so the winds must be stronger than the cloud.

7. But the wind is not able to move a human being when he is standing on the earth, so the human being must be stronger.

8. But the human being when intoxicated is not able to control himself, so intoxication must be stronger.

9. But when a human being sleeps, his sleep is able to take care of his intoxication, so sleep must be stronger than intoxication.

10. But a person with anxiety is not able to sleep.

Therefore, the strongest thing Allah created in this world is anxiety and worry.

Worries and anxieties can destroy a person's life.
They are indeed the strongest things created by Allah.

What can I do to prevent worrying?

The barrier to worry is praying to Allah with the Dua made by Muhammad (Peace be upon him) in the Hadith. The Dua is:

'O Allah, I seek refuge with You from anxiety and grief, and I seek refuge with You from inability and laziness, and I seek refuge with You from cowardliness and stinginess, and I seek refuge with You from being overpowered by debts and men.'

Summary

In this Hour we have completed verses 18-19 from Surah Baqrah, Alhumdulillah! Let's continue pondering what we have learnt so far in our salah. Remember to use the Quran to benefit you and not misuse it.

For grammar we studied Passive Verbs. Try to master how to form these by studying them and you will easily become familiar with the process.

So far we have learnt 205 words that come in the Quran 24,230 times. Alhumdulillah!

Workshop

The quiz questions and the exercises are provided to further your understanding. Don't worry if you can't answer all of the questions in the quiz. Try your best to answer as many as you can. See Appendix A to check your answers.

Quiz 23

1. What is the purpose of the signs of Allah?
2. What is the strongest thing created by Allah?
3. What is the solution for being not worried in life?
4. Form Passive verbs for the following verbs in both the Past and Present Tenses. Don't worry about the meanings of these words.

فتح   نصر   ضرب

Exercise

Insert the CD-ROM accompanying this book in your drive. Select the appropriate folder and do the quiz for this Hour. You may do the quiz as many times as you like in order to further your understanding.

23

Hour 24

At the end of this Hour you will have learnt

212 New Words	**Our Aim 200 Words**
25,093 Total Words	**Our Aim 25,000 Words**

Surah Baqrah Verse 20 and Broken Plurals

In this Hour we will continue with Surah Baqrah and study Verse 20. This is the last verse we will study for this course. In this verse Allah is talking about one of His attributes: that of His power over all things.

Let's make Dua to Allah and let's approach this Hour in the firm belief that Allah will make this Hour easy for us.

The highlights of this Hour include:

- Surah Baqrah verse 20
- Grammar – Broken Plurals
- Advice and guidance

Surah Baqrah Verse 20a

In this verse Allah is talking about His power over all things.

Table 24.1.1

يَكَادُ	الْبَرْقُ	يَخْطَفُ	أَبْصَارَهُمْ
Almost	*the lightning*	*snatches away*	*their sight.*

There are two new words in this verse.

Table 24.1.2

New Word	يَكَادُ
Almost	
يَكَادُ	Means "almost" i.e. "when something is about to happen".

Table 24.1.3

الْبَرْقُ	
the lightning	
بَرَق	Means "lightning". See Table 23.2.10.

Table 24.1.4

New Word	يَخْطَفُ
snatches away	
يَخْطَفُ	Means "he snatches away". It comes from the *masdar* (خَطَفٌ) which means "to snatch away".

24

Table 24.1.5

أَبْصَارَهُمْ
their sight.
أَبْصَارَ   Means "eyes". See Table 17.2.9.

Surah Baqrah Verse 20b

This is a continuation of the previous verse.

Table 24.1.6

فِيهِ	مَشَوْا	لَهُمْ	أَضَاءَ	كُلَّمَا
in it	*they walk*	*for them*	*it flashes*	*Whenever*

There are three new words in this verse.

Table 24.1.7

New Word	كُلَّمَا
	Whenever
كُلَّمَا Means "Whenever".	

Table 24.1.8

New Word	أَضَاءَ
	it flashes
أَضَاءَ	

Means "it flashes". It comes from the *masdar* (إِضَاءَةٌ) which means "to flash", "to light up".

Table 24.1.9

لَهُمْ
for them
لَ   Means "for". See the Hour 5 grammar lesson on Prepositions.

Table 24.1.10

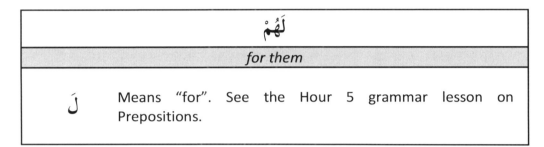

New Word	مَشَوْا
	they walk
مَشَوْا Means "they walk". It comes from the *masdar* (مَشْي) which means "to walk".	

Table 24.1.11

فِيهِ
in it
فِي   Means "in". See the Hour 6 grammar lesson on Prepositions.

Surah Baqrah Verse 20c

This is a continuation of the previous verse.

Table 24.1.12

قَامُوا	عَلَيْهِمْ	أَظْلَمَ	وَإِذَا
they stand	on them	it darkens	and when

There are two new words in this verse.

Table 24.1.13

وَإِذَا
and when
إِذَا   Means "when". See Table 6.3.4.

Table 24.1.14

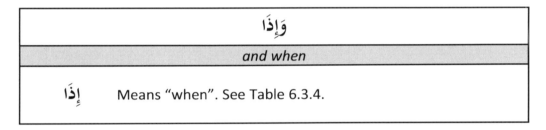

New Word	أَظْلَمَ
	it darkens
أَظْلَمَ	Means "it darkens". It comes from the *masdar* (إِظْلَام) which means "to become dark".

Table 24.1.15

عَلَيْهِمْ
on them

عَلَي	Means "on". See the Hour 6 grammar lesson on Prepositions.
هِمْ	Means "them". See the Hour 3 grammar lesson on Possessive Adjectives.

Table 24.1.16

New Word	قَامُوا
	they stand

قَامُوا	Means "they stand". It comes from the word (قِيَام) which means "to stand".

Surah Baqrah Verse 20d

This is a continuation of the previous verse.

Table 24.1.17

وَأَبْصَارِهِمْ	بِسَمْعِهِمْ	لَذَهَبَ	شَاءَ اللّٰهُ	وَلَوْ
and their sight.	their hearing	He would certainly take away	Allah willed	and if

There are two new words in this verse.

Table 24.1.18

New Word	وَلَوْ
	and if
لَوْ	Means "if".

Table 24.1.19

New Word	شَاءَ اللهُ
	Allah willed

شَاءَ   Means "He willed".

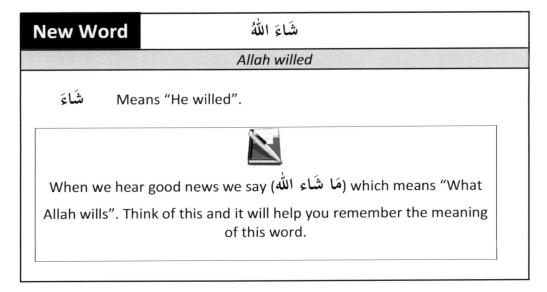

When we hear good news we say (مَا شَاءَ الله) which means "What Allah wills". Think of this and it will help you remember the meaning of this word.

Table 24.1.20

لَذَهَبَ
He would certainly take away

لَ   Means "certainly"

ذَهَبَ   Means "he went". See Table 22.2.11.

Table 24.1.21

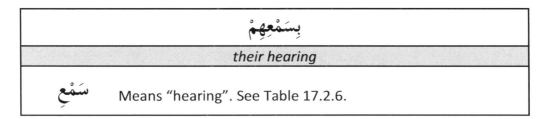

بِسَمْعِهِمْ
their hearing
سَمْعٌ   Means "hearing". See Table 17.2.6.

Table 24.1.22

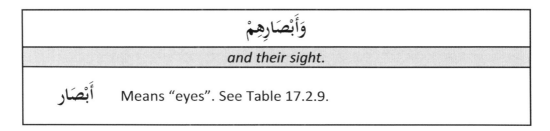

وَأَبْصَارِهِمْ
and their sight.
أَبْصَار   Means "eyes". See Table 17.2.9.

Surah Baqrah Verse 20e

This is a continuation of the previous verse.

Table 24.1.23

قَدِيرٌ	شَيْءٍ	كُلِّ	عَلَى	إِنَّ اللهَ
has power	*thing*	*all*	*over*	*Indeed Allah*

There are three new words in this verse.

Table 24.1.24

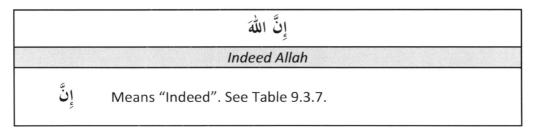

إِنَّ اللهَ
Indeed Allah
إِنَّ   Means "Indeed". See Table 9.3.7.

24

Table 24.1.25

عَلَى	
over	
عَلَى	Means "on". See the Hour 6 grammar lesson on Prepositions.

Table 24.1.26

New Word	كُلٌّ
	all
كُلٌّ	Means "all". [In English we would use 'every'.]

Table 24.1.27

New Word	شَيْءٍ
	thing
شَيْءٍ	Means "thing", "object".

Table 24.1.28

New Word	قَدِيرٌ
	has power
قَدِيرٌ	Means "All Powerful". This is an Active Participle verb. It comes from the *masdar* (قُدْرَة) which means "power", "strength".

Lessons derived from this Verse

Common misconceptions

Many people believe that Allah can do anything and everything. Unfortunately we teach this misconception to our children. Nowhere in the Quran does Allah say that He can do anything and everything. Instead the Quran says that Allah has power over all things, but He will only do Godly things. For example, Allah will never commit an injustice, as the Quran says "Allah is never unjust in the least degree," (Quran 4:40). Allah will never make a mistake, as the Quran says "Allah never errs," (Quran 20:52). So Allah has power over all things but He will only do Godly things, He will never do ungodly things.

Do you know why we get exhausted when handling calamities?

When Allah says that He has power over all things, we should not belittle Allah's power. Many times we disregard the power of Allah and look for help elsewhere. Allah's help is guaranteed, and He will never let us down, so let's take all of our affairs to Allah.

The reason why most of us become exhausted when handling calamities is because we try to carry everything on our own shoulders, when we should go to Allah and asking Him to take care of all of our affairs. We need to ask Allah for help. Instead of putting so much time and energy into the calamity. we need to put that time and energy into asking Allah to take care of our calamities. When we do that, Allah takes care of all of our affairs and He gives us this world and the hereafter.

Don't think you cannot bear a calamity

Many people think they cannot bear calamities. Allah says in the Quran that "Allah does not place a burden on a soul greater than it can bear," (Quran: 2:286). So never think "I cannot bear this calamity." If you were not able to bear it, Allah would not have given this calamity to you.

Don't carry everything on your shoulders by yourself.
Let Allah carry it for you, and focus your heart on one thing and that is Allah.

Practice what you have Learned

أَبْصَارَهُمْ	يَخْطَفُ	الْبَرْقُ	يَكَادُ
their sight.	snatches away	the lightning	Almost

فِيهِ	مَشَوْا	لَهُمْ	أَضَاءَ	كُلَّمَا
in it	they walk	for them	it flashes	Whenever

قَامُوا	عَلَيْهِمْ	أَظْلَمَ	وَإِذَا
they stand	on them	it darkens	and when

وَأَبْصَارِهِمْ	بِسَمْعِهِمْ	لَذَهَبَ	شَاءَ اللهُ	وَلَوْ
and their sight.	their hearing	He would certainly take away	Allah willed	and if

قَدِيرٌ	شَيْءٍ	كُلِّ	عَلَى	إِنَّ اللهَ
has power.	thing	all	over	Indeed Allah

Don't forget to ponder over the meaning in your next Salah. Pause after every verse, imagine the response from Allah, and try to build humility and love for Allah in your Salah.

Revision of vocabulary words studied

Meaning	Arabic Word
almost	يَكَادُ
he snatches away	يَخْطَفُ
whenever	كُلَّمَا
it flashes	أَضَاءَ
they walk	مَشَوْا
it darkens	أَظْلَمَ
they stand	قَامُوا
he willed	شَاءَ
all	كُلِّ
thing	شَيْءٍ
all power	قَدِيرٌ

Phew! Alhumdulillah!

We have completed verse 20 of Surah Baqrah. Without Allah's help it would not have been possible, so let's say Alhumdulillah! Let's start to ponder over what we have learnt so far in our salah. This was our last verse for this course. Remember to understand the message from this verse, ponder over it, implement it and also spread it.

Take a Break!

Grammar – Broken Plurals

In this lesson you will learn various forms of Broken Plurals. In the Hour 2 grammar lesson we studied how to form plurals by adding (ون) or (ين) at the end of the noun. However sometimes plurals are formed in a very different pattern, and that's why they are called Broken Plurals.

There are many different patterns of Broken Plurals in Arabic grammar.

Table 24.2.1

Broken Plural Pattern Examples		
Singular	**Plural**	**Meaning**
أُمَّةٌ	أُمَمٌ	community
كِتَابٌ	كُتُبٌ	book
بَحْرٌ	بِحَارٌ	sea
جِلْدٌ	جُلُوْدٌ	skin
صَاعِقَةٌ	صَوَاعِقُ	thunder-claps
فَقِيْرٌ	فُقَرَاءُ	poor
يَتِيْمٌ	يَتَامَى	orphan

Study these Broken Plural patterns and see if you can come up with a few examples of your own from the vocabulary you have learnt so far. If you cannot remember any, you may go back and see if you can find any words with these patterns of Broken Plurals.

24

Advice and guidance from the Author

If Allah wants He can punish us immediately

In this verse Allah is saying that if He willed He would certainly take away the faculties of hearing and seeing. If Allah wants to, He can punish us immediately for our sins. However Allah gives us chances over a certain period of time. Once that period is over there are no more chances. Once your time is up, it's up!

Be grateful for Allah's blessings

We need to be grateful for everything Allah has given to us, for things like the faculties of hearing and sight, and countless blessings. Unfortunately many people are very ungrateful to their Lord Allah. Allah says in the Quran "Very few of my servants are grateful to me," (Quran 34:13). Let us be counted among those people who are grateful to Allah.

Components of being grateful to Allah

1. To ponder and reflect over the bounty in your heart. i.e. you visualize the bounty and you are fully aware of it.
2. As you visualize it, gratitude must manifest itself in what is being said, so you are constantly engaged in praising Allah.
3. Using these bounties in ways that are only pleasing to Allah.

Summary

This is our last Hour and we have completed verse 20 from Surah Baqrah, Alhumdulillah! Let's continue pondering what we have learnt so far in our salah. Remember to be grateful for the blessings of Allah which have been bestowed upon you.

For grammar we studied Broken Plurals. Try to master these patterns by studying them and you will easily become familiar with them.

We have achieved the aim of this course which was to learn 200 words that occur in the Quran almost 25,000 times. Alhumdulillah! Do not stop here, study the section "What Next".

Workshop

The quiz questions and the exercises are provided to further your understanding. Don't worry if you can't answer all of the questions in the quiz. Try your best to answer as many as you can. See Appendix A to check your answers.

Quiz 24

1. Is it true that Allah can do anything and everything?
2. Why do we get exhausted when handling calamities?
3. What are the minimum requirements for showing gratitude for Allah's blessings upon us?
4. Name at least three Broken Plurals from the vocabulary you have studied in this course.

Exercise

Insert the CD-ROM accompanying this book into your drive. Select the appropriate folder and do the quiz for this Hour. You may do the quiz as many times as you like in order to further your understanding.

24

What Next?

This 24-hour tutorial has given you a good foundation for Mastering Quraning Arabic. This means that your learning must not stop here, in fact it must continue. When you build the foundations of a building, you need to build the structure on this foundation. If you don't build the structure, then the building is incomplete. Similarly, what we have done, has given you a good solid foundation for you to build upon, so don't stop here: instead, continue. So, what is the way forward?

Quite simply, you have learnt 25,000 words from the Quran -- which is just over 30% of the words used in the Quran. So, many words in the Quran are repeated. When you open the Quran, each page will contain many repeated words; there will only be some words that you will need to learn the meaning of. For example, if you continue with verse twenty one of Surah Baqrah, there is only one new vocabulary word in this verse, the other words are all repeated.

So you can continue with the rest of the Quran, studying a few verses from the Quran every day, learning the words you do not know and adding them to the foundation we have already laid in this book.

PART V

Appendixes

A Answers

B Using the CD –Rom

C Using the Website

APPENDIX A

Answers

Quiz 1

1. It is compulsory to understand the Quran because the Quran is the message from our creator Allah and every human being must know and understand the message of his creator.
2. Anyone who does not understand Quranic Arabic.
3. Your goal in this course is to understand the message of the Quran, implement it, and spread it.
4. Our plan in this course is to learn 200 vocabulary words which occur in the Quran almost 25,000 times. This is just over 30% of the words in the Quran.
5. The three steps for success are: 1) Ask help from Allah 2) Strive and struggle in His path 3) Learn techniques and do the training which this course provides for you.

Quiz 2

1. There are many benefits, but the main one is that it is a protection from Shaitan.
2. Surah Shifa, Hamd, Salah, Umm Al-Kitab (the Mother of the Book).
3. To make plurals we can simply add (ون) or (ين).
4.

   غَافِلُوْنَ   عَارِفُوْنَ   صَالِحُوْنَ   نَاصِرُوْنَ

5. There are four principles: 1) The person is more important than the point. 2) Being kind is more important than being right. 3) Mean what you say and say what you mean. 4) Don't be harsh.

Quiz 3

1. One who prepares himself for the hereafter is a wise person.
2. Worship means to follow the commands of Allah.
3. There are two conditions of worship: 1) to do that act for the sake of Allah. 2) to do that act by emulating Prophet Muhammad (Peace be upon him).
4. Talismans and amulets are not allowed in Islam.
5.

طَعَامُهُ   صَلَاتُهُ   قَلَمُهُ   رَبُّهُ

Quiz 4

1. A masdar is a verbal noun.
2. Guidance is of two types. The first is the guidance of Islam, and second is guidance of firmness and continuity of performing the deeds.
3. The first group is those that Allah has bestowed His favours upon, the second group is those who have earned Allah's wrath and the third group is those who have gone astray.
4. Prophets of Allah, the truly faithful, martyrs and righteous people.
5.

مُشْرِكَاتٌ   مُتَصَدِّقَاتٌ   خَاشِعَاتٌ   قَانِتَاتُ

6.

طَعَامُهُ   صَلَاتُهُ   قَلَمُهُ   رَبُّهُ

Quiz 5

1. This Surah is protection from black magic and protection from Shaitan.
2. Remembrance of Allah.
3. The Quran.
4. Shaitan would withdraw because you have recited the Quran.

Quiz 6

1. From the evil of what Allah created, from the evil of night, from the evil of those who blow knots, and from the evil of the envier when he envies.
2. There is nothing that Allah created 100% evil. There is always some good in everything.
3. Envy of those to whom Allah has given knowledge of the Quran and the Hadith and he spreads it day and night; and of those upon whom Allah has bestowed wealth and he gives it away in the path of Allah day and night.
4. People envy because of their love for the world.

Quiz 7

1. Allah is One and only, He is absolute and eternal, He begets not nor is He begotten and there is nothing like Him.
2. We know them how Allah described them, the form is unknown, believing in it is obligatory, and asking questions regarding this is an innovation.
3. Prophet Muhammad (Peace be upon him) told one of his companions "your love for this surah will enter you into Jannah". This Surah is also equivalent to a third of the Quran.
4. Certain Arabic words cannot be translated into English due to the complex nuances of the word in Arabic.

Quiz 8

1. Allah punished both of them because they intended to hurt Prophet Muhammad (Peace be upon him).
2. No, as long as you have wealth in your hand and not in your heart.
3. This depends on our response to that calamity.
4. If we leave pious and righteous offspring they will pray for us when we are in our graves.

Quiz 9

1. It is the last surah to be revealed and it is equivalent to one fourth of the Quran.
2. Arabic words are based on a root system, whereby various words with related meanings are formed from a root word.
3. Prophet Muhammad (Peace be upon him) would start his day by praising Allah.
4. You end up creating a negative environment around you which is not healthy.
5. Past tense forms for the following verbs:

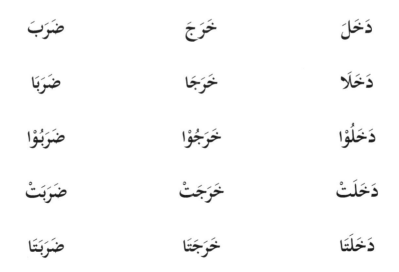

دَخَلَ	خَرَجَ	ضَرَبَ
دَخَلَا	خَرَجَا	ضَرَبَا
دَخَلُوْا	خَرَجُوْا	ضَرَبُوْا
دَخَلَتْ	خَرَجَتْ	ضَرَبَتْ
دَخَلَتَا	خَرَجَتَا	ضَرَبَتَا

ضَرَبْنَ	خَرَجْنَ	دَخَلْنَ
ضَرَبْتَ	خَرَجْتَ	دَخَلْتَ
ضَرَبْتُمَا	خَرَجْتُمَا	دَخَلْتُمَا
ضَرَبْتُمْ	خَرَجْتُمْ	دَخَلْتُمْ
ضَرَبْتِ	خَرَجْتِ	دَخَلْتِ
ضَرَبْتُمَا	خَرَجْتُمَا	دَخَلْتُمَا
ضَرَبْتُنَّ	خَرَجْتُنَّ	دَخَلْتُنَّ
ضَرَبْتُ	خَرَجْتُ	دَخَلْتُ
ضَرَبْنَا	خَرَجْنَا	دَخَلْنَا

Quiz 10

1. There is no compromise when it comes to tawheed issues.
2. We should not forget that we are dealing with other human beings.
3. This surah is a protection from shirk, which is the biggest sin in Islam.
4. It is equivalent to one fourth of the Quran and Prophet Muhammad (Peace be upon him) would tell his companions to recite it before going to sleep.
5. Past tense forms for the following verbs:

رَكِبَ	تَعِبَ	بَرِحَ
رَكِبَا	تَعِبَا	بَرِحَا
رَكِبُوا	تَعِبُوا	بَرِحُوا
رَكِبَتْ	تَعِبَتْ	بَرِحَتْ
رَكِبَتَا	تَعِبَتَا	بَرِحَتَا
رَكِبْنَ	تَعِبْنَ	بَرِحْنَ
رَكِبْتَ	تَعِبْتَ	بَرِحْتَ
رَكِبْتُمَا	تَعِبْتُمَا	بَرِحْتُمَا
رَكِبْتُمْ	تَعِبْتُمْ	بَرِحْتُمْ
رَكِبْتِ	تَعِبْتِ	بَرِحْتِ
رَكِبْتُمَا	تَعِبْتُمَا	بَرِحْتُمَا
رَكِبْتُنَّ	تَعِبْتُنَّ	بَرِحْتُنَّ
رَكِبْتُ	تَعِبْتُ	بَرِحْتُ
رَكِبْنَا	تَعِبْنَا	بَرِحْنَا

Quiz 11

1. It is a river in paradise.
2. It's a river, whose banks are of gold and it runs over pearls, its water is whiter than milk and sweeter than honey.
3. Those who innovate in religion will not be permitted to drink.
4. You can love Him by following His commands.
5. Present tense forms for the following verbs:

يَنْصُرُ	يَدْخُلُ	يَخْرُجُ
يَنْصُرَانِ	يَدْخُلَانِ	يَخْرُجَانِ
يَنْصُرُوْنَ	يَدْخُلُوْنَ	يَخْرُجُوْنَ
تَنْصُرُ	تدْخُلُ	تَخْرُجُ
تَنْصُرَانِ	تدْخُلَانِ	تَخْرُجَانِ
يَنْصُرْنَ	يَدْخُلْنَ	يَخْرُجْنَ
تَنْصُرُ	تدْخُلُ	تَخْرُجُ
تَنْصُرَانِ	تدْخُلَانِ	تَخْرُجَانِ
تَنْصُرُوْنَ	تدْخُلُوْنَ	تَخْرُجُوْنَ

تَخْرُجِيْنَ	تَدْخُلِيْنَ	تَنْصُرِيْنَ
تَخْرُجَانِ	تدْخُلَانِ	تَنْصُرَانِ
تَخْرُجْنَ	تَدْخُلْنَ	تَنْصُرْنِ
اَخْرُجُ	اَدْخُلُ	اَنْصُرُ
نَخْرُجُ	نَدْخُلُ	نَنْصُرُ

Quiz 12

1. Prophet Muhammad (Peace be upon him) said, "The one who cares for an orphan and myself will be together in paradise like this," and he held his two fingers together.
2. One who repulses the orphan and does not encourage feeding the poor.
3. Those who are neglectful with their prayers, those who show off and those who refuse to meet neighborly needs.
4. Present tense forms for the following verbs:

يَنْعِمُ	يَحْسِبُ	يَضْرِبُ
يَنْعِمَانِ	يَحْسِبَانِ	يَضْرِبَانِ
يَنْعِمُوْنَ	يَحْسِبُوْنَ	يَضْرِبُوْنَ

437

تَنْعِمُ	تَحْسِبُ	تَضْرِبُ
تَنْعِمَانِ	تَحْسِبَانِ	تَضْرِبَانِ
يَنْعِمْنَ	يَحْسِبْنَ	يَضْرِبْنَ
تَنْعِمُ	تَحْسِبُ	تَضْرِبُ
تَنْعِمَانِ	تَحْسِبَانِ	تَضْرِبَانِ
تَنْعِمُوْنَ	تَحْسِبُوْنَ	تَضْرِبُوْنَ
تَنْعِمِيْنَ	تَحْسِبِيْنَ	تَضْرِبِيْنَ
تَنْعِمَانِ	تَحْسِبَانِ	تَضْرِبَانِ
تَنْعِمْنَ	تَحْسِبْنَ	تَضْرِبْنَ
اَنْعِمُ	اَحْسِبُ	اَضْرِبُ
نَنْعِمُ	نَحْسِبُ	نَضْرِبُ

Quiz 13

1. Food and safety

438

2. The one who awakens safe in his bed, healthy in his body, who has enough to sustain him for his day, then it is as if he has gained the entire world.

3. Not only through our lips, but our actions must demonstrate we are grateful to Allah.

4. Use the Present Tense Form, delete the Prefix, add إ or أ as a prefix and finally add *Sukoon* at the end.

5. Imperative Tense forms:

اِفْتَحْ   اُنْصُرْ   اِضْرِبْ

Quiz 14

1. There is no intelligence like planning.
2. Ask for good in this world and in the hereafter.

3. Use the Present Tense Form, add لَا as a prefix and finally add *Sukoon* at the end.

4. Negated Verb forms:

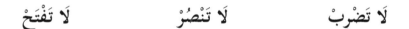

لَا تَفْتَحْ   لَا تَنْصُرْ   لَا تَضْرِبْ

Quiz 15

1. Belief, rituals, character and actions.
2. The Quran.
3. Through knowing who Allah is and loving Allah.
4. These are the Superlative forms:

أَجْمَل   أَصْغَر   أَنْصَر

اَجَامِل	اَصَاغِر	اَنَاصِر
جُمْلَى	صُغْرَى	نُصْرَى
جُمْلَيَات	صُغْرَيَات	نُصْرَيَات

Quiz 16

1. These are the characteristics of guided and successful people:
   - be conscious of Allah (have taqwa);
   - believe in the unseen;
   - establish the salah;
   - spend from what Allah has provided you;
   - believe in what was revealed to the Prophet Muhammad (Peace be upon him);
   - believe in what was revealed before him (all previous scriptures); and
   - have complete and certain conviction in the Hereafter

2. If he can do the new change for a period of twenty one days.
3. Those which benefit humanity.
4. Comparative forms:

اَرْخَص مِنْ	اَجْمَل مِنْ	اَحْسَن مِنْ

Quiz 17

1. يَا مُقَلِّب الْقُلُوبِ ثَبِّتْ قَلْبِي عَلَى دِينِكَ

2. Whether you warn them or not, it does not make any difference to them.

3. فَاعِلٌ and فَاعِلَةٌ

4. Active Participle verbs:

فَاتِحٌ	نَاصِرٌ	ضَارِبٌ
فَاتِحَةٌ	نَاصِرَةٌ	ضَارِبَةٌ

Quiz 18

1. The three points which make up imaan are:
   - It must be demonstrated through speech
   - Believed in the heart
   - Demonstrated through limbs i.e. through actions.

2. They deceive Allah by outwardly showing belief in Allah and concealing their disbelief.

3. The different patterns of Active Participles learnt in this lesson are:

مُفْعِلْ	فَعَّال	فَعُوْل	فَعِيْلٌ

4. The Active Participles for the verbs are:

مُفْعِل	فَعَّال	فَعُوْل	فَعِيْل
مُقْسِط	جَبَّار	وَدُوْد	قَدِيْر
مُنْعِم	قَهَّار	صَبُوْر	عَظِيْم

Quiz 19

1. When he speaks, he lies; when he is trusted, he proves dishonest; and when he promises, he breaks his promise.
2. Rectifying means to correct bad actions and make up for them. Reforming means to enhance the goodness of the good and eliminate the evil.
3. Fear and grief are the two greatest things that destroy a person's life.
4. مَفْعُوْلٌ and مَفْعُوْلَةٌ
5. Passive Participles for the verbs:

مَفْتُوْحٌ	مَنْصُوْرٌ	مَضْرُوْبٌ
مَفْتُوْحَةٌ	مَنْصُوْرَةٌ	مَضْرُوْبَةٌ

Quiz 20

1. Allah will not give you the ability to repent.
2. Three points for respecting the companions are:
   - Love them and respect them from your heart
   - Love them and respect them with your tongue
   - Love them and respect them by following them.
3. مَفْعَل and مَفْعِل
4. If the middle letter of present tense is (ﹷ), then we use the pattern (مَفْعَل) otherwise we use (مَفْعِل)
5. Nouns of Place for the verbs:

Quiz 21

1. When his right foot is in paradise.
2. Jin kind and human kind.
3. They misguide you by taking you away from those things which bring people closer to Allah.
4. Sentences using the Interrogative Particles:

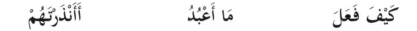

Quiz 22

1. This World is imperfect and will never last whereas the Hereafter is perfect and will last forever.
2. You know by opening the Quran and Hadith and checking.
3. Characteristics of hypocrites are:
   - They make mischief here on earth; they practice corruption.
   - They try to deceive Allah and the believers.
   - They have doubts about the *deen*.
   - They lie constantly.
   - They mock the believers.
   - They are two-faced: they say one thing to the believers and something else to their friends.
4. Darkness of doubts, darkness of disbelief and hypocrisy.

Quiz 23

1. To direct a human being to Allah.
2. Anxiety and worry.
3. The solution is to make the Dua mentioned in the hadith.

4. Passive Verbs:

Quiz 24

1. No. Allah has the power over all things, but He will only do godly things.
2. The reason why we get exhausted is because we try to handle everything ourselves.
3. Minimum requirements are to ponder and reflect over His bounty in the heart, to be constantly engaged in praising Allah and to use these bounties only in ways that are pleasing to Allah.
4. Broken plurals from this course:

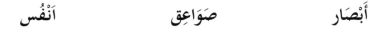

APPENDIX B

Using the CD-ROM

The CD-ROM that accompanies this book contains all the author's Quizzes and Presentations for each Hour of this course.

Windows Installation Instructions

1. Insert the CD-ROM into your CD-ROM drive.

2. From the Windows desktop, double-click the My Computer icon.

3. Double-click the icon representing your CD-ROM drive.

4. Copy the folder on to your desktop.

5. This folder contains Quizzes and PowerPoint Presentations for each Hour.

APPENDIX C

Using the Website

If you don't have access to a CD-ROM drive, you can always access the materials on my website at www.irga.co.uk

Website Instructions

1. Logon to www.irga.co.uk

2. Select courses and Training from the menu.

3. Click on 'Access Material' under 'Learn Quranic Arabic' section.

4. Put in your code: [**46240**] and you will get access to all the Quizzes and PowerPoint Presentations for each Hour of this course.